Experiencing the Father's Love

A Daily Encounter with Him

365-Day Devotional

BOOKS BY JACK FROST

———◈———

Experiencing the Father's Embrace

From Spiritual Slavery to Sonship

Unbound: Breaking Free From Life's Entanglements

EXPERIENCING THE FATHER'S LOVE

A DAILY ENCOUNTER WITH HIM

365-DAY DEVOTIONAL

JACK FROST

DESTINY IMAGE® PUBLISHERS, INC.
PO Box 310, Shippensburg, PA 17257-0310
"Promoting Inspired Lives."

This book and all other Destiny Image and Destiny Image Fiction books are available at Christian bookstores and distributors worldwide.

Cover design by Eileen Rockwell
Interior design by Susan Ramundo
For more information on foreign distributors, call 717-532-3040.
Or reach us on the Internet: www.destinyimage.com

ISBN 13 HC: 978-0-7684-1484-4
ISBN 13 EBook: 978-0-7684-1485-1
TP (POD) ISBN: 978-0-7684-1648-0
LP ISBN: 978-0-7684-1649-7

For Worldwide Distribution, Printed in the U.S.A.
1 2 3 4 5 6 / 20 19 18 17

INTRODUCTION

Behold, I am going to send you Elijah the prophet before the coming of the great and terrible day of the Lord. And he will restore the hearts of the fathers to their children, and the hearts of the children to their fathers, lest I come and smite the land with a curse (Malachi 4:5-6).

Then comes the end, when He delivers up the kingdom to the God and Father, when He has abolished all rule and all authority and power (1 Corinthians 15:24).

We are living in possibly the greatest moment since the beginning of time, when God has begun to restore all things to His sons and daughters in order to prepare them for a great end-time revival. These verses imply that all things began with the Father, and in the end, all things will end with a deeper revelation of the Father.

In the January 1990 issue of *Charisma* magazine, a prophetic voice to the world was asked: "What do you believe the decade of the 1990s holds for the church?" His answer: "I believe the church is about to experience a revelation of the Fatherhood of God. A new wave of evangelism will result as millions of prodigals will see the Father's love in the church again."

In the late 1980s, much of the Church had grown lukewarm or complacent in their love for God. Much of it was because we sought to consume the blessings of God upon our own lusts for position, power, or possessions. We continued in our duty, as the voice of the Lord grew dim. We applied our energies to ministry and religious activity. There was a lack of experiential understanding of Father God's love for His children; thus, many sought for various levels of His love and intimacy through works.

In the early part of the 1990s, Father began drawing us back home to Him by releasing renewal upon the Church once more. *Now*, the Church is being prepared to become the Father's house so that millions of prodigals and pre-Christians will see Father's love, compassion, and forgiveness in us, and thus will desire to come home to Father God. We no longer are just learning about Father's love; many are actually experiencing Father's love breaking forth in their area of need: *"The love of God has been poured out within our hearts..."* (Rom. 5:5). It is no longer enough to just teach on God's love; we are living in an hour when we are to minister out of our deep personal experiences in Father's affectionate love.

Jack Frost was an accomplished sea captain as well as a charismatically powerful Bible teacher and founder of Shiloh Place Ministries. He was an ordained minister for the Salvation Army and pastor of evangelism at Evangel Cathedral in Spartanburg, South Carolina. His three books touched hearts, minds, and spirits worldwide. In 2007, Jack passed into Heaven after a battle with cancer.

Excerpts from his very popular books are the basis for this exceptionally inspirational devotional.

Part I
Experiencing the Father's Love

JANUARY 1

I LOVE YOU!

"Son, I love you. Everything is going to be all right." It was 1972. Because of an LSD overdose, I lay in a semi-comatose state in a hospital bed in Daytona Beach, Florida. My dad was cradling me in his arms and running his fingers through my shoulder-length hair, telling me—his rebellious, misfit son—that he really loved me.

This can't be happening, I thought to myself as I listened to the faint beeping of medical equipment. My dad was telling me he loved me! This was the same overpowering dad who months earlier had shoved me to the floor in our home, grabbed a pair of scissors, and violently cut off my hippie-style hair after telling me I was a disgrace to the family. Now he was tenderly whispering to me about love, forgiveness, and acceptance. Even though I was in a drug-induced fog, his words sank deep into my soul. "Son, I love you."

But God demonstrates His own love toward us, in that while we were yet sinners, Christ died for us. (Romans 5:8)

PRAYER TO ENCOUNTER YOUR FATHER
Father, I thank You for accepting me as Your son in spite of my old behavior patterns. You see me through Your eyes of Love. Lord, thank You for exampling a true Father's love to me through the gift of Jesus.

GOD IS THINKING OF YOU!

For years I had tried unsuccessfully to be the tough man my father wanted me to be. Yet as I lay in that hospital bed at a time of ultimate failure, dad was holding me in his arms and expressing love for me. He was not aware that I could hear his voice or that I could feel his arms around me. I had been willing to stop being my father's son, but my father was not willing to stop being my father. His commitment to me was greater than my commitment to him.

That was perhaps my first glimpse of Father God's unconditional love—and of His desire to express His affection to me, even though I had felt I had failed miserably. However, it would be several more years before I would take the first step to receive that amazing love.

I'll [God] *show up and take care of you as I promised and bring you back home. I know what I'm doing. I have it all planned out—plans to take care of you, not abandon you, plans to give you the future you hope for.* (Jeremiah 29:11 MSG)

PRAYER TO ENCOUNTER YOUR FATHER
Father, every time I feel as though I have failed I chose to believe that I was small and unworthy of Your love. I have strived to believe Your promise and Your plan for my future. Help me believe, Lord God.

JANUARY 3

REVIVE THE SPIRIT AND HEART

Dad was a respected man in our community, and his athletic abilities—particularly his skills as a professional tennis instructor, won him acclaim. I tried to meet my dad's expectations in sports and perform well enough to earn his approval, but I was awkward with a tennis racquet and never seemed to impress him. I felt like such a failure, I wanted Dad's approval. I did not realize that an ungodly belief (stronghold) was growing stronger and stronger in me. I was slowly being consumed by a deep fear of failure and rejection, a fear that caused me to feel worthless.

This ungodly belief produced unhealthy results in my 20s when I became a commercial snapper and grouper fishing boat captain. Driven by a relentless desire to prove myself, I aspired to become the best fisherman on the Southeastern coast of the United States. Everything I did in life began to revolve around my dream to become what people in the fishing business call "top hook." I desired my father's approval above anything else in my life in order to believe I belonged and was loved.

But you belong to God the Father, my dear children. (1 John 4:4a NLT)

PRAYER TO ENCOUNTER YOUR FATHER
Father, I welcome Your acceptance. I thank You that I belong to You because You have created me in Your image as Your child. I thank You that I never have to perform for Your love or acceptance.

JANUARY 4
"Top Hook"

Like my father, I had to be the toughest and the best. And like my father, I developed a fierce temper. Any member of my crew who caused us to lose fish or who disappointed me in any way faced the brunt of my anger. I became known as Captain Bligh of the Carolina coast. I was a screamer and a tyrant. People did not want to mess with Jack Frost in those days.

I would often risk the lives of the crew by spending a week or more off the Carolina coast in the winter, riding out 40 to 60 mph gales and 20- to 30-foot seas in a 44-foot boat so we could claim the coveted prize—**top hook**. I was driven by my fear of failure and by a cruel ambition that left no room for compassion for anyone. I did not realize that deep inside, I was consumed by an unconscious desire to win my father's approval. That nagging void had become a cancer that was eating me alive. I have never been told that love should be a gift not a reward for performance so I demanded performance in order for my crew or anyone else in my life to feel accepted by me.

Pride goes before destruction, and a haughty spirit before stumbling.
(Proverbs 16:18)

PRAYER TO ENCOUNTER YOUR FATHER
Father I ask You to forgive me of pride and how I have treated those You sent me to love. Lord. Come close and help me see what is the source of my pride, anger, and frustrations and change me into Your image and help me to understand how You see me and my peers.

TRUE JOY AND FREEDOM

Everything changes when God's overwhelming love finally breaks through. At 27 years of age, my life was in shambles. I had been addicted to drugs, alcohol, and pornography for more than ten years. My anger was out of control, constantly wounding my wife, son, and others with condescending words and looks.

In a desperate attempt to escape the pain, I took my fishing boat out to sea one day. I cried out to God for three days, "O God, please do something. I've hurt everyone around me. I'm miserable. It's like something inside me is pushing me to the edge of insanity. I feel like I am being poisoned from the inside. Please help me."

While listening to the secular song "Jesus is Just Alright With Me, by the Doobie brothers, during my lowest point in life, I encountered the unconditional love of God for the first time. Instantly His presence broke the chains of alcoholism, drug addiction, and pornography. The burden of sin lifted, and I felt true joy for the first time. I tasted God's goodness. But it would take years for me to find total deliverance from the fear of failure and the aggressive striving that had made me such a driven man.

In kindness he takes us firmly by the hand and leads us into a radical life-change. (Romans 2:4 The Message)

PRAYER TO ENCOUNTER YOUR FATHER

Father take me by Your hand of mercy and shower me with Your unconditional love. Forgive me for my behaviors that have alienated those I love from me. Thank You, Jesus.

WINNING APPROVAL

After my conversion, I became active in church life and quickly learned that my tendency toward performance operated well in a religious environment. I simply transferred my ungodly beliefs, my fear of failure, and my aggressive striving into church work. I thought that the best way to win God's approval and acceptance was to do things for Him and also to win the favor of the Christians around me.

It seemed to be perfectly natural to express my love for God by building my identity through hyper-religious activity. But this false understanding of God's character came with a high price. After working so hard to please Him, I had no lasting joy, no peace, no rest, and no energy left to convince my wife and children that I loved them more than ministry.

Am I now trying to win the approval of human beings, or of God? Or am I trying to please people? If I were still trying to please people, I would not be a servant of Christ. (Galatians 1:10 NIV)

PRAYER TO ENCOUNTER YOUR FATHER

Father, Forgive me for striving for acceptance from those who You have placed in my life. May Your grace, mercy, and faithfulness be absorbed into my being today and every day as I develop Your nature in me. Help me to express Your love to those same people.

JANUARY 7

AN EMPTY HEART

As I began to pastor a small church, my childhood filter system for earning love and acceptance translated ministry into an aggressive zeal to win souls and build the fastest-growing church in our denominational district. Just as I had been willing to do anything to be the best fisherman in the Southeastern United States, now—as a Christian leader—I wanted to achieve my spiritual goals so I would receive the praises of people.

My commitment to "the ministry" was far greater than my commitment to my wife, my children, or any other loving relationships. Everything I did was tainted with a passive anger. My countenance became stern and serious, and my preaching became legalistic and demanding. I focused on biblical truth, but my heart was empty of love. I knew the theology of God's love, but I had not experienced it in my relationships. I could quote verses in Scripture about His unconditional acceptance of us, but it was a foreign concept to me. So because of my lack of knowledge, my wife and family often felt like I have given to ministry what was rightfully theirs; my first affections therefor leaving them with an empty heart also.

But from there you will seek the Lord your God, and you will find Him if you search for Him with all your heart and all your soul. (Deuteronomy 4:29)

PRAYER TO ENCOUNTER YOUR FATHER

Fill my heart with You and Your love, mercy, and grace. I ask You to show me how to love my family first and to give to them what is rightfully theirs; my first affection, love, and attention.

A NECKLACE OF PRIDE

Earlier on as a young Christian leader I began comparing myself to others in ministry, thinking they were more blessed or more gifted than I was. This fostered a competitive attitude, rooted in jealousy, that made it almost impossible for me to relate to other ministers or to anyone in spiritual authority in a healthy way. I became a master of disguises. I would sit at ministers' conferences with a smile on my face but underneath my clever religious mask, I viewed successful church leaders with an attitude of rivalry and judgmentalism. I couldn't stand the thought that they might be successful. If they were blessed, I felt deprived. If they experienced some form of failure, I secretly rejoiced. My heart was sick with pride!

Therefore, pride is their necklace; the garment of violence covers them. (Psalm 73:6)

PRAYER TO ENCOUNTER YOUR FATHER

O Father, search my heart and cut out any pride that is making me spiritually and physically sick. I am totally available to You, Lord, for whatever transformation is needed to keep me near You.

JANUARY 9

BAD HABITS

A couple of years after realizing my issue with pride, I acknowledged my need for healing and went through some deep, healing prayer ministry to uncover the roots of anger, drivenness, and lack of intimacy. This experience impacted so many areas of my life that my wife, Trisha, and I spent the next seven years teaching seminars about emotional healing in many churches throughout the country. I thought I was free!

Trisha and I were effective in ministering to pastors and other church leaders as we helped them find healing in their marriages and families. But I soon realized that my own deep struggle with performance orientation was not resolved. Even after we began the healing prayer ministry, I would often fall back into my old habit patterns of aggressive striving.

For where jealousy and selfish ambition exist, there is disorder and every evil thing. (James 3:16)

PRAYER TO ENCOUNTER YOUR FATHER
You know that habits are hard to break, Father—and bad habits even harder. Help me to keep my heart open to the nudging of the Holy Spirit and Jesus, my perfect role model. I ask You to continue to remind me how to be the person who represents You to the world.

JANUARY 10
THE HYPOCRITE

Outwardly, I was a Christian of moral integrity and godly character. I never had a moral failure and I was an aggressive pursuer of God, praying and reading the Bible for two or three hours a day and doing all the right religious things. But inwardly, I lacked the ability to express love at home, was joyless, had no inner peace, and was driven by spiritual ambition because my identity and value systems were built on position, power, and performance. My faithfulness, duty, and service were not a response of true love to God; they flowed instead from a desire for personal gain and reward.

I could not see the bondage I was in, but my family could! Daily my wife had to wear her own disguises, suppressing the guilt and anger she constantly felt because her need for intimacy and emotional bonding wasn't being met. After twenty years of living like this, Trisha was dying inside and I still needed to change. How to change became my new challenge.

> *When you pray, you are not to be like the hypocrites; for they love to stand and pray in the synagogues and on the street corners so that they may be seen by men. Truly I say to you, they have their reward in full.* (Matthew 6:5)

PRAYER TO ENCOUNTER YOUR FATHER
Father, I pray for eyes to see how others are being affected by my acts, words, and attitude. Please open my eyes, heart, and mind to others' needs and desires. Give me the wisdom to meet those needs and desires.

JANUARY 11
"THE LOOK"

My children didn't fare any better than Trisha. As more legalism crept into my life, the more unyielding and joyless I became as a Christian parent. My three children could never do things well enough for me. I would tell them I loved them, but I constantly pointed out every mistake and shortcoming. I lacked the ability to express love, tender affection, and grace and mercy when they fell short. My attitude of superiority eroded any possibility of trust and intimacy.

Then our 17-year-old son and 14-year-old daughter had closed their spirits to any affection, correction, or advice I tried to offer them. They stopped looking me in the eye because they feared **"the look"** of rejection I often gave. My pride produced a desire in them to rebel. And worst of all, they wanted nothing to do with the angry, legalistic God I modeled to them.

And they were bringing even their babies to Him so that He would touch them, but when the disciples saw it, they began rebuking them. But Jesus called for them, saying, "Permit the children to come to Me, and do not hinder them, for the kingdom of God belongs to such as these." (Luke 18:15-16)

PRAYER TO ENCOUNTER YOUR FATHER
You, heavenly Father, are the only perfect Parent. Yet You give me everything I need to be a good parent to the children You have entrusted to me. May I use every sense, talent, and skill to raise godly children who love and respect You, Lord.

A HAUGHTY SPIRIT

Even though my family life was in shambles, God was still at work. While I was attending a spiritual renewal conference, He began bringing me fresh revelation of His power and grace. There were times when I spent hours weeping at the altar. Yet during these dramatic encounters, I never equated His presence with what I know now as God's *phileo* love—His "demonstrated, natural affection" (see John 16:27). I tended to view God's anointing as His power—or His supernatural ability to do great things. I had no idea that His anointing could actually be a demonstration of His unconditional affection for me.

I was so locked into the trap of performance orientation that I still did not break free from my aggressive striving—even after a powerful visitation of God's Spirit! In fact, at that point, the more favor and visibility in ministry, my addition to hyper-religious activity grew even stronger!

I will silence those who secretly want to slander my friends, and I will not tolerate the proud and arrogant. (Psalm 101:5 Passion Translation)

PRAYER TO ENCOUNTER YOUR FATHER
Father am I blind? Am I just going through the motions of Christianity? I pray that isn't so, but if there is any haughtiness in me, show me and help me destroy it.

THE GOLDEN CALF

My wife and children knew I was worshiping a golden calf of self-centered religious pride. The ministry was all I talked about and lived for, all that brought a smile to my face. I felt inadequate at expressing love and care for my family, so I gave myself to what I could do well—the ministry.

Thinking that it was Trisha who had the real problem, I took her to a conference on emotional healing. During a prayer session, I knelt beside her and someone began to pray, "Father God, take all the men in this room who were never held by their fathers. Hold them close right now. Give them the love their fathers did not know how to give."

The presence of God fell on me immediately. It felt as if hot, liquid love was pouring into my soul. I began crying like a baby. Such displays of emotion were not normal for me. But my mask was off now.

He saw the calf and the dancing; and Moses' anger burned, and he threw the tablets from his hands and shattered them.... He took the calf which they had made and burned it with fire, and ground it to powder, and scattered it over the surface of the water. (Exodus 32:19-20)

PRAYER TO ENCOUNTER YOUR FATHER
Father, burn every idol out of my life, grind to powder everything that keeps me from experiencing Your embrace, scatter every hurt in my past that is preventing me from feeling Your love for me.

JANUARY 14
BREAKTHROUGH!

Suddenly I realized that now, thirty-four years later, my heavenly Father was meeting the deepest need in my heart for a natural demonstration of a father's affectionate love. I had a direct encounter with the *phileo (brotherly love)* of God. As I lay weeping, Father God entered that dark closet of my childhood and held me in His arms. The Holy Spirit washed away much of the guilt, shame, fear of failure and rejection, fear of intimacy, and the fear of love.

My breakthrough finally came! I had never realized how deeply in bondage I was to striving and fear. I had never lowered the walls of protection enough to receive personally a natural demonstration of His love and affection in some of my deepest areas of pain. Every time I looked into my wife and children's eyes because of my lack of tenderness, the tears of repentance would flow. Then I would plead for forgiveness for the times I had harshly misrepresented Father's love to them.

Hope does not disappoint, because the love of God has been poured out within our hearts through the Holy Spirit who was given to us. (Romans 5:5)

PRAYER TO ENCOUNTER YOUR FATHER

Father, I ask You to enter the dark closet of my childhood and hold me in Your arms. I trust You to wash away any guilt, shame, and fears that may be lurking within me. I accept Your grace to make me whole.

BAPTISM OF LOVE

I knew the healing would not come instantly. My children's hearts had been closed to me for years. But now, the brokenness I was experiencing began to open their spirits. Four months after I received this unusual baptism of Father's love, my daughter, Sarah, gave me an essay she had written for her English class. It was titled, "The Greatest Influence in My Life Is…":

The greatest influence in my life is my daddy! Through him, I have seen the eyes of Jesus and felt His unending love! Not very long ago, my daddy was a man to fear. He was Captain Bligh off the H.M.S. Bounty. Now he is as gentle as a lamb, not to mention just as loving. Through watching my daddy change from being a hard man to being tender, he has influenced me to change. His new patience has helped bring me through a very difficult year. Seeing my father love and cherish God, like never before, has done miracles for me….

Love always protects, always trusts, always hopes, always perseveres. Love never fails. (I Corinthians 13:7&8a)

PRAYER TO ENCOUNTER YOUR FATHER
Daddy, thank You for meeting me at the place I need You the most. I am excited about the transformation You are making in me and look forward to every aspect of being fully embraced by Your great love and Your righteous discipline.

WALLS CRUMBLE WITH LOVE

In spite of the breakthroughs I experienced with my children, something in me seemed to hold back from pursuing deeper levels of intimacy with Trisha. I always kept my emotions and feelings under control around her.

During a Father Loves You conference, through the supernatural leading of the Holy Spirit, it was discerned that around age ten I had constructed thick walls of protection in my soul when my father and mother were having extreme difficulties in their marriage. Then what seemed like a river of God's love broke through my fears of intimacy, and the walls I built so long ago began to crumble.

When I arrived home from the conference, I ministered my love to Trisha in healing prayer. She wept for hours as Father took her back to some points of deep wounding in her youth, comforting her with His healing love. The love of God washed away hidden barriers and took us into deeper depths of love for each other.

C'mon God love us with all you've got. That's what we are depending on.
(Psalms 33:22 The Message)

PRAYER TO ENCOUNTER YOUR FATHER

Father, all earthly marriages have ups and downs—I pray that You will bless my marriage, my spouse, and my children. Lead me to a depth of love that reveals Your vast compassion.

LOVE RESTORES

As Father's love has brought restoration of intimacy to my marriage and family, it has changed my whole philosophy of ministry as well. I am no longer striving to be holy or to win God's favor. I don't want to do anything to hinder the intimate, loving relationships that God has given me. Ministry is no longer something that I have to work or strive for; comparisons, competition, and rivalry are fading away. Spiritual ambition is now but a shadow.

Most of the time I am motivated by a deep gratitude for being loved and accepted unconditionally by my Father. Ministry is simply an overflow of the love of God that flows freely through my marriage and family. As I receive His natural demonstration of affection for me, His precious *phileo* love, then I simply give it away to the next person I meet.

> *For this very reason, make every effort to add to your faith goodness; and to goodness, knowledge; and to knowledge, self-control; and to self-control, perseverance; and to perseverance, godliness; and to godliness, mutual affection; and to mutual affection, love.* (2 Peter 1:5-7 NIV)

PRAYER TO ENCOUNTER YOUR FATHER
Thank You, Father, for this new day when I can welcome You once again into my life's journey. Walk along with me, show me Your way, and I will be Your good and faithful son who is a quick learner.

LOVE ONE ANOTHER

Do you know what it means to love God wholeheartedly? Is love for God reflected in faithful Bible reading, rigorous prayer, or strict holiness? I think not. What reveals a genuine love for God is my ability to convince my family and others of my love for them. Without this, everything else finds its rewards in self-love. Doing great things—even religious things like preaching, winning souls, performing miracles, or feeding the poor—all have their own rewards. And we can do these things out of wrong motives. But the Bible tells us that we cannot say we love God if we do not love each other (see 1 John 4:7-8,20).

Do you desire to experience more fully God's love for you? Would you like to encounter His unconditional affection? This devotional contains many of the truths I have experienced and learned about Father's love since I was touched so deeply by Him. As you read and contemplate, I pray you will do much more than develop a healthy theology. I pray you will experience Father God's affectionate embrace, feel His unconditional acceptance, and hear His tender words of love in deeper ways than you have ever known.

If anyone boasts, "I love God," and goes right on hating his brother or sister, thinking nothing of it, he is a liar. If he won't love the person he can see, how can he love the God he can't see? The command we have from Christ is blunt: Loving God includes loving people. You've got to love both.
(1 John 4:20-21 The Message)

PRAYER TO ENCOUNTER YOUR FATHER
Father, I pray for Your warm embrace to surround me. I pray that I will share that loving embrace with others—physically, emotionally, and spiritually.

Prayer of Faith

Perhaps you have not taken the first step toward intimacy with God by seeking forgiveness for your sins against love and inviting God into your life. The way to the Father's love is through His Son. Or perhaps you have accepted salvation and desire to refresh your commitment. You may want to pray this simple prayer of faith.

I believe Jesus is the Son of God and that He died for me on the cross so that my sins will be forgiven. I believe He rose from the dead so I will have eternal life. I believe Jesus is seated with Father God so that I, too, may have intimacy with the Father. I ask You, Jesus, to forgive me of my sins. I invite You to come and dwell in my heart and reveal Father's love to me. Thank You for sacrificing Your life for me and making a way for me to come home to God's love.

If you prayed that prayer for the first time, I encourage you to find someone you know who is a Christian and tell that person. I also encourage you to find a church to attend that teaches God's love, mercy, and grace toward His children—you.

> [Jesus said] *"You don't have to wait for the End. I am, right now, Resurrection and Life. The one who believes in me, even though he or she dies, will live. And everyone who lives believing in me does not ultimately die at all."* (John 11:25 MSG)

Prayer to Encounter Your Father

It is hard for me to understand a gift so great after all my wrongs and sins I've committed. But I do accept Your gift of salvation, Father God. Thank You, Jesus, for Your ultimate sacrifice to redeem me.

FAITHFUL LOVE HEALS

After Nicolae Ceausescu's dictatorship ended in Romania in 1989, the world was horrified to learn that thousands of Romanian children had been forced to live in poorly managed, state-run orphanages. The youngsters were unwanted at birth and completely neglected when they arrived at these crude institutions. But when communism collapsed in Eastern Europe, Westerners rushed into the country to adopt these love-starved children.

But in the mid-1990s, the adoptive parents learned firsthand what psychologists had already predicted. These children, who had never known the love of a father or mother, and who had never been held, consoled, or shown any form of affection, had been mentally and emotionally crippled beyond repair. They developed uncontrollable anger, severe hyperactivity, learning disorders, and compulsive tendencies such as lying, stealing, or hoarding food.

Sadly, many of these children are still struggling with incredible psychological trauma. Others did not live to see their 12th birthdays. They died simply from a lack of expressed love!*

Then Jesus said to her, "O woman, your faith is great; it shall be done for you as you wish." And her daughter was healed at once. (Matthew 15:28)

PRAYER TO ENCOUNTER YOUR FATHER

How tragic it is when children are abused and neglected in this world. Thank You, heavenly Father for never neglecting me, Your child. You yearn to love me intimately—may I always be open to receiving Your love.

---

*Dean Ornish, MD, *Love and Survival: The Scientific Basis for the Healing Power of Intimacy* (New York: HarperCollins Publishers, Inc., 1998).

JANUARY 21

COMPASSION

Some studies have shown that people recover from illness quicker if they have a human being—or even a pet—to supply that tenderness. Caring words, friendship, affectionate touch—all of these have a healing quality. Why? Because we all were created by God to receive and express love. If we do not receive it and learn to give it away, we may suffer emotionally and relationally and never reach our God-given potential.

I understand this today, but there was a time in my life when I thought I could live without love. My father was the same way. He was part of the self-made World War II generation. He knew what it meant to claw and scrape through economic hardship without anyone else's help. He was a survivor. He had closed his heart to love so that he couldn't feel the pain that throbbed inside his soul. And he passed that pain on to me like some kind of inherited disease. Being emotionally detached became part of my personality.

For the Lord your God is a compassionate God; He will not fail you nor destroy you nor forget the covenant with your fathers which He swore to them. (Deuteronomy 4:31)

PRAYER TO ENCOUNTER YOUR FATHER

Father, it is too easy to shut out people rather than let them into my life. I know this is not Your will for me—or for them. I pray that right now my heart will be open and loving to everyone You bring into my life.

JANUARY 22
AS I HAVE LOVED YOU

By the time I was 12 years of age, I had decided that I didn't need anybody. By age 24, I was captain of my own fishing boat. I was strong, self-confident, and detached. I learned to be successful, provide for my family, and build my reputation. I loved it when people said, "Man, how did you survive that storm? How did you stay out on the ocean for so many days?" I didn't need intimacy with another person. It was just me and the sea. Because I couldn't bond in healthy relationships, I bonded to the ocean and to my career as a commercial snapper fisherman.

When I accepted Jesus, I still didn't know how to bond in healthy relationships, and I began searching for another counterfeit affection. I found it in the ministry. There is nothing easier than self-deception. I thought love was about what we do. I didn't know that we were created by God to receive love and to express love.

> *A new commandment I give to you, that you love one another, even as I have loved you, that you also love one another. By this all men will know that you are My disciples, if you have love for one another.* (John 13:34-35)

PRAYER TO ENCOUNTER YOUR FATHER
Teach me, Father, to become dependent on You. Show me, Lord, how to bond with You, which will lead me to love and serve others—giving You all the glory for my good works.

JANUARY 23
THE GREATEST OF THESE

Because we were born into a sinful world, and because our sinful nature was bent toward believing the worst about God—rather than choosing to know Him as the loving Father He is—we find that receiving His love and giving it away to others is a struggle even after we initially come to accept God's plan of salvation. Our minds need to be renewed by the Holy Spirit until we truly can say as the apostle John declared, *"And so we know and rely on the love God has for us. God is love. **Whoever lives in love lives in God, and God in them**"* (1 John 4:16 NIV).

Notice that it does *not* say that God lives in the person who preaches eloquently or who attends church every week or who fasts 50 days every year. It does *not* say that God lives in the person who prays faithfully every day or who knows the mysteries of God or who wins souls. It says that God lives in the person who lives in love.

> *...but do not have love, I am nothing.* (1 Corinthians 13:2b)

PRAYER TO ENCOUNTER YOUR FATHER
All this emphasis on love makes me feel uncomfortable. I'm not used to focusing on love. Lord, help me to reveal love more openly for my family, friends, colleagues, and especially You.

LOVE IS NOT

Are you comfortable with love? Are you continually filled with the understanding of how much Father loves you? Are you aware that Father takes delight in you and that He thinks good thoughts about you all the time? (See Jer. 29:11.) Do you realize that He feels nothing but perfect love when He thinks about you? First Corinthians 13:5 (NKJV) tells us that *"love thinks no evil."* Many of us struggle through life because we are afraid to receive and give love. We are basically afraid of intimacy (into-me-see).

At the core of our fear is deception. We find it difficult to love because we have believed a lie about God. The enemy, who is described as *"the father of lies"* in John 8:44, continually lies to us about the loving nature of Father. If the enemy of our souls can convince us that God has rejected us, is upset with us, or has withdrawn from us because of some sin we committed, he knows we will hide from God and try to live our lives performing well enough to earn His love, thus increasing the depth of our guilt and shame.

> [Love] *does not dishonor others, it is not self-seeking, it is not easily angered, it keeps no record of wrongs.* (1 Corinthians 13:5 NIV)

PRAYER TO ENCOUNTER YOUR FATHER

Father, I seek greater understanding of Your love. I understand that I don't have to fear being close to You any longer. I refuse to listen to the enemy's lies and trust only in You alone.

JANUARY 25
IN OUR IMAGE

Understanding the following four principles, you can break through the lies and fears that prevent you from truly knowing and believing that God loves you unconditionally.

Key #1: Self-image helps determine our depth of intimacy.
You were created in God's image, and God is love. If you are uncomfortable with God, you are uncomfortable with love. If you are uncomfortable with love, you are uncomfortable with yourself. If you are uncomfortable with yourself, you are going to be uncomfortable with others. If you do not believe you are lovable, you may find it difficult to receive God's gift of unmerited love and favor. And it may be difficult to enjoy healthy relationships with others if you view yourself differently from the way God views you.

In whose image do you walk? If you derive your self-worth from how well you do your job or from some kind of spiritual achievement or ministry success, then your self-image is wired to what *you do* instead of what *Jesus did* for you on the cross.

Then God said, "Let us make mankind in our image." (Isaiah 66:9 NIV)

God is love. (I John 4:8b)

PRAYER TO ENCOUNTER YOUR FATHER
Please help me extract my self-worth and self-esteem from You, Father, not the world. Only You love me unconditionally—and I am made in Your image.

IN OUR IMAGE
KEY #1, CONTINUED

Do you see yourself as created in God's image and a lover of other people? When you are away from your family, do you think about them, waiting for the moment when you can wrap your arms around them again? Are you able to share openly and honestly with your spouse about your deepest hurts and struggles? Are you free to shower praise and affection on your children? Are you able to encourage them—or do they know only of your correction, criticism, and disapproval? Are you free to love friends and family members around you?

Or have you bought into the lie that says you do not need to express love? Men in particular struggle with this ungodly belief. When I start talking about intimacy, tenderness, and emotional vulnerability, many guys head for the door. Many men would prefer to live their lives inside a thick suit of armor—always pretending, always with their guard up, never sharing their true feelings. They have become numb to love. They bought a lie that says men don't feel, men don't cry, men don't get in touch with their emotions. Some men even believe that it is not masculine to be tender and loving but Jesus wept. He wept at loss, He wept at man's unbelief but He never shamed us or ever never stopped loving us.

Jesus wept. (John 11:35)

PRAYER TO ENCOUNTER YOUR FATHER
Father, help me shed my thick suit of armor, help me to stop pretending, show me how to love others as You love me. Break my heart when to know when I am criticizing instead of encouraging.

IN OUR IMAGE
KEY #1, CONTINUED

Without love we have nothing because we are not abiding in God. Apostle Paul says, *"And if I give all my possessions to feed the poor, and if I surrender my body to be burned, but do not have love, it profits me nothing"* (1 Cor. 13:3). Why would someone give all their possessions to feed the poor and yet not make such sacrifices from a motive of love? Why would they go to the mission field and die in some developing country and yet not demonstrate affection and love for their own family members? Why would a successful preacher give all of his time to the ministry and yet neglect or even abuse his wife and children?

These people would do these things because they are trying to earn love and acceptance by their actions. They are trying to earn God's approval because they don't truly understand His love. They have believed a lie, and it has helped warp their self-image. A Pharisee once came to Jesus to find out what the most important commandment was. He probably thought that he could earn Jesus' approval. He must have been surprised when instead, Jesus said, *"You shall love the Lord your God with all your heart, and with all your soul, and with all your mind.' This is the great and foremost commandment. The second is like it, 'You shall love your neighbor as yourself.' On these two commandments depend the whole Law and the Prophets"* (Matt. 22:37-40).

> *You shall love the Lord your God...and love your neighbor as yourself....*
> (Matthew 22:37-39)

PRAYER TO ENCOUNTER YOUR FATHER
May I follow these two commandments of Yours from this moment until the day I come home to be with You Father.

In Our Image
Key #1, Continued

Jesus said it is all about love, but we want to make this Christian life about everything else. We want it to be about rules or spiritual formulas or how we can impress God or win His favor. We have put the Great Commission before the Great Commandment.

Born-again, Spirit-filled people who are eager to learn the latest spiritual truths and jump through the latest spiritual hoops have never learned the Bible's most elementary lesson. In churches across this country, thousands upon thousands of Christians who grew up singing the kindergarten chorus "Jesus Loves Me, This I Know" have not experienced this truth to the deepest depths of their core need—**receiving God's love and giving it away to the next person they meet**.

> *But a Samaritan, who was on a journey, came upon him; and when he saw him, he felt compassion, and came to him and bandaged up his wounds, pouring oil and wine on them; and he put him on his own beast, and brought him to an inn and took care of him. On the next day he took out two denarii and gave them to the innkeeper and said, 'Take care of him; and whatever more you spend, when I return I will repay you.' Which of these three do you think proved to be a neighbor to the man who fell into the robbers' hands?" And he said, "The one who showed mercy toward him." Then **Jesus said to him, "Go and do the same."*** (Luke 10:33-37)

PRAYER TO ENCOUNTER YOUR FATHER
Father, I did grow up singing that song—and I will start today to experience the truth of that fundamental song. I ask for You to open my eyes each day to see those whom You have called me to example Your great Commandment to. To receive Your love and give it away to the next person You prompt me to love.

INTIMACY

Key #2: Recognize your need for intimacy.
As much as you may think that you need to be independent and self-sufficient to survive, you were not created to live apart from God or others. Even Jesus Himself, who was the very image of God, was dependent on His Father. John 5:19 tells us that *"the Son can do nothing of Himself, unless it is something He sees the Father doing."* Through this humility and dependence, Christ has been given all dominion and authority.

My brother and I had the opportunity to really talk for the first time in thirty years. We were in the hospital with my father, discussing his impending death, and the conversation turned to the paths our lives had taken. My brother said to me, "You know, one thing I can say is that nobody has ever given me anything. Everything I've ever gotten has been because I've worked hard to get it." Thinking back over my own life, I responded, "Yeah, that's what happened to me, too." We were priding ourselves on our self-sufficiency and our independence, but we did not realize that that attitude is completely contrary to the nature God wants us to have. Both of us have struggled with intimacy and expressing love throughout much of our lives.

> *Then Jesus came to them and said, "All authority in heaven and on earth has been given to me."* (Matthew 28:18 NIV)

PRAYER TO ENCOUNTER YOUR FATHER
I realize now, Father, that everything I have and will have is because You allowed it. You are the Source of everything good in my life. Thank You.

INTIMACY
KEY #2, CONTINUED

Have you bought into the idea that you should be able to pull yourself up by your own bootstraps and take care of yourself without help from anyone else? Would you rather close yourself off from other people than take a chance on really getting to know them? If so, it is a sin against love, believing that your self-sufficiency is all that you need. It may seem easier to focus on taking care of your own problems and surviving in a dog-eat-dog world, but in the long run you will have missed out on what is most important in life.

As human beings we have been created by God with the need for intimacy—to know and to be known. And His perfect plan is to provide us with a way to meet that need—fellowship with Him and with each other. Why do we need to be intimate, loving beings? Because we were created for love! But before we can truly abide in this love that God has for us, we are to first recognize that our need for such love exists. We are to realize that we cannot meet all of our needs on our own. We cannot control our emotions and destiny without it having harmful generational impact.

But showing love to a thousand generations of those who love me [God] *and keep my commandments.* (Exodus 20:6b)

PRAYER TO ENCOUNTER YOUR FATHER
Father, with Your guidance, I want to learn how to love so that my legacy will be pointing to You and You alone.

INTIMACY
KEY #2, CONTINUED

When God created Adam, He placed him in the Garden of Eden. God was so pleased with this creation that He called it *"very good"* (Gen. 1:31). Adam's needs were provided for: wonderful food to eat, a beautiful garden to enjoy, and unhindered, intimate fellowship with his Creator. Adam walked with God every day, with no shadow of sin separating them. Yet the Lord God knew this was not enough, saying, *"It is not good for the man to be alone; I will make him a helper suitable for him"* (Gen. 2:18). He then began to bring all the beasts of the field, the birds of the sky, every living creature, before Adam to see what he would call them. This was not just to give Adam something to do in his spare time. God had a purpose—to show Adam his need for intimacy.

Why do you suppose Eve was not created at the same time as Adam? Wasn't God smart enough to realize that man would be lonely? Didn't He know that He'd eventually have to create Eve? Of course God did. **But He wanted Adam to have an understanding of his need.** Before Eve was created, Adam's relationship with God became cemented, but he had also been created with the need for intimacy with another human being. When Adam began to understand that need, he was later able to truly love and cherish the woman God brought to him.

Now the man called his wife's name Eve, because she was the mother of all the living. (Genesis 3:20)

PRAYER TO ENCOUNTER YOUR FATHER
Father, Your wisdom and knowing of everything amazes me continually. I yearn to understand intimacy in relationships and the need for them. Help me to be able to love those You love and have sent to me to love and cherish.

INTIMACY
KEY #2, CONTINUED

For many years, I kept my relationship with God separate from my wife. For seven years, I prayed two, sometimes three hours a day, with my wife shut out of my prayer closet. It was just God and me, together waiting for her to get her life straightened out. I believed I was the holy and righteous one because I was doing all the right, religious things, but all the while I was unconsciously neglecting my relationship with my wife.

God wants us to have fellowship with Him, but a true relationship with God will not come at the expense of intimacy with our spouses and families. If you spend ten to eleven hours a day ministering to other people, but you spend very little time each day ministering to your spouse, your life is dangerously out of balance. I may have been focusing on a right relationship with God, but I had not recognized the deep need I had for true intimacy with my wife and family.

> *The Man said, "Finally! Bone of my bone, flesh of my flesh! Name her Woman for she was made from Man." Therefore a man leaves his father and mother and embraces his wife. They become one flesh. The two of them, the Man and his Wife, were naked, but they felt no shame.* (Genesis 2:23-24 MSG)

PRAYER TO ENCOUNTER YOUR FATHER
Thank You, Lord, for my spouse (or for my future spouse). I will commit to finding true intimacy with her and with my family—for this is Your desire for Your family.

FEBRUARY 2

RISKS AND TRUST

Key #3: Embrace your responsibility for intimacy.
Many relationship problems we experience are a result of our unwillingness to know others and be known. This usually happens because we have been hurt or disappointed at some point in our lives, and we don't want to take that risk again. So we either deny our need for intimacy, or we place the blame on someone else—the person who hurt us.

Do you find yourself holding back in your relationships, unwilling to share your true self with your partner or mate? Have you been hurt in the past and find it difficult to trust? Are you afraid of further disappointment if you allow yourself to love again? Jesus came to restore our capacity for love and intimacy, despite all the many times we may have been hurt. In Jesus, we inherit all the things that had been lost in the Fall—not only healing, joy, and salvation, but also our capacity to love fully and to be loved. By accepting God's plan of salvation, you will receive all kinds of blessings, but if you don't have love and intimacy in your relationships, you have missed out on the fullness of what Jesus died for—to restore you to intimacy. It is your responsibility to choose to allow intimacy to become a priority in your life.

> *For the Holy Spirit makes God's fatherhood real to us as He whispers into our innermost being; "you are God's beloved child." And since we are His true children, we qualify to share all His treasure, for indeed we are heirs of God Himself.* (Romans 8:16-17 The Passion Translation)

PRAYER TO ENCOUNTER YOUR FATHER
I choose right now, Father, to accept and allow intimacy to be a priority in my life. Help me to understand that You see me as Your child, therefor Your heir. I thank You that I have full access to Your kingdom, as Your child and joint heir with Jesus.

FEBRUARY 3

RISKS AND TRUST
KEY #3, CONTINUED

As Christians, what is the most important question we can ask of ourselves? How much of the Scripture have I studied? How many Bible conferences have I attended? How much faith do I have? All of these things are important, but they are not as important as the burning question: "Father, how can I receive Your love and give it to the next person I meet?" When I first began to ask myself that question, I tried to ask it daily. Then I learned that I needed to ask it hourly. Now I seek to ask it of myself every ten or fifteen minutes. I can't wait to demonstrate Father God's love to everyone I meet, and especially to my wife and family, because this attitude begins at home. If you are showing love to everyone else but denying true intimacy with your spouse, you are not embracing your full responsibility for walking in Father's love.

In our modern Christian culture, the responsibility for intimacy has often fallen upon the female members of the household. The lie that men aren't supposed to feel or be tender and caring if they are to be considered masculine has pervaded even our church circles. Many Christian men shy away from the vulnerability that comes from sharing not only their emotions, but also their spiritual lives, with their wives and families. And when that happens, women often take up the slack.

With tender humility and quiet patience, always demonstrate gentleness and generous love toward one another, especially toward those who may try your patience. (Ephesians 4:2 The Passion Translation)

PRAYER TO ENCOUNTER YOUR FATHER
Father I thank You that each member of my household is vital to the success of this family. I ask that Your love will permeate our home and then spill out into our neighborhood and relationships.

FEBRUARY 4

RISKS AND TRUST
KEY #3, CONTINUED

When the Fall occurred in the Garden of Eden, both Adam and Eve sinned before God. But there was a difference between the two of them. Paul tells us in Second Corinthians 11:3 that *"the serpent deceived Eve by his craftiness,"* but in Romans 5:14, he tells us that Adam willfully sinned. Adam and Eve were both faced with the serpent; Eve fell under satan's web of deception, but Adam sinned willfully. Although Eve had also sinned, Adam was the one God first held responsible. But when confronted with his sin, he turned the blame onto the woman—and at that point, the door for male irresponsibility in intimacy was opened wide.

Too many Christian men struggle with fears: fear of rejection, failure, giving love, receiving love, and fear of intimacy. They find a false sense of security in their careers, or even their ministries, because they do not want to face the uncomfortableness and insecurity they might experience if they were truly vulnerable with their wives. But God has called husbands to love their wives as Jesus loves the Church. Jesus sacrificed His very life for His Bride; how many of us men are willing to sacrifice our self-love to meet the emotional needs of our wives? Both men and women are to understand the importance of fostering intimacy in their lives and assume responsibility for taking the steps necessary to achieve it.

Then the Lord God called to the man, and said to him, "Where are you?" (Genesis 3:9)

PRAYER TO ENCOUNTER YOUR FATHER
Father, am I hiding from You? Am I hiding from my spouse and family behind my career or ministry? Expose me, Lord, bring me out from my hiding place into Your presence.

FEBRUARY 5
WORTHY

Key #4: Being who God created you to be.

So many of us base our self-worth on the things we do and what we can achieve, rather than who we are. This was a deception I struggled against for many years. I constantly asked myself, *How many people have been set free under my ministry this week? How many hours have I spent in the Word and prayer? How many people have I witnessed or ministered to this week?* I began to live my life by the numbers. When I began to focus so strongly on what I had or had not achieved, I fell off center of God's love, away from the focus He wanted me to have. And that affected all of my relationships because it short-circuited my ability to be vulnerable with others.

Do you base your self-worth on how well your career is going? Do you need other people to praise your accomplishments in order to feel good about yourself? Let me ask the question another way. If you didn't get that promotion, or if you lost your job altogether, would you still feel good about yourself because you know in your heart that you are God's favored child? Would you live your life giving His love away to others? If you can't answer yes to these questions, you might be basing your self-worth on your own accomplishments rather than on who God created you to be—a gift of His love to others.

> *The women sang as they played, and said, "Saul has slain his thousand and David his ten thousands." Then Saul became very angry, for this saying displeased him...."* (1 Samuel 18:7-8)

PRAYER TO ENCOUNTER YOUR FATHER

Father, I don't want to compare myself to others, but it comes so naturally. Please infuse me with Your supernatural wisdom to see myself as You see me, a gift of Your love.

FEBRUARY 6

HEALTHY RELATIONSHIPS

The four keys I have shared with you are important to help you break through the deceptions about intimacy into which you may have bought. They can help you begin to foster genuine intimacy in your relationships. But I have learned that you can't withdraw from the bank what hasn't already been deposited there. If you have never received genuine unconditional love in your own life, it may be difficult for you to demonstrate that kind of love to others. And if you have experienced not just a lack of love, but also any kind of abuse, you may think it impossible for you to foster healthy relationships. Until you have an encounter with Father God and allow His unconditional, affectionate love to fill the hurt and empty places in your heart, it may be difficult to pour out love to others.

Before we can have genuine relationships with others, it is helpful to first experience the healing comfort of our heavenly Father in those areas of hurt and rejection in our souls (mind, will, emotion, and personality). You may have forgiven those people in your past who hurt you. You may have even experienced deliverance from inner vows you made as a result of those painful events. But have you allowed Father God to wrap His loving arms around you and comfort you in those areas in which you have never felt comfort before?

I am not saying this as though I were issuing an order but to stir you to greater love by mentioning the enthusiasm of the Macedonians as a challenge to you. (2 Corinthians 2:8)

PRAYER TO ENCOUNTER YOUR FATHER

Hello, Father. It's me again. And I'm still trying to be the person You want me to be. I realize I can't do that without the help of the Holy Spirit. I give You permission to stir me with the enthusiasm to example Your love for others through me.

PRAYER FOR AN OPEN HEART

If you want to experience intimacy and fulfillment in your life, begin by opening your heart to the Father and praying this prayer:

Father God, I believe that I have been created for love, to experience Your healing love, and to share that love in my relationships with others. It's not enough to have success in my life or in my ministry if I don't have a relationship built upon expressed love with You or with my spouse and family.

I renounce the lie that I am not a lover, that I cannot open up my emotions or allow myself to be hurt again. Instead, I ask You to wrap Your arms around me, to comfort me in those areas of hurt and pain, and to fill me up so that I can in turn share Your love with those around me. I choose to love my family as Christ loves the Church and gave Himself for her.

I make a commitment to ask myself hourly, "Father, how can I receive Your love and then give it away to the next person I meet?" I want to live my life as an expression of Your love, no longer focusing on my own worldly successes, but allowing Your character to shine through me to others. In Jesus' name, amen.

...and the Lord opened her heart to receive Paul's message. (Acts 16:14b The Passion Translation)

PRAYER TO ENCOUNTER YOUR FATHER
Repeat the prayer above and meditate on the sentence that seems the most meaningful to you right now.

FATHER'S INFLUENCE

"Jack," Trisha said, "I love you, and I love Sarah, but if you don't hurry up and come home to deal with her, you may not have a daughter when you finally get here!" When I asked her what had happened, she replied, "I'm so tired of her negativity and mood spells. I honestly can't take living in the same house with her anymore! I need you to come home." I told Trisha that I could not cut my trip short and didn't want to deal with it harshly over the phone.

When I first accepted the Lord, my life was transformed, and I was set free from drugs, alcohol, and pornography—all at one time—never to return. But I easily fell into law and legalism. Becoming a legalistic holiness pastor, I preached hellfire and brimstone to my congregation. I valued obedience over relationship.

This was the dad Sarah expected to meet when I arrived home. But driving back, the Holy Spirit prompted me to handle the situation in a different way, not with my usual lack of grace, but with the unconditional love of Father God. With that on my heart, I prayed the entire way home, "God, I really want to be a representation of Your love, not of the home environment I grew up in. I want to handle it the way You would handle it, demonstrating Your fatherly comforting heart to Sarah."

The Lord is slow to anger and abundant in lovingkindness, forgiving iniquity and transgression; but He will by no means clear the guilty. (Numbers 14:18)

PRAYER TO ENCOUNTER YOUR FATHER

Father, I ask for wisdom and grace when faced with unpleasant situations or puzzling problems. I thank You in advance for always being available to hear my prayers.

FEBRUARY 9
SOOTHING WRATH

Continuing the Sarah story from yesterday, when I arrived home, it was mid-morning, and no one was home but my daughter. As I walked through the front door, she was waiting for me with a look of dread, failure, and utter dejection on her face. She knew she had blown it.

This time, however, I didn't come down on her immediately; I didn't even give her that you-have-been-such-a-disappointment-to-your-father-again look. Instead, I invited Sarah to go swimming. For an hour we swam, played, and laughed, but all the while, Sarah was waiting for the hammer to fall. By the time we returned to the house, the rest of the family was home. Acceptance, laughter, and play had caused Sarah to relax. As I began unpacking my suitcase, I could hear her singing in the shower, "I've got the joy, joy, joy, joy down in my heart…and I'm so happy, so very happy…." Trisha immediately looked at me and said, "Can you believe **what a difference the presence of the father makes** in the house?"

When you fail and know you deserve the rod of judgment, what does the presence of the Father represent to you? Do you picture God as the great policeman in the sky, waiting to pounce on any infraction of the law you may commit? Or is He your loving Daddy who brings the joy back to your heart, whom you can't wait to spend time with, and who can't wait to spend time with you?

Our mouths were filled with laughter, our tongues with songs of joy. Then it was said among the nations, "The Lord has done great things for them." (Psalm 126:2)

PRAYER TO ENCOUNTER YOUR FATHER
Father, I sometimes think of You as a harsh disciplinarian, yet deep in myself I know You are the most kind, loving, and understanding Father I could ever dream of having. Thank You!

Necessary Discipline

I did discipline Sarah later that day for her attitude and the way she had treated her mother and brothers. But I did it with honor, acceptance, and love. When most Christians sin, they cringe, as Sarah did, expecting the full brunt of an angry God's wrath upon their heads. Most of us, when we have failed, picture Father wagging His finger in our face in disapproval, rather than envisioning His running toward us with arms wide open, eager to welcome us back into His presence. (See Luke 15:20.)

God certainly disciplines us, but not in a way that imparts shame, fear, or accusation. His motivation behind discipline is His vast and eternal love for us. (See Heb. 12:6-10.) He does it for our good and betterment because He wants the very best for us. *"There is no fear in love; but perfect love casts out fear, because fear involves punishment…"* (1 John 4:18).

For many years, I believed in and vigorously preached that sinners are protected from the wrath of Father God only by the compassionate nature of Jesus, who paid for our sins on the cross. This almost schizophrenic view of the nature of God—that Jesus loves us but His stern Father is perpetually angry with us—has been ingrained in the mindset of many Christians.

My dear child, don't shrug off God's discipline, but don't be crushed by it either. It's the child he loves that he disciplines; the child he embraces, he also corrects. (Hebrews 12:6 MSG)

Prayer to Encounter Your Father

Father, it seems I lean on a loving relationship with Jesus, but can become apprehensive when considering intimacy with You. Forgive me. I ask You to help me to be able to receive Your discipline as correction to my behavior because You do actually love me.

FEBRUARY 11
TRUST HIM

If you walked into a church service and spotted someone you knew was angry with you, you would probably head to the opposite side of the church to look for a seat. When there is a grudge being held or an ongoing disagreement, the people involved usually find a way to conveniently avoid one another, sometimes for years—even in marriages.

When we believe that God is angry with us, it is not easy for us to accept His love or draw near to Him. When we commit a sin, we think, *Oh, what a holy God He is! And, oh, what a wretched sinner I am!* Our image of God directly contrasts with the image we have of ourselves. When we feel ashamed or guilty, we often run and hide as Adam did in the Garden of Eden.

Because we immediately dread God's wrath falling on our heads when we sin, we cannot freely run to Him for forgiveness; instead, we run to anything that seems safe and from which we can derive comfort. For some people, their addictions provide a safe and familiar environment, but running to addictions can also cause them to spiral dangerously into a cycle of sin from which it is difficult to break free. For others, hyper-religious activity brings a sense of penance and gives false relief, thus offering a sense of comfort.

Trust in the Lord with all your heart and do not lean on your own understanding. In all your ways acknowledge Him, and He will make your paths straight. (Proverbs 3:5-6)

PRAYER TO ENCOUNTER YOUR FATHER
Correct my incorrect perspective of You and help me to see You as You are—trustworthy, faithful, and loving.

THE NATURE OF FATHER GOD

Are you afraid to come before God and freely confess your sin? Do you instead try to forget about what you have done, perhaps drowning your guilt in alcohol or some other addiction? Or, as I did, throw yourself into a religious frenzy, trying to atone for your sin and appease an angry God with your good works and religious disciplines and duty? If you follow any of these deadly cycles, you may be being influenced by a religion of fear and intimidation, and you need a new God for your old problems. You need a new image of God!

Religion has misrepresented the nature of Father God and portrayed Him to be something He is not. The idea that Father is the vengeful arm of the Trinity and that Jesus is the compassionate One pleading for our undeserved pardon, is not just harmful to our relationship with God, but it runs totally contrary to the teaching of Jesus.

To gain a true picture of Father's feelings toward His children, it is best to turn to the One whose purpose it was to show us the Father. Jesus spent three years in ministry, demonstrating His Father's heart of compassion as He forgave sinners, healed the sick, and raised the dead. But even after all that time, Philip, one of Jesus' closest followers, echoed a sentiment that many Christians today would still say, *"Show us the Father, and it is enough for us"* (John 14:8).

[Jesus said] *"If you had known Me, you would have known My Father also; from now on you know Him, and have seen Him."* (John 14:6b&7)

PRAYER TO ENCOUNTER YOUR FATHER

Dear heavenly Father, when I think of You, I will think of Jesus and the Holy Spirit, as You are Three in One. May I encounter the whole of You right now, today!

THE NATURE OF FATHER GOD
(CONTINUED)

From yesterday's story, Jesus' response to Philip is very telling: *"Have I been so long with you, and yet you have not come to know Me, Philip? He who has seen Me has seen the Father…Do you not believe that I am in the Father, and the Father is in Me? The words that I say to you I do not speak on My own initiative, but the Father abiding in Me does His works"* (John 14:9-10).

Jesus is the image of the invisible God and the exact representation of God's nature (see Col. 1:15; Heb. 1:4). The nature of the Father is the same as that of Jesus: He is love. Even when we sin, Father still loves us, and He longs to be the One to whom we run for comfort and forgiveness. God is love, and His perfect love casts out all fear (see 1 John 4:18). Everything Jesus did on earth shows us the heart of the Father—a heart of love and compassion, not one of wrath and judgment.

When we have an accurate understanding of the nature of our heavenly Father, we don't possess an unhealthy fear of Him; we don't have to jump through hoops to earn His love. The religion of fear will have no hold on us; and even when we sin, we can still crawl up into the lap of Father God and seek His love and forgiveness.

He is the image of the invisible God, the firstborn of all creation.
(Colossians 1:15)

PRAYER TO ENCOUNTER YOUR FATHER
Thank You, Jesus, for being the very image of our God, for being the most perfect role model we could ever hope to imagine.

YOU'RE GOD'S HAPPY THOUGHT!

The following Scriptures demonstrate how, in Christ, you are Father God's "happy thought." They reveal His true nature and thoughts toward you. As you meditate on these verses, allow the Holy Spirit to begin to transform your image of Father into that of a loving Daddy who longs to care for you. You may even want to copy these verses and stick them on a mirror or your fridge. Or better yet, memorize them!

- Psalms 139:17—How precious are your thoughts toward me, how vast is the sum of them.

- Psalms 40:5—Many o Lord my God, are your wonderful works, which you have done and your thoughts toward us cannot be recounted. They are more than can be numbered.

- Jeremiah 29:11 (Amplified Bible)—For I know the thoughts and plans that I have for you, says the Lord, thoughts and plans for welfare and peace and not for evil, to give you hope in your final outcome

- I Cor. 13—Love thinks no evil.

PRAYER TO ENCOUNTER YOUR FATHER

Father I have never thought about how much You think about me personally. It seems unfathomable that You could think of me so often but Your word says You do. I thank You for Your plan for my life and how You have thought through each detail of my purpose. I ask You to remind me daily of this.

FATHER GOD'S MY HAPPY THOUGHT!

The following are more verses to absorb as your own, to contemplate, and possibly memorize.

- And the Holy Spirit's **intense cravings** hinder your old self-life from dominating you. (Gal. 5:16 The Passion Translation)

- My Father loves me just as much as He loves His Son, Jesus. *"I in them and You in Me, that they may be perfected in unity, so that the world may know that You sent Me, and loved them, even as You have loved Me"* (John 17:23).

- Even when I have sinned, Father loves me and asks me to sit beside Him. *"But God, being rich in mercy, because of His great love with which He loved us, even when we were dead in our transgressions, made us alive together with Christ (by grace you have been saved), and raised us up with Him, and seated us with Him in the heavenly places in Christ Jesus"* (Eph. 2:4-6).

- My Father wants me to overflow with His love. *"and to know the love of Christ which surpasses knowledge, that you may be filled up to all the fullness of God"* (Eph. 3:19).

- James 5:11b The Message, God Cares, He cares right down to the last detail.

PRAYER TO ENCOUNTER YOUR FATHER

Father I have never thought about Your having intense cravings for relationship with me. I thank You for the plan You had to deliver me from my old fleshly behaviors. I thank You that You think of me daily and that You care right down to the last detail of my daily living.

HAPPY THOUGHTS
(CONTINUED)

- Troubles do not separate me from God's love. *"Who shall separate us from the love of Christ? Shall tribulation, or distress, or persecution, or famine, or nakedness, or peril, or sword? But in all these things we overwhelmingly conquer through Him who loved us"* (Rom. 8:35,37).

- In God's love I am hidden from sin. *"For you have died and your life is hidden with Christ in God"* (Col. 3:3).

- I am filled with God's power, love, and a sound mind. *"For God has not given us a spirit of fear, but of power and of love and of a sound mind"* (2 Tim. 1:7 NKJV).

- In God's love I find grace and mercy. *"Let us therefore draw near with confidence to the throne of grace, that we may receive mercy and may find grace to help in time of need"* (Heb. 4:16).

- Father's perfect love for me displaces my fears. *"There is no fear in love; but perfect love casts out fear, because fear involves punishment, and the one who fears is not perfected in love"* (1 John 4:18).

- The evil one has no right to touch me while I am in my Father's arms. *"We know that no one who is born of God sins; but He who was born of God keeps him and the evil one does not touch him"* (1 John 5:18).

PRAYER TO ENCOUNTER YOUR FATHER
When I am fearful or anxious about some this or that, Your Word brings immediate comfort through the presence of the Holy Spirit. Lord God, how can I ever thank You enough.

FEBRUARY 17
FATHER'S GOOD PLEASURE

Several years ago, I was visiting my father in Florida, and we spent some time on the golf course. I was struggling with my swing when, finally, my dad handed me one of his clubs and said, "Try this. See how well you hit with it."

When I used that club, I hit the ball longer and straighter than I ever had before. I understood why when I realized that the club Dad had handed me had a $350 price tag! But when my father saw how well the club worked for me, he said without any hesitation whatsoever, "Take it, son. It's yours." It was in my father's heart to bless his son.

Later, I took my son, Micah, out to the golf course to play with my new set of clubs. He was 19 and in a difficult, rebellious phase of life. That particular day he was playing very poorly, and although his dream was to one day be a golf pro, on that day I was "eating his lunch." Frustrated and angry, he began to complain, "You got those new Ping clubs. It's no wonder you're winning!" His attitude became worse and worse until finally I got off the golf cart and switched my golf bag with his.

"Son, my clubs have become yours," I said to him. "You own them now. Do your best with them—that's all I ask." I did keep that new 300 dollar putter though Ha!

Do not fear, little flock, for it is your Father's good pleasure to give you the kingdom. (Luke 12:32 NKJV)

PRAYER TO ENCOUNTER YOUR FATHER
As it is Your good pleasure to bless me, I pray, God, that You will show me how and when to bless others. I want to be a giver—not just a taker in life. I also know that You will never withhold any good thing from my life.

FATHER'S CHARACTER

Even though Micah had a miserable attitude and had done nothing to deserve my generosity, I gave him my brand-new set of golf clubs, worth almost a thousand dollars. I did it because it's in the heart of a father to bless his children. I wanted my son to be blessed, to have more and better things than me, in spite of his attitude.

That is also the nature of Father God. He sends rain on the just and the unjust. He blesses the deserving and the undeserving, simply because it is His character to love. Although He disciplines His children, Father does not judge or condemn them (see John 5:22-24). Father is patient, Father is kind, and is not jealous; Father does not brag and is not arrogant, does not act unbecomingly; He does not seek His own, is not provoked, does not take into account a wrong suffered, does not rejoice in unrighteousness, but rejoices with the truth; bears all things, believes all things, hopes all things (1 Cor. 13:4-7).

When you come to believe that you truly are Father God's happy thought, you will be able to run freely to Him when you sin or when you experience times of distress. He will become your own happy thought because you have encountered firsthand His perfect love and acceptance, and His unconditional love displaces our fears of intimacy.

Truly, truly, I say to you, he who hears My word, and believes Him who sent Me, has eternal life, and does not come into judgment, but has passed out of death into life. (John 5:24)

PRAYER TO ENCOUNTER YOUR FATHER

Father I want to encounter You, in Your image. I want this to become my highest priority. I want to feel Your embrace, Jesus, this really is my desire.

WHAT ABOUT...

There are those who say, "What about God's anger in the Old Testament?" Love is passionate, and in the Old Testament we see a loving Father passionately protecting His children from those wanting to defile, corrupt, and hurt them. Others say that this theology makes God too common and lessens people's awe and fear of Him.

May I ask you—which Father would you have more respect for: an angry One or a loving, forgiving One? Which God does your family want to be most like? To which God would sinners be most attracted? With which God would Jesus want you to spend eternity? If you have not found perfect peace and rest in Father God's unconditional love, then you may have a false image of who He is and what Heaven will be like!

Father God, I come before You today and humbly ask You to forgive me for judging You wrongly and allowing misrepresentations of who You are to affect my perceptions of You. I have allowed religion, that is based on performance and fear, to color my thoughts toward You. I have sought to please You and gain Your acceptance through my good works. I thought You were angry with me and disappointed in me because I wasn't good enough to deserve Your love. My focus has been on religion and my performance instead of on my relationship with You. Please help me gain a new understanding of Your unconditional love for me.

For the Lord your God moves about in your camp to protect you and to deliver your enemies to you. Your camp must be holy, so that he will not see among you anything indecent and turn away from you. (Deuteronomy 23:14 NIV)

PRAYER TO ENCOUNTER YOUR FATHER

Lord, I understand now that You are not angry with me, You are longing for deep fellowship with me because You love me so much. I worship You, Father.

FEBRUARY 20

REBELLION

When I was 18 years of age, my father gave me a haircut that changed my life. Once a sergeant in the war, Dad was a strict military man, and that training and experience carried over into the way he related to his family. He loved us and there was no question that he would have given his own life for ours, but he also demanded obedience—unconditional and immediate—to his rules. These rules covered almost every area of our lives, right down to the way we wore our hair.

Because of my father's military background, I was never allowed to grow my hair long; I always had a flattop or crew cut. During my late teen years, Dad wasn't home much, so I decided to let my hair grow, hoping he wouldn't notice. Just as it had grown out enough to begin to touch the back of my collar, he came home one day and happened to notice my unruly locks. Immediately the command was issued, "You will have that hair cut off by tomorrow morning!"

I told my father what I thought of his rules and that I absolutely was not cutting my hair. I have never hit the floor so fast in my life, before or since! My father took me down and forcibly cut off my hair himself. He mistakenly thought that was the best way to control the rebellion that was festering in my heart.

For rebellion is as the sin of divination, and insubordination is as iniquity and idolatry. (1 Samuel 15:23)

PRAYER TO ENCOUNTER YOUR FATHER
Too often, Father God, my rebellious nature prevents me from being close to You, my family, and even cooperative with my coworkers. Purge rebellion from me, please.

HIDING FROM GOD

Unfortunately, Dad's discipline regarding my hair had the opposite effect, and when I got up from the floor with considerably shorter hair, I called my father every name I could think of. Shortly after that, I packed my bags and left my parents' house, essentially refusing to remain my father's son and severing all ties with him.

Not too long after leaving home, I got a job in a head shop (a place where drug paraphernalia was sold) on Main Street in Daytona Beach, Florida. It was the decade of the '70s, and this particular head shop, with its dark lighting and perpetual haze of drug-induced smoke, resembled a black cave. It was the place everyone went to smoke a joint and get stoned, and I joined in every chance I got.

But even though I had ceased being my father's son in my heart, he never ceased being my father in his. At that time, he was a mailman, and ironically, his route took him down Main Street every day, right past the head shop where I was "working" at getting stoned. He passed by every day and would come in looking for his son. And each time he showed up, I went farther back into the cave to light up another joint. I rejected my father every single day for over a year.

They heard the sound of the Lord God walking in the garden in the cool of the day, and the man and his wife hid themselves. (Genesis 3:8)

PRAYER TO ENCOUNTER YOUR FATHER

Father, I pray with all my heart that I am not hiding from You in any area of my life. Search me and show me where I am shirking my responsibility as Your child.

FATHER PURSUES

As wounded by my rejection as he was, my dad never stopped pursuing me. He knew where I was living—a communal home with several other hippies—and many times he came by and saw my motorcycle out front. He would stop, come to the front door, and try to talk to me, but I would not receive him. In over a year, he had to have been rejected by me at least four hundred times, yet he continued to pursue me.

A broken, wounded father, whose last visible contact with his son had been an angry dispute culminating with his being called every name in the book, continued to seek a relationship with his son. If my earthly father, who himself had been abused in his youth, had that depth of love and commitment to me, how much more does Abba Father, our heavenly Father who is perfect love, pursue restoration and intimacy with His wayward children?

Eventually, my relationship with my father was restored, but only because of his relentless commitment to restore a relationship with his son. He was a prodigal father and a reflection to me of my heavenly Prodigal Father.

The LORD appeared to us in the past, saying: "I have loved you with an everlasting love; I have drawn you with unfailing kindness. (Jeremiah 31:3 NIV)

PRAYER TO ENCOUNTER YOUR FATHER

Father, open my heart to Your everlasting love even when I am upset with You. Give me the grace I need to forgive and forget my disappointments in our relationship. Pursue me, heavenly Father with Your everlasting love that draws men to change.

HUMILITY OF MIND

During the 1980s and early 1990s, many Christians began to value God for what they could receive and what He would do in their lives, and not for intimacy and love. Many began to hear about healing, so thousands would flock to crusades to receive that blessing from the Lord. Then, a different manifestation of power would begin in another church, and thousands would flock there to receive that portion of their perceived inheritance. For some, chasing after one demonstration of God's power or another became more important than fostering an intimate relationship with the Father and allowing His love to transform their families.

An attitude began to fester among many of these Christians that God somehow owed them the benefits of healing and financial prosperity because it was part of their inheritance in Christ, but they did not pursue the way of love. Many ministers began to compare themselves to each other; seeing the power and favor of God in some ministries, others became caught up in ambition, pride, or jealousy. They wanted the same power of God to be displayed in their own ministries, not in order to bless the people, but to receive the honor and favor that such ministers seemed to have.

Often, immature Christians seek the blessings of their relationship with God rather than hungering for God Himself, but this attitude, if continued long enough, will eventually lead us into a distant land, far from home and away from Father's protection and care.

Then he said, "There was once a man who had two sons. The younger said to his father, 'Father, I want right now what's coming to me.'" (Luke 15: 11-12)

PRAYER TO ENCOUNTER YOUR FATHER
Father, be with me today as I choose to not be selfishly ambitious, prideful, and jealous. These traits too often show up in my day-to-day life, God. I repent and ask for forgiveness.

FEBRUARY 24

"GIMME"

Have you said, "I want to do this myself. I want to control this on my own. God, give me what You owe me and then let me do things my own way." As soon as we reach that point, we begin drifting away from Father's embrace, and begin consuming God's blessings on our own lusts.

Throughout the '80s and early '90s, many took the inheritance of God but did not seek His heart for intimacy. There were times when we demanded the blessings from God—healing, the gifts of the Spirit, His power demonstrated in signs and wonders—and in His graciousness, God did give us what we asked for. But the end result was an eventual drought in the spiritual life of the Church.

When Christians value the Father more for what He can do for them than for intimacy and love, they eventually begin to seek to fulfill their own selfish desires rather than enjoy the relationship they have with God. Then, in order to fill the void that has been created, they seek comfort or identity in one or more of the counterfeit affections—power, possessions, position, people, places, performance, or passions of the flesh. This vicious cycle can continue until they realize that what they are lusting for will not satisfy them and that they have an unmet need for love and intimacy that only Father God's embrace can fulfill.

The younger of them said to his father, "Father, give me the share of the estate that falls to me." So he divided his wealth between them. And not many days later, the younger son gathered everything together and went on a journey into a distant country, and there he squandered his estate with loose living. (Luke 15:12-13)

PRAYER TO ENCOUNTER YOUR FATHER
Father, will You reveal the idols in my life. I pray, Lord, that You will destroy them and then fill me with Your blessings only.

LIFE IN THE PIGPEN

How do well-meaning children of God fall into such unclean states? I have spent the past twenty years ministering to wounded Christian leaders and their wives. Rarely a week goes by that I do not find myself talking with someone who has found him or herself involved in an immoral situation, and not one of them had planned on drifting into that sin.

Every day disappointments can cause even the most well-meaning Christians to lose their sense of love and intimacy with the Father. Eventually they drift away from Father's embrace and straight to the place they said they would never go; the pigpen. The place of shame and self-condemnation, becomes their new home until they recognize that where they are truly longing to be; back in their Father's embrace.

Until you value intimacy and love more than what God can do for you, you will continue to have a void in your heart. Some try and fill the void with alcohol, drugs, or even with religion instead of finding true intimacy with Father.

> "Father, I've sinned against God, I've sinned before you; I don't deserve to be called your son ever again." But the father wasn't listening. He was calling to the servants, "Quick. Bring a clean set of clothes and dress him. Put the family ring on his finger. My son is here—given up for dead and now alive!" And they began to have a wonderful time. (Luke 15:21-22)

PRAYER TO ENCOUNTER YOUR FATHER

I am living in a pigpen and don't realize it, I have lost my sense of love and intimacy with You. I thank You that I can run back to Your loving arms.

WHAT LOVE!

What love this prodigal father had for his son! What love our heavenly Father has for us! Before the son had ever left home, his father had already forgiven him. The love he had for his son was not based upon the son's behavior. He was simply waiting for his son to return so that he could fully express his affectionate love. Before you take even one step outside the covering of your heavenly Father, He has already forgiven you. Paul has told us that even *"if we are faithless, He remains faithful; for He cannot deny Himself"* (2 Tim. 2:13). Not only will He forgive you, but He will also run to you as soon as you take one step back toward His love. He reminds us in Jeremiah 31:3, *"I have loved you with an everlasting love; therefore I have drawn you with lovingkindness."* It is Father who is prodigal, whose love is recklessly extravagant, who is ready to pour out undeserved blessings, grace, and mercy on our lives.

When we have failed, Father does not approach us with a heavy rod of correction. He runs to us with His arms outstretched, ready to welcome us back into His embrace with all the fullness of His forgiveness and love; but sometimes our own attitude can hold us back. The shame of what we have done or the embarrassment of our failures still lingers even after we experience God's forgiveness.

> *So he got up and came to his father. But while he was still a long way off, his father saw him and felt compassion for him, and ran and embraced him and kissed him.* (Luke 15:20)

PRAYER TO ENCOUNTER YOUR FATHER
Thank You, thank You! Father—thank You for loving me so very much and for welcoming me back with open arms when I repent and ask for forgiveness!

FEBRUARY 27
I HAVE SINNED

Many children of God are living under the burden of self-condemnation from past sins they may have committed. They are playing the shame game, a cycle that began at the time of the very first sin in the Garden of Eden. When a Christian falls into sin, there is an immediate sense of failure, of not measuring up to God's expectations. That failure leads to shame and embarrassment for not being perfect, and guilt for having violated God's law. Shame and guilt lead to fear—fear of being found out, fear of rejection, fear of God's wrath—and the natural reaction to fear is to hide.

When Adam and Eve sinned in the Garden of Eden, they were caught in this cycle, which culminated in their hide-and-seek game with God (see Gen. 3:7-10). Their shame and embarrassment caused them to sew fig leaves together to hide their nakedness. Today, Christians do not use literal fig leaves to hide their sin from God, but they may use hyper-religious activity, or spiritual fig leaves, to cover themselves.

But if we turn our hearts toward Father's house, He will run toward us and welcome us back into His embrace. He exchanges our fig leaves of shame for royal robes of righteousness. He places His ring back on our finger, restoring us to the place of full heirs in His household.

I will get up and go to my father, and will say to him, "Father, I have sinned against heaven, and in your sight; I am no longer worthy to be called your son…" (Luke 15:18-19)

PRAYER TO ENCOUNTER YOUR FATHER
Father, am I wearing fig leaves to cover my sin? I ask You to search me then and see if there is any wounded way in my heart and show it to me so I can respond to Your love that changes my behavior.

FEBRUARY 28
THE HOMECOMING

How does a homecoming take place? The prodigal son parable demonstrates six simple principles we can apply to restore the relationship of intimacy with the Father that was lost because we valued Him for what He could do for us and not for intimacy and love.

1. *Come to your right senses.* If you have received Jesus as your Savior, you are a son or daughter of the Father of creation. Even if you are living in a pigpen of impurity and sin, understand that is not where you belong. Come to your senses! Your Father loves you and is eagerly awaiting your return to His house. If you are afraid to approach an angry God who is pointing His finger of judgment in your face, you don't have an accurate understanding of God's compassionate love. The younger son realized that he had a prodigal father, one who loved him unconditionally and who couldn't wait to welcome him home.

2. *Confess your sin.* Declare as the rebellious son declared, "I have sinned against heaven and in your eyes." His attitude changed from one of self-love to one of humility. Jesus tells us that we are to humble ourselves and become like little children in order to enter God's Kingdom, and that *"whoever then humbles himself as a child, he is the greatest in the kingdom of heaven"* (Matthew 18:4). Homecoming is difficult without humility, but when we humble ourselves in repentance, we will be exalted into Father's presence.

> But the father said to his slaves, "Quickly bring out the best robe and put it on him, and put a ring on his hand and sandals on his feet; and bring the fattened calf, kill it, and let us eat and celebrate; for this son of mine was dead and has come to life again; he was lost and has been found." And they began to celebrate. (Luke 15:22-24)

PRAYER TO ENCOUNTER YOUR FATHER

Father, I ask You to help me understand this nature of Yours that seems to be willing to forgive me of my sin and harsh judgments against You and others. I repent of my selfish desires that don't line up with Your purpose for me as Your son/daughter. Please direct my mind to always have my "right senses" in gear so that I can understand Your heart.

THE HOMECOMING
(CONTINUED)

3. *Forgive your earthly parents for any hurts or issues of the past.* Our earthly parents are only human, and they are bound to make mistakes. Often these mistakes color our later views of God and affect our ability to perceive Him as a loving and forgiving heavenly Father. By practicing a lifestyle of forgiveness and releasing your parents to God, you will actually free yourself from your past and begin a journey of experiencing unhindered intimacy with God. This is Father's embrace.

4. *See Father's house as your source of love.* The lifestyle of the pigpen could not meet the needs of the discontent son. Even with the inheritance he had received, he was still left wanting because he lacked a relationship with his father. You will not find true fulfillment in counterfeit affections, no matter how appealing they may seem at first. Don't expect your husband or wife, your career, hobbies, or religious activities to satisfy you if you aren't also fostering an intimate relationship with God that is built upon His grace and evidenced by intimate relationships with others.

> *And he said to him, "Your brother has come, and your father has killed the fattened calf because he has received him back safe and sound." (Luke 15:27)*

PRAYER TO ENCOUNTER YOUR FATHER

I know that only You can fill the void in my life, Father. Only You know my innermost desires and failings and potential. Fill me with Your Holy Spirit and help me to see You as my source of love!

THE HOMECOMING
(CONTINUED)

5. *Anticipate Father's embrace.* Most Christians expect the rod of judgment when they fail. Even if they do summon up the courage to approach God with their sin, they do so while cringing in fear or shame. But they don't realize that their deepest moment of failure is when Father most desires their homecoming. He grieves for their pain, and His compassion is endless. He is waiting with open arms to embrace His wayward sons and daughters as they return to Him.

6. *Return to the presence of the Father.* The spirit of adoption (being placed in Father's presence) was released over you when you were born again (see Rom. 8:15). You became God's favored child, and He will not deny His name that was stamped upon you. The prodigal Father eagerly awaits your return. He is waiting for you to exchange your fig leaves of shame for His love. He lives to take away your shame. (See 1 Peter 4:8; Heb. 2:11; 11:16.)

> *When this son of yours came, who has devoured your wealth with prostitutes, you killed the fattened calf for him.* (Luke 15:30)

PRAYER TO ENCOUNTER YOUR FATHER

Heavenly Father, I know I can do nothing to make You love me more than You already do. I know that I don't deserve that love—except for what Jesus did when He showered the world with Your love with His redeeming blood. So I invite Your presence to embrace me and to help me to understand this great love so I can respond to it and share it with others.

MARCH 3

FORGIVENESS

One night, at 2:30 a.m., the phone rang in my father's house. My dad answered and heard the words he had dreaded for months: "Mr. Frost, we have your son here at the hospital." I had taken an overdose of "orange sunshine," the LSD of choice at that time. For five days, I lay in a drugged, semi-comatose state. My father never left my side, and I miraculously recovered with no permanent damage. The only thing I remember in those five days is hearing my dad say over and over again, "Son, I love you. Everything's going to be all right."

As wounded as my earthly father was, and at the time when I had brought the greatest pain, failure, and shame to his life, he still forgave me and actively sought to restore our relationship. He loved me as much in my day of disgrace as he did in my day of grace!

How much more do you think your heavenly Father pursues you and longs to welcome you back into His loving embrace? Hear the words He is whispering to you: My child, I love you. Return to Me. I live to take away your shame. Everything is going to be all right.

> For I am convinced that neither death, nor life, nor angels, nor principalities, nor things present, nor things to come, nor powers, nor height, nor depth, nor any other created thing, will be able to separate us from the love of God, which is in Christ Jesus our Lord. (Romans 8:38-39)

PRAYER TO ENCOUNTER YOUR FATHER

Father, I long to return to Your house. I confess my sin. Please forgive me for valuing my inheritance and the things I hope to gain for myself more than I value an intimate relationship with You. I also ask You to forgive me for judging those responsible to love me that did not know how to love because they had never received the right kind of love themselves.

MARCH 4

HE WILL RESPOND

When pursuing an experiential encounter with Father's love, it is difficult to process His love as fast as you want because there are often barriers, hindrances that will slow you down. Pride, counterfeit affections, hidden core pain from the past, unforgiveness, unresolved conflicts, shame, judgmentalism, and aggressive striving are some of the major hindrances. Often, as Christians, we think that we have put all these issues behind us.

The Father desires that His love begin to lift you above the circumstances that have held you back from experiencing intimacy and love. Remember that a river always flows to the lowest point. It flows to those who have been deeply wounded by the sins of others and to those whose own sins have left them clothed with guilt and shame. It flows most freely to those who are meek and lowly of heart and who will come to the Father like a little child in need of Daddy's comforting love.

> *Then some children were brought to Him so that He might lay His hands on them and pray; and the disciples rebuked them. But Jesus said, "Let the children alone, and do not hinder them from coming to Me; for the kingdom of heaven belongs to such as these." (Matthew 19:13-14)*

> *He will respond to the prayer of the destitute; he will not despise their plea. (Psalm 102:17 NIV)*

PRAYER TO ENCOUNTER YOUR FATHER

Father, I need a deep scrubbing to wash away the stench of my past and prepare me for the future You have for me. I invite Your presence to cleanse me from my past .

MARCH 5
SLOW TO ANGER

In 722 B.C., God's people, the nation of Israel, were finally taken into captivity by the wicked, degenerate nation of Assyria. For many years they had been threatened by this, their most dreaded enemy. One of the greatest illustrations of repentance and God's compassionate love recorded in the Old Testament took place during this time. The Assyrians, some of the most depraved people on the planet, were a race of unrepentant idolaters, sexual fornicators, and ruthless murderers—a bloodthirsty and savage people who sacrificed their own children to false gods and who took pleasure in tyrannizing the nations they conquered.

As He often does, God dealt with the situation in an unexpected way—He appointed His prophet Jonah to travel to Nineveh, the capital city of Assyria, and call the people there, essentially Jonah's enemies, to repentance. Of course, Jonah's refusal and subsequent disobedience in fleeing to Tarshish has made him a rather infamous character in our Sunday school classes. In the story of Jonah, he has a not-so-surprising change of heart in the belly of the fish. After he is spit back up onto the beach, he follows God's command and becomes the first missionary to the people of Nineveh.

> *But it greatly displeased Jonah and he became angry. He prayed to the Lord and said, "Please Lord, was not this what I said while I was still in my own country? Therefore in order to forestall this I fled to Tarshish, for I knew that **You are a gracious and compassionate God, slow to anger** and abundant in lovingkindness, and one who relents concerning calamity."* (Jonah 4:1-2)

PRAYER TO ENCOUNTER YOUR FATHER
Father, before You allow me to be swallowed whole by a huge problem that is the result of my disobedience to You, please knock me on the head a couple of times so I say yes to Your request.

MARCH 6

GOD'S COMPASSION

Jonah's motives in pursuing this ministry weren't rooted in God's grace and love. Jonah never wanted his mission to Nineveh to be successful. He strode through the city streets, loudly proclaiming, "Yet forty days and Nineveh will be overthrown" (Jonah 3:4). But the king and the people of Nineveh heeded Jonah's message. To his utter displeasure, they dressed themselves in sackcloth and ashes, declared a fast of repentance, and began to cry out to God for mercy. Jonah believed God would spare Nineveh, but he lacked the compassion for the people (see Jonah 4:1-2).

The heart of the Father is always responsive to those who truly turn to Him, no matter how far from Him they have strayed or how wicked and depraved they might be. God relented from the catastrophe that He had planned for the Assyrians. Instead, He forgave the people of Nineveh and welcomed them into His presence.

One would think that Jonah would have been pleased to see his ministry succeed. But he was suffering from the "older brother syndrome." After Nineveh's repentance, he threw a colossal pity party and became angry because God was not going to punish the Assyrians in the way he felt they deserved. Jonah thought his anger was justified, but God's response to him demonstrates the compassion the Father has for all people and His desire for the lost to come home (Jonah 4:10-11).

> *Then the Lord said, "You had compassion on the plant for which you did not work and which you did not cause to grow, which came up overnight and perished overnight. Should I not have compassion on Nineveh, the great city in which there are more than 120,000 persons who do not know the difference between their right and left hand, as well as many animals?"* (Jonah 4:10-11)

PRAYER TO ENCOUNTER YOUR FATHER

Lord, who am I to judge others? I'm no one but a sinner myself. Keep me from being self-righteous—from being a miserable example of a Christian.

Sin Against Love

The Bible doesn't tell us Jonah's response to God's reprimand. We can only hope that he recognized that his attitude was wrong and experienced a homecoming of his own with the Father. But the question for us to ponder is this: When God wanted to bring revival to the most wicked city on earth, with whom did He have more trouble—the people of Nineveh or the man of God sent to that city? We may think that revival comes only when the hearts of sinners turn to God, but the hearts and motives of Christian leaders must also be prepared.

Jonah was exhibiting the older brother syndrome that we may acquire when we see God bestow His blessing on those whom we feel don't deserve it. These sins of the older brother may in reality be a greater hindrance to the Kingdom of God than are the sins of the younger son. While the younger brother may commit sins of immorality and violate God's laws of behavior, the older brother commits perhaps the greatest sin of all—a sin against love.

Previously, we discovered that the younger son in actuality had a compassionate, forgiving father waiting to welcome him home with open arms. But the younger son too often has an older brother also waiting for him back in the father's house with a not-so-welcoming attitude. What would have happened to the younger son if the older brother had approached him before the compassionate father did?

> *This is war, and there is no neutral ground. If you're not on my side, you're the enemy; if you're not helping, you're making things worse.* (Matthew 12:30 MSG)

Prayer to Encounter Your Father
Father, I don't want to be like the older brother who was envious and not compassionate toward his brother and actually making matters worse. I also don't want to judge his behavior toward me so Father will You deal with my heart and change me.

MARCH 8
TIME TO CELEBRATE

The final part of the parable of the prodigal father demonstrates where many Christians can be found, especially many who are involved in some kind of ministry. They may be the most loyal, hard-working, and dutiful workers in their Christian service. From all outward appearances, they seem to be the holiest, most virtuous members of the church, but a closer examination of their hearts tells a different story. Jealousy, anger, pride, spiritual ambition, self-righteousness, and sullenness are often lurking just below the surface in these souls that lack an experiential revelation of the Father's love. Many have the attitude of the older brother, the good son, and their sin against love can misrepresent Father God's heart in far greater ways than the more blatant sins of the rebellious son.

The attitude of the father toward the older brother is the same as the attitude he has toward the younger son: His loving compassion entreats him to change his attitude and join in the party. The older brother has left the father's house just as surely as the younger son left, and the father realizes that both of his sons need a homecoming. The younger son had physically lived in a distant land, but the heart of the older brother was much more distant from a loving home. But the father still invites him to come home, to change his attitude and join in the joyous celebration.

> His father said, "Son, you don't understand. You're with me all the time, and everything that is mine is yours—but this is a wonderful time, and we had to celebrate. This brother of yours was dead, and he's alive! He was lost, and he's found!" (Luke 15:31-32 MSG)

PRAYER TO ENCOUNTER YOUR FATHER
How distant is my heart from You Father? I want this intimacy that Your word illustrates so well. Help me change my attitude and celebrate with You!

THE STRAIGHT AND NARROW

When I first came into the Father's house, my heart was filled with so much joy and love that I wanted to spread it to everyone I met. I was a rebellious son who had entered into the welcoming embrace of Father God, and I experienced the joyous homecoming found in Jesus Christ. At that time, I was living on the sea 20 to 25 days a month—it was just God and me out under the stars. I didn't know anything at all about the Christian lifestyle; all I knew was that I longed to spend time in the presence of my Father. I would weep for hours, overwhelmed by His love and forgiveness. I realized that I wanted to share this overwhelming love with others, so I decided to become a minister. I left the life of the sea and enrolled in a traditional Bible school to learn all the things I needed to know about ministry.

I soon began to drift further and further into the attitude of the older brother. In Bible school, I began to learn the disciplines of the Christian faith: prayer, the study of the Word, witnessing and evangelism, fasting, and tithing. I began to slave faithfully in the fields of the Father, and I was always striving to live up to my own exacting standards. I never allowed one moral failure in my behavior, not one slip-up or negligence of integrity in my actions.

*Enter through the narrow gate. For wide is the gate and broad is the road that leads to destruction, and many enter through it. But **small is the gate and narrow the road that leads to life**, and only a few find it.* (Matthew 7:13-14 NIV)

PRAYER TO ENCOUNTER YOUR FATHER

Father It is so easy to drift off the path the You laid out for me. I had rules but I love boundaries. Detours seem to be more fun or lead to faster success. Father, steer me back on the path that leads to You, and a closer relationship with understanding Your direction, Your way, Your path.

MARCH 10
FOR FATHER'S GLORY

I became so proficient in every task I was given in Bible school that when I finally graduated and was sent out into the ministry, I was immediately given the position of a senior pastor. I quickly learned how to please the governing board of my denomination: grow the membership of my congregation, and increase the financial income of my church. By my second year in the ministry, I had the fastest-growing church in my denominational district. At the annual pastors' conference, I was brought to the platform and given a plaque for my service.

When we begin to serve God for the praise of man or to find identity in what we do, no matter how great the call of God is on our lives, no matter how powerful the gifts or the anointing flow in our ministry, that underlying attitude of self-love can begin to produce a hidden resentment and anger, fueled by a fear of rejection and a fear of failure. There is nothing wrong with practicing the Christian disciplines of tithing, fasting, prayer, Bible study, or witnessing. These can help us grow and mature and are outward expressions of the intimate relationship that we are cultivating with our heavenly Father. But as I was learning these disciplines in a rigid holiness environment, I was filtering them through the system of love that I had learned in my childhood.

Fear and intimidation is a trap that holds you back. But when you place your confidence in the Lord, you will be seated in the high place. (Proverbs 29: 25)

PRAYER TO ENCOUNTER YOUR FATHER
Father, may my motives and goals be to serve You and give YOU all the glory for any and every accomplishment in my life. I thank You that Your desire for me is not to be afraid of man but to respond to Your love and acceptance. I thank You that Love is a gift not a reward for performance.

SOBER JUDGMENT

Christian disciplines, when motivated by unconditional love, can bring great blessings to the Church and be an important witness to those outside the faith. But when they were poured through the filter system that I had carried over from my childhood, they created a burden too heavy for me to bear. No amount of fasting or study or servitude can earn the love of the Father, especially when the motivation behind these actions is based on a desire for personal gain and reward.

As the weight of pleasing the Father became heavier and heavier on my shoulders, I sought release from the burden, by looking down on others not as disciplined as I was, in order to make me look good. I spent a great deal of time and energy on achieving excellence in myself, and I came to expect that same level of commitment from my family, my congregation, and everyone else around me. When I placed my exacting standards on other people and found them to be lacking, my own ego was inflated and my spirituality seemed that much more holy, more pious, and more perfect than theirs. I was blind to my own self-deception.

> *For by the grace given me I say to every one of you:* **Do not think of yourself more highly than you ought**, *but rather think of yourself with sober judgment, in accordance with the faith God has distributed to each of you.* (Romans 12:3 NIV)

PRAYER TO ENCOUNTER YOUR FATHER

As You know, Father, the human ego can grow to be enormous. Place in me a check of some sort that will alert me to any exaggerated ego growth. I repent of pride within my own abilities to get things done my way and I ask You for the humility to look at how You see me. I ask You to help me become interdependent on You.

OUR RIGHTEOUS JUDGE

The older brother syndrome creates its own cycle that takes the sincere but gullible participant down a subtle path of self-destruction that, if left unchecked, ultimately leads to a cold heart void of love, tenderness, or compassion. The key to breaking the cycle is to recognize the symptoms early enough to thwart its development. The sins of the older brother can cause severe damage in the Church if allowed to continue, because the sins against love and compassion are the most harmful to needy people seeking forgiveness and healing. It is a great tragedy when wayward younger brothers and sisters who are on the verge of repentance and restoration to the Father are shut out by the self-righteousness of those who profess the name of Christ.

As soon as the older brother or good son drifts away from the Father's house because of a negative attitude of self-love, jealousy, or judgmentalism, an emotional and spiritual distance is immediately created between him and his Father. Any distance from God's love will gradually gravitate to law and legalism, and it will lead to feelings of insecurity, because it is the unconditional acceptance of the Father that gives us our true value and self-worth.

Judge me, O Lord my God, according to Your righteousness. (Psalm 35:24)

PRAYER TO ENCOUNTER YOUR FATHER
With Your help, Father, let it never be said of me that I caused anyone to turn away or even have a sour opinion of Christ. Help me guard my words and actions against self-righteousness and the love of law.

COMPARING IS NOT WISE

Deeply intimate relationships with other people are possible only between individuals who are secure in God's love, because the foundation of such relationships is love, trust, and commitment. As soon as distance from God's unconditional love and insecurity begins to occur, intimacy with others becomes very difficult because we treat others in the way we feel about ourselves. Whatever we feel that we have to do to feel valued by God, then others will have to do the same to feel valued by us.

The second step in the cycle takes place when the person tries to regain the intimacy that has been lost by aggressively striving to gain the acceptance and approval of others. The older brother was driven to slave in his father's fields to earn his position in the family; what he didn't realize was that his position was already secure, no matter what he accomplished in life.

When people believe that their value is based on their performance and what others, including God, think of them, it leads directly to the third step: competition. They must become better than anyone else in order to receive the Father's love. When a minister reaches this stage, he or she can become overly concerned with the church across the street or how the ministry measures up when compared with the other ministries in town. When the comparison to others comes up short, as it eventually will, the inevitable result is envy, the fourth step in the vicious cycle.

We do not dare to classify or compare ourselves with some who commend themselves. When they measure themselves by themselves and compare themselves with themselves, they are not wise. (2 Corinthians 10:12 NIV)

PRAYER TO ENCOUNTER YOUR FATHER

Father, in reality, there will always be others richer and smarter and more attractive than I am. There will also always be people poorer and dumber and less attractive than I am. Comparing myself with others is futile—With Your help I will try and stop, today.

COMPARING IS NOT WISE
(CONTINUED)

Unhealthy competition leads to feelings of ill will toward those in the same line of work. Not everyone can receive the plaque for the fastest-growing church or be salesman of the year, but most want it for the recognition it brings. The real problem comes when we believe that to truly be accepted, or important in life, we must be the one to earn it. If we aren't able to achieve what we believe we must, we may begin to judge ourselves, the fifth step in the cycle. And finally, because of the guilt that we feel for coming up short, we put on a cloak of defensiveness and judgmentalism, and the need to be right becomes more important than fostering healthy relationships.

This final step seals the hardness of heart of the older brother. Most older brothers are right; they are usually the most loyal, hardest-working, best performers in the church. But often they would rather prove their rightness than promote intimate relationships. They value obedience over relationship, and they use that self-righteousness to justify their negative attitudes. And it results in an attitude of superiority and condescending tones. At that point, other people begin to feel devalued—the family suffers first, then the other members of the Body of Christ. And sadly, this attitude of the older brother keeps younger or rebellious sons from returning to the Father, perhaps the worst consequence of all.

God is not a respecter of persons! (Romans 2:11)

PRAYER TO ENCOUNTER YOUR FATHER
Father help me not to think more highly of others than I do myself. I also ask that You forgive me for judging those who try and make me feel inferior when Your word tells me that we are all Your favorite kids.

MARCH 15
I Want to Be Like You

About six months after my change of legalistic heart, our daughter called from school, asking if she could bring a friend home. I was surprised, because before I had a revelation of love, my children rarely brought friends home. I readily agreed. Then she said, "Well, Dad, I just need to prepare you, Erica has orange hair and a cat collar around her arm and earrings in strange places."

That took me back, but I composed myself and replied, "Why do you want to bring this girl into our house, Sarah?" My daughter's answer surprised me, "Because she's so hurt. Her own father is a drug addict and left her family years ago. I want her to meet you, Dad. I want her to see what having a loving and tender father is like."

For six weeks, Erica was a daily guest in our home, and each week, something changed in her appearance. Her natural hair color returned; the collar and earrings in strange places disappeared; and eventually Erica gave her heart to Christ. Erica was led home to the Father because I had relinquished the attitude of the older brother and instead was motivated by love and compassion for a lost and hurting little girl.

Bad people loved to hang out with Jesus. Good people wanted to kill Him. How do the lost and hurting feel around you? Do they sense your compassion and concern, or do they feel devalued, shamed, or belittled?

God spoke: "Let us make human beings in our image, make them reflecting our nature…" (Genesis 1:26 MSG)

We are being transfigured into His Image as we move from one brighter level of glory to another. And this glorious transfiguration comes from the Lord who is the Spirit. (2 Corinthians 3:18 The Passion Translation)

PRAYER TO ENCOUNTER YOUR FATHER
Father I ask You to help me see and understand the image of You in each individual person You assign to me to love.

OLDER BROTHER SYNDROME

Any Christian discipline that you practice or any theology that you hold *not* rooted and grounded in the love of the Father will gradually cause you to gravitate toward a love of the law. This legalism may have disastrous consequences: Families may be destroyed, ministries may be lost, and revivals may be quenched because of the sin of the older brother.

Do you notice any of the symptoms of the older brother syndrome in your heart? Are you aggressively striving to gain the approval of God or other people? Do you find yourself constantly competing to be the best in your career or in your service to God at the cost of dishonoring or devaluing others? Do you require perfection in those around you and mete out a judgmental or a devaluing attitude when this perfection is not achieved? Do you have a greater love of the law than you do of the needs of people? If so, you may be cultivating the attitude of the older brother, and you are in need of a homecoming with your Father.

Until I let go of the striving, jealousy, and rivalry in my heart, I led a life of frustration and resentment. No promotion was ever enough. No acknowledgment or accolade would completely satisfy. The success of others would frustrate me, and my feelings of servitude only increased as I moved further and further from dwelling in the Father's embrace.

> *The older brother became angry and refused to go in. So his father went out and pleaded with him. But he answered his father, "Look! All these years I've been slaving for you and never disobeyed your orders. Yet you never gave me even a young goat so I could celebrate with my friends."* (Luke 15:28-29)

PRAYER TO ENCOUNTER YOUR FATHER
Father there have been times where I have been guilty of having an older brother attitude. I ask You to forgive me for not believing that I am loved because I am me. I have been designed uniquely as Your child and I choose to believe that I am loved as much as any of my siblings...physical or spiritually.

MARCH 17

FREE AND UNDESERVED

The love of God is a gift; it is free and undeserved. There is nothing you can do to be loved by Him any more than you already are. And there is nothing you can do to lessen His love. God's love is unconditional, but if it is not experienced on a level that brings healing to the childhood hurt and anger at not feeling unconditionally loved, a resentment and critical attitude is often the result. When that childhood frustration encounters the laws and rules of religion, an environment is created in which the older brother syndrome may flourish.

Before I received the life-changing revelation of the Father God's love, I would be out on the road ministering, slaving for the Lord, for weeks at a time, and my resentment and frustration would often overflow onto my wife and family when I arrived home. Trisha knew she had better be on time to the airport to pick me up when my flight came in. If she was late, she had better have a good reason. Traffic was not a good enough excuse.

My demands and condescending tones were constant and unrelenting. To everyone outside of my family, I appeared to be holy and righteous, a man of integrity, but to my wife and children I lacked grace and mercy. As the "older brother," I was more concerned with people's performance than with intimate, healthy, loving relationships.

But the fruit of the Spirit is love, joy, peace, patience, kindness...
(Galatians 5:22)

PRAYER TO ENCOUNTER YOUR FATHER
Your love is free and undeserved, Father. Thank You for this gift that I too often take for granted and don't appreciate. Thank You for loving me as I become the person You intended when You created me.

TRUE HOMECOMING

How was I able to relinquish this attitude and lifestyle and experience a true homecoming to the Father's house? The transition from the love of the law to embracing the law of love required a repositioning of my heart, attitudes, and core values.

1. First of all, I came to an awareness of my sin. I noticed symptoms of the older brother syndrome in my life, and I realized I was in need of a homecoming with my Father.

2. I moved to a state of repentance. I needed a change of heart so deep that it reached to my core attitudes of self-love, resentment, and envy. I saw how deeply I had hurt those around me with my legalism and demeaning tones. I began to understand how much it wounded my children when I valued my work and ministry over time spent with them. When my heart began to break because I felt the pain that I had caused, I was ready for the homecoming to the Father's house.

3. I asked for and received forgiveness from God for believing the lie about His nature that says I must work to gain more of His love and acceptance. I relinquished the anger, jealousy, criticism, and judgmental attitudes to which I had clung so fiercely, and I allowed His Spirit to transform my very nature and character.

> *Jesus said, "The first in importance is, 'Listen, Israel: The Lord your God is one; so love the Lord God with all your passion and prayer and intelligence and energy.' And here is the second: 'Love others as well as you love yourself.' There is no other commandment that ranks with these." (Mark 12:30-31 The Message)*

PRAYER TO ENCOUNTER YOUR FATHER

Father, I want to transition from love of the law to embracing the law of love so I can reposition my heart, attitudes, and core values. I know I can count on You to assist me in this transformation!

True Homecoming
(Continued)

4. I needed to seek forgiveness from those whom I had hurt. This is the principle of restitution—going to those to whom I had misrepresented the Father's love. When the revelation of God's love changed my heart, I realized the pain I had inflicted on those I love, and I set things right by apologizing. When I relinquished the attitude of the older brother, being right no longer mattered as much as the restoration of the important relationships in my life.

5. Finally, in humility, I began to find my Father waiting with His arms outstretched to embrace me and to bring me back into His house of peace and rest.

Anticipate the homecoming your heavenly Father has planned for you. He understands your hidden core issues, your need for affirmation that may stem from issues in your childhood. He sees the secret place in your heart that cries out for the unconditional love of a father, for the affirmation and affection that only He can provide. His compassion and mercy are available to you; He longs to bring you back into His house and for you to join in the celebration and the joy of the feast. He is not ashamed or angry at your misrepresentation of His love. He wants you in His loving embrace!

Jesus said, "The first in importance is, 'Listen, Israel: The Lord your God is one; so love the Lord God with all your passion and prayer and intelligence and energy.' And here is the second: 'Love others as well as you love yourself.' There is no other commandment that ranks with these." (Mark 12:30-31 The Message)

Prayer to Encounter Your Father
My heart is full of Your love and mercy and compassion—I thank You that You find me worthy of such precious gifts from You, Father.

MARCH 20
GOD CALLS YOUR NAME

If you need this homecoming with your Father, pray this prayer and begin to return to the joy of your first love:

Heavenly Father, I come before You with a repentant heart. I realize that I have been like an older brother in Your house, placing the love of the law above the law of love in my heart. I recognize that my attitude has been one of superiority, resentment, competition, striving, and jealousy, and I see the damage this has caused to my relationship with You and my relationship with the people I love. I realize how much I require others to perform for my acceptance and love. I have sinned against love!

Father, I turn from these attitudes and return to Your heart of love and compassion. Restore to me the joy of my salvation when I was motivated by my love for You and my gratitude for Your sacrifice. I want to serve You with a pure heart, motivated by Your compassion and love for others. Thank You for welcoming me back into Your house and allowing me to join in the celebration. In Jesus' name, amen.

I will give you the treasures of darkness and hidden wealth of secret places, so that you may know that it is I, The Lord, the God of Israel, who calls you by your name. (Isaiah 45:3)

PRAYER TO ENCOUNTER YOUR FATHER
Father, I forgive all of the "older brothers" who prevented me from experiencing a homecoming with the Father. I'm so excited and thankful to have been welcomed home by You!

MARCH 21

I WANT TO LOOK LIKE YOU

"Dad, the kids made fun of me all day long! Everybody laughed at my ears. I never want to go back to school again!" Our son was experiencing a wound, one that could potentially last a lifetime. I immediately took him in my arms, held him tight, and told him how handsome he was.

Then I showed him what I looked like when I was his age. We looked like identical twins, and I asked him, "Who do you want to look like when you grow up, Joshua?" He answered without hesitation, "I want to look just like you, Dad!" "Then, son, you never have to worry about what anybody says again. You are your Dad's beloved son, and I love you. You are going to be the most handsome man when you grow up!"

My son never had to go through the suffering I went through, because when I faced the taunts of other children, my own father never comforted or protected me. He was not able to express love, comfort, or affirmation when I needed it the most, and as a result, I often experienced pain and rejection. Fortunately, a revelation of Father's love for me helped to break the cycle of pain, and I was able to comfort Joshua when he needed it. Instead of carrying that wound throughout his life, the pain never entered his heart.

For he knew all about us before we were born and he destined us from the beginning to share the likeness of his Son. This means the Son is the oldest among a vast family of brothers and sisters who will become just like him. (Romans 8:29 The Passion Translation)

PRAYER TO ENCOUNTER YOUR FATHER
Father I want to "look like You," I have lots of bumps and blemishes, but one by one with Your help I will be conform to Your perfect image.

FATHER ISSUES

Unresolved father issues from childhood can often be a major cause of emotional pain later in adulthood. Adult pain is often wired to childhood pain. Many family counselors believe that the majority of a child's identity is formed through the father–child relationship. When that relationship becomes skewed, children may grow up with difficulties relating to other male authority figures later in life. And when they come to Christ and become born again, the issues that they have with their earthly fathers can easily transfer to the new relationship they have with their heavenly Father.

In the parable of the rebellious son that Jesus told in Luke 15, both of the sons had father issues. To whichever brother we can relate, whether we are running from God by living a life of addictions and immorality or striving to please Him with our hyper-religious activity but not allowing Him to touch our heart, our relationship with God can be highly influenced by the relationship we had with our earthly father. Our anger, fear, and distrust, which is often rooted in our hidden core pain, easily spills over into many areas of our lives—our marriages, our families, our careers, our ministries, our walk with God—and the effects can greatly hinder a life of intimacy and love.

> *Behold, I will send you Elijah the prophet Before the coming of the great and dreadful day of the Lord. And he will turn the hearts of the fathers to the children and the hearts of the children to the fathers.* (Malachi 4:5-6)

PRAYER TO ENCOUNTER YOUR FATHER

Father, I want to be restored to You Father first but also to my earthly father. Help me to understand his pain and what he could not give me. Forgive me for judging his lack, forgive me for judging my brothers and I ask You to restore our relationships.

FOUR BASIC EMOTIONAL NEEDS

All human beings have four basic emotional needs. As children, we look to our parents, and from three years of age and older, we especially look to our fathers to meet these needs for us. The family is the place where children learn how to relate to the world, and the lessons learned there are ones carried throughout a lifetime.

When these four needs go unmet in childhood, it becomes very difficult for a person to develop healthy relationships with God or with other people later in adulthood.

1. *The need for unconditional expressed love.* It is not enough for a father to provide shelter, food, and clothing for his children. It is not even enough for a father to have loving feelings for them. Those feelings must be communicated and expressed in a way that is meaningful to the child. Every child is different, and each one will experience love in a different way. One child may need extra time spent playing with him and his favorite toys; another will crave physical touch, hugs, and kisses, or being cuddled on Daddy's lap. Fathers who spend the time to get to know their children will learn to express their love to them in the way that means the most.

Lord I passionately love you I want to embrace you. Psalms 18:1 (The Passion Translation)

PRAYER TO ENCOUNTER YOUR FATHER
Father I know I need to be loved by You. I ask You to help to receive Your love for me and then to give it first to my family and then the world. Help to understand how to love the way You love.

FOUR BASIC EMOTIONAL NEEDS
(CONTINUED)

2. ***The need to feel secure and comforted.*** Every child needs to feel safe, both physically and emotionally. A father can provide a secure environment by putting locks on the doors and keeping his children safe from the monsters in the closet. But children also need to know that their families and households are emotionally safe and that they always have a safe place in their father's heart, no matter how much they fail. Explosive anger and rage are frightening experiences for many children, and too often they become a reality. They need an atmosphere of unconditional love and acceptance so that their emotional well-being is secure.

3. ***The need for praise and affirmation.*** Even adults want other people to say good things about them. Children especially need this from their parents, and many sons and daughters spend their lives trying to gain the approval of their fathers. Dr. James Dobson, founder of Focus on the Family, stated that it takes at least forty words of praise to counteract just one word of criticism in a child's heart. Many fathers have the best of intentions, and they try to be tough on their kids to help prepare them for the "real" world. But children will become better prepared for life when their self-esteem and value are recognized and encouraged by their fathers, more so than if they live under the shadow of constant criticism.

You will be secure, because there is hope; you will look about you and take your rest in safety. (Job 11:18 NIV)

I promise I will never leave you comfortless or abandon you as an orphan. I will come back to you. (John 14:18 The Passion Translation)

PRAYER TO ENCOUNTER YOUR FATHER

Father, I pray that my family will feel safe and secure because of their faith and my faith in You. May we all give You the praise You deserve, as I give them the praise and affirmation they deserve.

FOUR BASIC EMOTIONAL NEEDS
(CONTINUED)

4. *The need for a purpose in life.* Fathers have a responsibility to cultivate their children's talents and gifts. Everyone needs to find a sense of value, a belief that their lives mean something and that they can make a difference. Children need to be told that they are special, that they have something unique to offer the world, and that they are a gift of God's love to their family and to the world.

Children look to their fathers to meet these four emotional needs, but unfortunately, no earthly father is perfect. Even the best of us fail to meet all our children's needs all the time. At some point, disappointments, hurts, and wounds will inevitably take place, and these may cause what I call "father flaws" to form in the hearts of our children. The leftover pain and wounds from childhood can create a lens through which adults later view the world and God.

Most earthly fathers will fall into one of six different categories: good father; performance-oriented father; passive father; absentee father; authoritarian father; abusive father. I am not trying to stir up old wounds, but help you identify where strongholds (destructive habit patterns of thinking) may be holding you back from intimacy and love.

> So we are convinced that every detail of our lives is continually woven together to fit into god's perfect plan of bringing good into our lives. For we are his lovers who have been called to fulfill his design purpose. (Romans 8:28 The Passion Translation)

PRAYER TO ENCOUNTER YOUR FATHER
Holy Spirit, reveal to me any unresolved hidden issues I may still have with my earthly father that may be affecting my ability to relate to my heavenly Father and to receive His affectionate love.

THE GOOD FATHER

My wife, Trisha, was raised in a "good home," and she had a good father throughout her childhood. He worked hard to provide for his family, and he loved and cherished her like a princess. But circumstances occurred that were beyond his control. When Trisha was about 12 years of age, he had a heart attack. He had been a truck driver for many years, but his health began to decline and eventually he was taken off the road. The family's finances suffered, and they sank from a middle-class income into poverty.

Trisha's father wanted so much to continue to provide all the things that his children had grown accustomed to, but year after year went by, and few promises were kept. Then his health continued to decline, despite fervent prayers for healing by their family, their pastor, and their church.

Trisha's father died when she was 20 years of age. Broken promises, disappointment, and grief all opened the door for hidden lies in Trisha's heart, despite the good intentions that her father had. She found it difficult to trust in a God to whom she had prayed so desperately for her father's health, only to be so deeply disappointed when he died. When she relinquished the pain, disappointment, and despair tied to her relationship with her dad, she could have a deep and intimate encounter with Father's comforting love and could move beyond her father issues into a joyous life of security, love, and intimacy.

If you, then, though you are evil, know how to give good gifts to your children, how much more will your Father in heaven give good gifts to those who ask him! (Matthew 7:11 NIV)

PRAYER TO ENCOUNTER YOUR FATHER
Thank You, Father, for being the most excellent Father. You have none of the imperfect qualities of earthly fathers. I choose right now to relinquish any pain or disappoint I hold against my earthly parents.

THE PERFORMANCE-ORIENTED FATHER

A primary root of depression is performance orientation. No one can ever do everything right all the time because we are only human beings, and we all experience failure. But after 20 or 30 years of constantly striving for perfection, fear and depression begin to creep into the heart of this adult son or daughter. They may be born again and filled with the Spirit, but they can still believe that God will be pleased with them only when they read the Bible enough or when they have prayed at least an hour a day. Eventually, if the pattern continues, they can collapse into spiritual burnout, unable to hear God's voice or sense His presence at all.

My own father set impossibly high standards for me in sports; he wanted me to be the greatest tennis champion in the world. But if I didn't hit the ball right, he would not even smile. If I hit it into the net too many times, he would become angry, and the look on his face told me exactly what he thought of me: I was not good enough to have a place in his heart. I carried that pain from my childhood over to my relationship with God until I experienced a deep revelation of His unconditional love for me—that there was nothing I could do to earn His approval, but that He was simply pleased with me being His own beloved child.

For the same love He has for His beloved Jesus He has for us. (Ephesians 1:6 The Passion Translation)

PRAYER TO ENCOUNTER YOUR FATHER

Heavenly Father, I want to know You and Your unconditional love for me. I know You love me the way You love Jesus, just because He was Your Son and nothing He did. Please forgive me for trying to perform for Your love. I ask You to heal me of all remnants of childhood pain that caused me to judge You like my earthly dad. I ask for the gift of compassion to understand the pain of others especially my earthly father.

MARCH 28
THE PASSIVE FATHER

The passive father makes no great demands on his children, but neither is there any overt rejection. He simply fails to be home even when he is home. He is not able to demonstrate love or affection, usually not intentionally, but because he himself never received these things from his own father. He does not experience life with his family; he simply lives his life under the same roof.

Many times these fathers are workaholics or military fathers, which require a man to put his emotions on the back burner in order to survive on the job. But when these men come home to their wives and children, they find it difficult to move their emotions forward to relate to their families in a loving and comforting way. Pastors and counselors sometimes also fall into this category; they often handle so many emotional situations throughout the day that when they come home they are exhausted. They have spent so much of their emotional energy helping other people that there is often nothing left for their own family.

When you have been raised in the home of a passive father, your relationship with God may be devoid of passion and joy. But walking in the Spirit should be an emotional encounter. It's all about love, joy, and peace (emotions) much more than it is about the study of doctrine or theory. God wants to touch our hearts and emotions; He wants to restore healthy emotions in our relationships even if your dad was so passive he was not able to example the love of Father God to you.

> *And these words, which I command thee this day, shall be in thine heart: And thou shalt teach them diligently unto thy children, and shalt talk of them when thou sittest in thine house, and when thou walkest by the way, and when thou liest down, and when thou risest up.* (Deuteronomy 6:6-7)

PRAYER TO ENCOUNTER YOUR FATHER

Sometimes I am emotionally drained from my work day, Father, I ask that You help me not to become a passive parent—unavailable for my family. Refresh me, God, when I am tired and empty.

THE ABSENTEE FATHER

Today in the United States, the absentee father is becoming more and more common. The absentee father is no longer physically present in the home. This could have been caused by a number of reasons: death, divorce, or abandonment. Children who have had an absentee father may face abandonment issues, and it may be very difficult for them to relate to God.

Even if they do foster a relationship with Him, there may be a sense of fear that at some point, He may not be there for them just as their earthly father wasn't. This can also result in striving to please God in order to appease an unconscious guilt they may feel for somehow being at fault for their father leaving. But the heavenly Father tells us, *"I will never leave you nor forsake you"* (Heb. 13:5 NKJV). These children need an experiential revelation of God's presence and unconditional love in their lives.

> *"At my first defense no one came to stand by me, but all deserted me. May it not be charged against them! But the Lord stood by me and empowered me to complete my ministry."* (2 Tim 4:16-17a The Passion Translation)

PRAYER TO ENCOUNTER YOUR FATHER

Father will You forgive me for judging my earthly father and spiritual authorities for not being there for the most important days in my life. I have developed a fear that You will not be there for the most important days either. I ask for You to help me identify and overcome the fatherless ways in me. I want to be love and be available for those who You have told me to example and be an influence of Your fatherly love to.

THE AUTHORITARIAN FATHER

Authoritarian fathers are more interested in the love of law than in the law of love. They go beyond the performance-oriented fathers and sternly demand immediate, unquestioned obedience from their children. There is no real emotional relationship that is fostered between the father and the child; the only emotions that seem to be present are intimidation, fear, and control.

These fathers are usually selfish; the entire life of the family must revolve around them and their needs. They do not recognize the unique individuality of each child; they may see them as pawns to be used for getting their own needs met. Children raised in such homes often see God as the Great Cop in the sky, a harsh authoritarian figure to be feared and obeyed rather than a loving Father to be enjoyed and cherished. They may strive so hard to meet His requirements that they feel more like servants rather than children whom Father loves.

> *Fathers, do **not exasperate your children**; instead, bring them up in the training and instruction of the Lord.* (Ephesians 6:4-5 New Living Translation)

PRAYER TO ENCOUNTER YOUR FATHER
Forgive me, Father, for all the times I have been an authoritarian parent. O also forgive my earthly father for all of his rules without relationship. I break agreement with that measuring stick that I can never attain to. I want to model Your perfect parenting to my children. Help me accomplish that goal. Thank You.

MARCH 31
THE ABUSIVE FATHER

Verbal, emotional, physical, or sexual abuse is becoming more and more common in families throughout the United States. If you have been abused in any of these ways, you often need more than just counseling or psychological therapy to be free of the deep pain and anger; you may need deep healing that can come only through the Holy Spirit pouring the love of God into your heart.

Abuse, especially sexual abuse, creates one of the deepest wounds a child can ever receive, for it often results in tremendous hidden core pain. It can violate the trust the child has placed in authority and can affect all his relationships for the rest of his life. Sexual abuse can leave children consumed with hidden fears and a deep distrust of God, pastors, other authority figures, and other men. It can create feelings of guilt and a profound sense of shame and unworthiness. It can leave children feeling as if they did something to deserve to be treated so badly. And underneath it all, there can be tremendous repressed anger, much of it focused on God for allowing the abuse to take place.

> *And hope does not put us to shame, because God's love has been poured out into our hearts through the Holy Spirit, who has been given to us.* (Romans 5:5)

PRAYER TO ENCOUNTER YOUR FATHER
Father abuse is the last thing I want to think about. I can't stand the thought of people, especially children, being abused. I ask You to heal my memories as I forgive my dad for any abusive behavior, whether physical, emotional, and sexual. Heal my broken spirits, Lord, in Jesus' name.

APRIL 1

Blame Game

Placing blame on your father for the problems you are having in life may increase your troubles and the sense of separation you feel from God. You may have been innocent of the wounding you experienced in your father's house, but you are accountable for your dishonor (disrespect) toward your father. Healing begins when you begin to forgive, take personal responsibility for present relational issues, and do not seek to blame others for them.

Many people feel wounded by feeling that their fathers have never blessed them. I believe that Father God wants to impart to us Father's blessing that we may have lacked, even as He blessed His Son at the Jordan River, saying, *"You are My beloved Son, in You I am well-pleased"* (Mark 1:11). Father also wants to affirm us for being His children. *"See how great a love the Father has bestowed on us, that we would be called children of God; and such we are..."* (1 John 3:1).

When we release our earthly fathers and begin to come to the Father as a little child in need of a father's love, we will begin to receive increasing revelation of Father God's love that is more powerful than any father issues we have carried through life. He will not ignore your cry for a father. No longer do you have to surrender yourself to the wounds within your father's house, for Father God is calling you to come home to Him.

> *Honor your father and mother (which is the first commandment with a promise), so that it may be well with you, and that you may live long on the earth.* (Ephesians 6:2-3)

Prayer to Encounter Your Father

Father, thank You that the door to Your house is always open to me and that I don't have to fear Your presence. Help me to understand how to honor my earthly father and mother. Forgive me for dishonoring them even when I felt I have reason to. I choose to be responsible for my actions and I chose to respond with forgiveness toward them instead of reacting to my pain.

APRIL 2
Healing Steps

Ways to heal:

- Choose to forgive your father for each way he hurt and disappointed you. Be detailed in speaking specific words of forgiveness for each moment of wounding that comes to mind. This may take some time. It is helpful to have a prayer partner lead you.

- Ask God to show you any specific memory that still influences your thought life, attitudes, or actions. Ask God to enter into that situation and bring comfort to the hurting child. Be still and quietly wait on God's love to touch that area.

- Lay your father at the foot of the Cross and release him. Lay at the Cross the pain, the anger, the bitterness, and the disappointments. Now turn and walk away.

- Turn to Father God and say, "I have nowhere to go for love. I know the door to Your house is always open. You said that You would not leave me like an orphan. I ask You, Father, to come to me now and reveal Your love and fatherhood for me. I choose to receive You as a Father to me. I choose to be Your child."

- Begin to pray, or have someone pray over you, the Scriptures about Father's love for you from "You Are Father's Happy Thought."

- Listen to music about Father God's love for you; let the message penetrate your heart as you sit quietly meditating on the Father's love. Spend time daily doing this, and allow His love to comfort you.

Father forgive them for they don't even know what they are doing. (Luke 23:34 The Passion Translation)

PRAYER TO ENCOUNTER YOUR FATHER

Please give me the courage to take these steps to heal any festering wounds, Lord. Just as Jesus had to ask You to forgive through Him when He was too hurt to forgive, so I ask You to forgive through me. I need You to do this with me Father. With You, all things are possible.

MOTHER ISSUES

Your relationship with your mother was your first experience with expressed love. Even in the womb, you either felt the emotional nurture and tenderness of your mother or you didn't, and those vital, tender bonding experiences helped form the way you felt about yourself, the world, and God. During the nine months spent in the womb and throughout the first two years of life, the mother figure is the most important figure in a child's life, having the strongest influence by the way she nurtures and expresses love to the child.

David demonstrated this principle in the Psalms when he declared to the Lord, *"Upon You I was cast from birth; You have been my God from my mother's womb"* (Psalm 22:10). Babies learn how to trust life, relationships, and even God when they are held, cuddled, fed, and nourished at their mother's breast. And without the mother's love, children may grow up with an inherent fear of relationships, and life that may be difficult to uproot. Storge, or family, love is demonstrated in three primary ways by mothers:

1. *Affectionate touch.* We were created for affection. Doctors have scientifically proven that without touch the body and the emotions become unhealthy. Touching someone says to them that they are important to you; they belong, and they have value. If we did not receive affectionate touch in the right way as a child, then in our teenage years we may allow ourselves to be touched in the wrong way.

And Jesus came to them and touched them and said, "Get up, and do not be afraid." (Matthew 17:7)

PRAYER TO ENCOUNTER YOUR FATHER

Father, I know that Mothers play such important roles in life—in every life. I will honor and respect my mother—whether living or passed—with my life, in conversations and deeds. I choose to forgive her for all the times she never touched me or for all the times that she touched me with a slap or inappropriately.

APRIL 4
MOTHER ISSUES
(CONTINUED)

2. *Eye contact.* The eyes are the windows of the soul where love is communicated to a child. They drink the love that flows to them from the eye contact with their parents. If children don't see understanding, loving looks in their parents' eyes, it can leave a wound that remains unhealed throughout life. They may feel awkward, insecure, separate, and out of place in their relationships.

3. *Tone of voice.* Babies learn to bond and trust when their parents look them in the eye and speak loving words in an encouraging, gentle, tender, and empathizing voice. Loving tones nurture the soul and help babies and children feel acceptance and value so they can walk free from the fear of rejection and failure.

When nurturing mothers walk into a room in which there is a baby, they seem to temporarily lose their sanity. They start babbling in baby talk, they "coo." When a mother picks up a baby, her tone, mannerisms, and everything about her changes; love and tenderness flow through her to the child. She does everything possible to meet the needs of the infant, and the baby senses that through her body language. She is demonstrating storge (family) love, and the child develops a godly belief that he or she will be comforted and that his or her needs will be met by others. In later years, they believe their needs will be met by God.

I will instruct and teach you in the way you should go. I will guide you with my eye. (Psalms 32:8 The Message)

PRAYER TO ENCOUNTER YOUR FATHER

Father, I never want to cause anyone, especially my family, to walk in the fear of rejection. I ask You to forgive me for each time I gave my child the look and for every time I spoke down to them or screamed at them to control them. I ask You to help me look at them, and speak to them in honoring tones and expressions of Your thoughts toward them. I also ask You to forgive me for judging my parents for how I was spoken to or for the look that sent the silent message to be that I had to perform for love.

APRIL 5
THE MOTHER HEART OF GOD

In the very nature of God, there is a mother's heart, the storge love that nurtures and comforts us in tenderness and compassion. This has been present since the beginning of time, even in the creation of the world.

How could God have created the female "in His own image" if there is not some aspect to His nature and character that is feminine? While I am not taking it to the extent that a few might, by saying that God is actually female, the nature of God does encompass both masculinity and femininity. The masculine heart cries out to do, to form and create, to initiate, to know wisdom, and to rationalize and intellectualize.

Men, while predominantly masculine, have a feminine part to their natures, and to reject it they often reject compassion, empathy, nurture, comfort, intimacy, and/or the ability to receive and give expressed love. In so doing, they can deny a portion of what God has created them to be, and thus they can easily give themselves over to finding their identity in performance, creating, and doing. They may begin to devalue emotions and intimacy; they may value logic and being analytical and intellectual over tenderness, affection, and warmth in relationships. Women likewise should not deny their masculine sides, or they may reject the analytical, intellectual aspects of their being.

In the image of God He created him; male and female He created them.
(Genesis 1:27 NKJV)

PRAYER TO ENCOUNTER YOUR FATHER
I have a problem understanding this aspect of Your image and of mine, Lord. I ask You to forgive me for each time I am demeaned the feminine nature in my life. I chose to forgive those especially my earthly mother for not bonding with me during my formative years. Because of that pain I have chosen to react with dishonor toward any mother figures in my life. I have closed my heart from femininity. I ask You to open my heart to basic trust again.

APRIL 6

ENMITY

Could there be some unholy scheme to destroy femininity on the earth? For 6,000 years, satan has had a special hatred for women. He has sought to destroy and devalue femininity in the hearts of humankind since the day in the Garden of Eden when the Lord God gave the woman (femininity—compassion, intimacy, communion, the ability to receive love) the power to defeat the enemy. The woman was not cursed; the curse was imposed upon satan that the woman would bring great harm to his kingdom. Satan now fears a person who walks in the intimacy that femininity brings forth; thus he seeks to wound us in our relationship with our mothers so that we reject femininity and a life of intimacy.

Could it be that it is easier for the world to value masculinity because the enemy has sought to make the world and religion value performance and productivity more than intimate, caring relationships? Could it be that the Church has lost some of its authority and power to overcome the evil one by putting a higher value upon masculine qualities (building and producing) than upon feminine qualities (communion and intimate, connected relationships)? Could it be that we need a healthier balance of both before we see a world revival?

So the Lord God said to the serpent, "Because you have done this, "Cursed are you above all livestock and all wild animals! ...And I will put enmity between you and the woman... (Genesis 3:14-15)

PRAYER TO ENCOUNTER YOUR FATHER

Father I ask You to show me the ways that I have chosen to dishonor femininity in my life. I ask You to forgive me for judging the females in my life as controlling always have to fight for a place to belong. I ask You to forgive me for not providing that place that they are honored. I choose today to honor the feminine as well as the masculine that both of them are Your image as Father.

APRIL 7

THE MOTHER WOUND

Breaches in the mother's love, whether they are caused intentionally or unintentionally, can leave wounds in a child's heart that can last a lifetime.

Our daughter, Sarah, was conceived during a very traumatic time. Our first child had already been born, but within a few months of his birth, he began having seizures that often caused him to stop breathing, which forced my wife to rush him to the emergency room, almost at the point of death. At that time, I worked on a fishing boat at sea twenty days or more out of each month. Trisha was left at home with a very sick child, and with very few sources of comfort in her life. Storms would blow through—nor'easters with very high winds—and she would know that I was out in dangerously high seas. She became consumed with fear, both for me and for our child, and as the situation wore on, she grew closer and closer to an emotional collapse.

Trisha's dream had always been to have a daughter. But when the doctor told her that she was pregnant with our second child, she nearly came unglued. "I can't be pregnant! I can't survive emotionally with what I am already going through—how will I be able to handle another baby?" When I arrived home from sea and she told me the news, I was thrilled. Another baby! I couldn't wait to have another child, and I couldn't understand Trisha's despair.

Yet you brought me out of the womb; you made me trust in you, even at my mother's breast. (Psalm 22:9 NIV)

PRAYER TO ENCOUNTER YOUR FATHER

Father, I thank You for giving me life but from the womb I have never felt like I belonged or was celebrated or welcomed to life. I choose to forgive my mom for rejection and sending me the message that I am an intrusion into her life. I ask You to forgive me for closing my heart to bonding to her as she tried to create an atmosphere of acceptance for me after my birth. I ask You Father to come and give me the nurture that I never experienced with my mom.

APRIL 8
A MOTHER'S HEART

"I don't want another baby right now! I can't handle it with you rarely home to help me!" She cried for three straight weeks. For nine months, Trisha carried Sarah in her womb, and her attitude rarely changed. It has been proven that the thoughts and emotions of the mother can affect a child in her womb—that what the mother thinks, experiences, and feels can influence the emotions of the baby inside her. At the moment of conception, a living spirit is created, and there is spirit-to-spirit communication between the mother and child in the womb. Habitual thoughts can create a response in the child in the womb. A mother who has been addicted to cigarettes need only think about smoking, and the heartbeat of the baby will begin to rise.

After nine months of experiencing her mother's emotional crisis, it was finally time for Sarah to come into the world. After twenty hours of excruciating labor, Sarah was delivered by an emergency caesarean section, a traumatic event for both mother and child. After the birth, Trisha went into a deep postnatal depression that lasted about a year. Throughout that time, the problems increased with my continual absence, our son's illness, and a newborn baby to take care of. Did Trisha love our daughter? Of course! She would have given up her own life for Sarah. But the emotional repercussions of those difficult times had seeded an ungodly belief in Sarah—a stronghold in her mind, will, and emotions.

Can a woman forget her nursing child and have no compassion on the son of her womb? Even these may forget, but I will not forget you. (Isaiah 49:15)

PRAYER TO ENCOUNTER YOUR FATHER
Father I ask You to forgive me for judging my mom for not providing a bonding experience with me in the womb. I have not understood completely why I walk into a room and expect to be rejected. I chose today to break agreement with the lie I embraced that I will never be celebrated or welcomed in any environment.

APRIL 9

HEALING WOUNDED HEARTS

By the age of two, Sarah would beat up any four-year-old she could find. She rejected all forms of affection, was antisocial, and defiant. Although she performed well in school, her attitude toward relationships and authority was lacking. She denied her femininity (bonding) and embraced only masculinity (performing). She had not allowed her femininity to be nurtured. Thus, she rejected bonding to her mother's love, even after Trisha was healed of depression and sought to do everything to make up for the storge love missing during those months of crisis.

When Sarah was nine years of age, we began learning many principles of healing for wounded hearts. Trisha and I ministered healing prayer to those wounded places in Sarah's heart that hadn't felt received by her mother. With the mothering touch of God's love, we watched a tomboy begin to transform into our beautiful daughter, feminine and soft. Now, her beauty is difficult to surpass. She is still self-motivated, always excelling in whatever she puts her hand to, but now she is also in touch with her womanhood and is warm and affectionate. As a result, her relationships with her mom, me, and others have become so much healthier.

I thank you Father for making me so mysteriously complex! Everything you do is marvelously breathtaking. It simply amazes me to think about it! How thoroughly you know me, Lord! You made me in a wonderful way.
(Psalms 139:14 The Passion Translation)

PRAYER TO ENCOUNTER YOUR FATHER
Father, I thank You that I have been created in such a wonderful way. I thank You for Your total acceptance of me. I choose to let go of the wounded messages that were unintentionally sent to me during my formative years. I thank You for the parents You gave me and I choose to embrace them with their faults.

APRIL 10
FAITH, LOVE, HOPE

Men tend to get irritated when we are asked to do something we don't know how to do. This leaves our families without a sense of love, comfort, value, and security. So we comfort ourselves (even as Christians) in our performance, addictions, compulsions, anger, isolation, insecurity, and fears of failure and rejection. I had filled my mind with knowledge, but years ago I had closed down a part of my heart to expressed love! As a small boy, my parent's marriage began to fall apart. The early years were good, but then everything seemed to go wrong. At about 12 years of age, I closed my heart and rebelled against receiving love and being a son. Something began to die inside of me.

We were created to experience love in order to be emotionally healthy! So many Christians are relationally unhealthy because they have not received the right kind of love—storge love. Storge is foundational to feeling secure and comforted. It quiets and brings rest to your soul and gives you vision and purpose in life. It makes you feel valued and gives you a sense that you belong. You begin to believe in yourself and develop faith to live and overcome. It equips you to conquer the fear of relationships and lowers walls of self-protection.

> *Every single moment you are thinking of me. How precious and how wonderful to consider that you cherish me constantly in your every thought. O God, your desires toward me are more than the grains of sand on every shore! When I awake each morning, you are still thinking of me.* (Psalms 139:17-18 The Passion Translation)

PRAYER TO ENCOUNTER YOUR FATHER
Father You are worthy of all my faith, love, and hope. I ask You to forgive me for shutting down and closing my heart to love out of the pain of not receiving Your storge love. I thank You that I can rest with who I am created by You.

BORN AGAIN

The ability for me to walk in pure, loving relationships was confined behind walls of fear and separation. Then, I attended a Father Loves You Conference. One of the prayer ministers ministered to me over my inability to receive or communicate storge love and the lack of comfort in my youth. She led the little boy within me in one prayer after another of repentance for each situation where I rebelled against being a son and against receiving love. For almost two hours I wept. Hidden core pain from the heart of the little boy began to surface. It was agonizing for me to submit to love and to have the walls of fear, separation, and isolation broken off my emotions and habit patterns of thought.

For weeks following that experience, it was as if I had been born all over again. It was as if the innocence and meekness of a little child were being restored to my emotions. My family saw an immediate change in my personality. I went from being serious and reserved to being more sensitive, comforting, and soft. I even found it easier to laugh and play with my children, which had been unnatural in the past. I began looking for every opportunity to give storge love away to my family. At first, they were suspicious. They wanted to see if they could trust me, if this was real and would last.

But Jesus said, "Let the little children come to me and do not forbid them for of such is the kingdom of heaven." (Matthew 19:14 NIV)

PRAYER TO ENCOUNTER YOUR FATHER

Sometimes I get tired of being a grown up with all the grown-up responsibilities. Today I ask You Father to help me to believe that You want to welcome me as a little child who needs to sit in Your lap for a while. Lift me up, Daddy.

COMFORT IN HIS ARMS

Even if you were physically or emotionally wounded as a child, you must not take on a victim mentality and believe that you are not responsible for any of your problems. You are the one who made the choice to turn to counterfeit affections to escape the pain or to turn to the mother heart of Father God for comfort and nurture and to experience His healing love. He longs for you to choose His love and to turn to Him no matter how much you have failed in the past. He loves you just the way you are; you do not have to do anything to experience His love for you. Does a little baby have to do anything to be loved? No! They need only choose to receive it!

Perhaps you need God's comfort or to experience His nurturing, mother love. Perhaps you never received storge love from your earthly mother, and the deep longing that has been left in your heart has caused you to turn to counterfeit affections to fill the void. Your mother may have forgotten or abandoned you, but God never has. No matter what type of mother you may have had, no matter how deeply she may have hurt or wounded you, God's unconditional love will always remember you, for you are written on the palms of His hands for all eternity.

> *For thus says the Lord, "Behold, I extend peace to her like a river, and the glory of the nations like an overflowing stream; and you will be nursed, you will be carried on the hip and fondled on the knees. As one whom his mother comforts, so I will comfort you; and you will be comforted in Jerusalem." (Isaiah 66:12-13)*

PRAYER TO ENCOUNTER YOUR FATHER

Father You know my earthly mother. You, Lord, know how she treated me and I treated her. I choose to forgive my mom for the hurts she caused in my life. Would You bring healing to any hurts either of us had or have—and help us rejoice in the state of forgiveness and gratefulness for each other!

COMFORT OTHERS

Now enter into the rest that you have been searching for all your life. Find a quiet place to sit, and let gentle, loving music play over you. Enter into Father God's mother heart as He gives you the things that your own mother was not able to give. Receive a mother's affirmation and acceptance pouring into you. Receive nurture and comfort. Receive Him playing all the games with you that your mother was not able to play. Receive Him taking all the seriousness out and pouring in playfulness and joy and displacing the intensity. Receive Him drawing you into a special place in His heart where you will never be forsaken or forgotten. Enter into His rest as His affectionate love casts out all fear.

Lord, I confess that I have turned to counterfeit affections rather than to You to seek the storge love that I needed to fill the void in my heart. Some of the choices that I have made have been wrong, and I repent from any impure thoughts, fantasies, or lust that I have allowed to breed in my mind and my emotions. Forgive me for not trusting You to meet all my needs.

I come to You now, lay my head on Your breast, and rest peacefully, knowing that You love and care for me.

Praise be to the God and Father of our Lord Jesus Christ, the Father of compassion and the God of all comfort, who comforts us in all our troubles, so that we can comfort those in any trouble with the comfort we ourselves receive from God. (2 Corinthians 1:3-4 NIV)

PRAYER TO ENCOUNTER YOUR FATHER

Father, I bring my longing to experience Your comforting, mothering heart to You. You are the only One who can meet the deepest need for storge love in my life. Thank You!

APRIL 14
DEEPER REVELATION

One time I was asked, "What three people have helped most to mature you and to release you in ministry?" At first I thought the answer was the friends in my life who had stood beside me and loved me through every trial and storm. But then I thought of several people who had not appeared to be loyal to me, those who sowed evil reports against me, those who tried to make themselves look good by exposing my faults and weaknesses to others, resulting in damage to my reputation and ministry.

I began to realize it is also some of the most hurtful, difficult relationships that have had some of the most dramatic impact for maturity and spiritual growth in my life. Without them, I may never have discovered some of the attitudes of pride, vindication, self-justification, and self-righteousness that I was full of. They helped me see how opinionated I was and how important it was for me to be right all the time in order to prove my self-worth! For years, for me to admit fault meant that I must be broken and deserving of rejection or punishment. Unknowingly, it was some of the more hurtful relationships that helped lead me into a deeper revelation of Father's embrace.

> *Blessed are you when people insult you and persecute you, and falsely say all kinds of evil against you because of Me.* (Matthew 5:11)

PRAYER TO ENCOUNTER YOUR FATHER

Wow! Lord, I never considered this angle in my life—that I actually was led to a deeper revelation of Your embrace by those who hurt me. Thank You; now I can see how You can make every encounter a blessing.

RIGHT OR RELATIONSHIP?

How many times have you valued being right over maintaining an intimate relationship with someone else and with God? How important has it been for you to have the last word? When you talk with your spouse or others, are you able to sit back and listen to what they have to say without constantly interjecting your own opinions? Are you afraid to show any weakness or vulnerability to family or peers? Do you portray yourself as the strong, but firm, authority who is always right?

The need to be right often creeps into our relationships in subtle ways. Because self-love is something that every one of us as human beings struggles with at some point in our lives, we have felt the need to prove ourselves better than someone else.

The core issue is usually insecurity and fear that is rooted in a love deficit. When insecurity is combined with a love of law, it can breed hypocrisy and a self-righteous attitude, the opposite of the Spirit of Christ, which is a meek and humble heart. It is meekness (no self-assertion) that enables us to enter into His rest and prepares our heart to experience Father's embrace. (See Matt. 5:5-11; 11:25-30.)

> At that time Jesus said, "I praise You, Father, Lord of heaven and earth, that You have hidden these things from the wise and intelligent and have revealed them to infants." (Matthew 11:25)

PRAYER TO ENCOUNTER YOUR FATHER
Wanting to be right is at the core of my being, Lord. I need the Holy Spirit to show me another way, the right way to respond.

APRIL 16

LAW OR GRACE

As Christians, it becomes very easy to value the letter of the law more than grace and mercy. It's funny how, in God's Word, He often turns what seems right and fair upside down. That is because satan, who is a legalist, demands what is right and fair. He demands payment for our sins and is constantly pronouncing us "guilty, guilty, guilty." But it is God who does not want to give us what we deserve—He wants to give us an undeserved, unmerited gift.

God is love; He is the opposite of satan. God's thoughts are positive, comforting, edifying, encouraging, accepting, valuing, and loving. Love *"thinks no evil"* (1 Cor. 13:5 NKJV). Grace, forgiveness, and innocence follow after His thoughts (see Jer. 29:11). Before I had this revelation, not knowing these truths brought much harm to my own life, family, and ministry. It hindered me from finding rest in Father's healing love. I acted more like God's policeman and developed accusatory thoughts or words about those I perceived had disappointed or hurt me. Then I became negative, critical, and devaluing toward them in my thought life. Unintentionally, my thoughts were coming into agreement with satan's thoughts! I entered into judgment, which hindered me from receiving healing and the blessings of God.

> *For sin shall not have dominion over you: for ye are not under the law, but under grace.* (Romans 6:14)

PRAYER TO ENCOUNTER YOUR FATHER

Am I acting like Your police officer, Lord? Am I judging people according to my warped perspective? I pray it isn't so. Correct me, Father, if I'm blind to this flaw.

VINDICATION

When people mistreat and disappoint us, it is only natural to feel hurt and wounded. But do we respond with God's grace? "Father, forgive them, for they know not what they are doing! They are acting out of their own hidden core pain and rejection! Help me to cover and restore relationship!" Or do we demand vindication, trying to justify and clear ourselves from blame? Do we try to make ourselves look good and innocent by exposing and talking about others' faults and thus making them look bad or in error?

Vindication can be one of the hungriest, most destructive appetites we possess. Vindication is rooted in demanding our rights and justice for the wrongs done to us! But God says, "Vengeance is Mine." It is His right, and it will cost us dearly to try helping Him out. When we do, God backs away from the situation and lets us handle things in our own fleshly, accusatory ways. Unknowingly, we are actually coming into agreement with satan and hindering ourselves from experiencing the intimacy of Father's embrace. When we decide we had better do something to help God straighten others out, we are definitely in need of God helping us!

Never take your own revenge, beloved, but leave room for the wrath of God, for it is written, "Vengeance is Mine, I will repay," says the Lord. (Romans 12:19)

PRAYER TO ENCOUNTER YOUR FATHER

Father, of course Your retribution is righteous and better than any petty, vindictive action I think someone deserves. I will begin, today, to remember that it is not my option to take my own revenge. Help me to remember that You think no evil of no one even when consequences for behaviors are in progress. I want to see others the way You do.

APRIL 18

BLESSING OR CURSE

We make the decision whether to receive mistreatment at the hands of others as a blessing or as a curse. God has promised a blessing if we respond with forgiveness and grace. But when we respond with accusation, vindication, fault-finding, or blame shifting, we then give satan a key to our front door; he can then come and go as he pleases in our house.

A study by Christian educator Mark Virkler reveals that 80 percent of most Christians' thoughts are negative. "They didn't value me! They didn't speak to me! They were not concerned with my need! They! They! They!" You can take most of your thoughts or conversations about a difficult person in your life, and in one way or another line them up under one of two categories: thoughts of restoration and relationship, or thoughts of vindication and exposure. One way leads to blessing; the other way releases a self-imposed curse. Satan wants us to inherit a curse. If the majority of our thoughts and conversations are in agreement with him, he has a right to release the curse.

Psalmist David put it so well: *"He also loved cursing, so it came to him; and he did not delight in blessing, so it was far from him. But he clothed himself with cursing as with his garment, and it entered into his body like water and like oil into his bones"* (Psalm 109:17-18).

Be angry, and yet do not sin; do not let the sun go down on your anger, and do not give the devil an opportunity. (Ephesians 4:26-27)

PRAYER TO ENCOUNTER YOUR FATHER

Blessing or curse? I'll take the blessing Father. I ask You to alert me every time I am choosing to think a negative thought about me or others. Help me to think no other thoughts than Your will for my life.

TRUTH OR CONSEQUENCES

God wants us to inherit a blessing. All we have to do is give the difficult person a gift that they may not deserve, a gift of forgiveness and grace.

It really comes down to whether we would rather be right or have relationship. How often our thoughts come into agreement with satan when we strive to be right in our relationships, especially at home. The biggest problem is, we usually are right about others' faults! But you can be right and have the wrong attitude, and you are dead wrong. Jesus didn't come to judge and accuse us; satan did (see John 3:17; 12:47; Rev. 12:10). Jesus didn't "grasp" for position or authority (see Philippians 2:5-8); satan did. Jesus sought to humble Himself. Satan sought to exalt himself (see Isaiah 14:12-14). Satan lost his position in God's presence. Christ was exalted to the right hand of the Father. When you choose the behavior, you choose the consequences!

> *Finally, all of you, be like-minded, be sympathetic, love one another, be compassionate and humble. Do not repay evil with evil or insult with insult. On the contrary, repay evil with blessing, because to this you were called so that you may inherit a blessing.* (1 Peter 3:8-9)

PRAYER TO ENCOUNTER YOUR FATHER
I remember the television game Truth or Consequences, Father. Oh how that has meaning to me after reading today's devotion. I choose Truth!

YOUR REWARD WILL BE GREAT

These verses imply that there is no blessing or reward when we do good to good people. Blessing comes when we do good to the people who hurt us. The blessing is being placed in Father's presence! We experience acceptance and unconditional love in the Father. We begin walking in a deeper intimacy with God and start taking on His spirit of grace, which releases intimacy in many of our relationships. We then start becoming more comfortable with love and forgiveness. This is the place where healing and the blessings of God begin to overtake you. What is the best way to make peace with a difficult person and enter into the blessing of Father's embrace?

> *But to you who are listening I say: Love your enemies, do good to those who hate you, bless those who curse you, pray for those who mistreat you. If someone slaps you on one cheek, turn to them the other also. If someone takes your coat, do not withhold your shirt from them. Give to everyone who asks you, and if anyone takes what belongs to you, do not demand it back. Do to others as you would have them do to you. If you love those who love you, what credit is that to you? Even sinners love those who love them. And if you do good to those who are good to you, what credit is that to you? Even sinners do that. And if you lend to those from whom you expect repayment, what credit is that to you? Even sinners lend to sinners, expecting to be repaid in full. But love your enemies, do good to them, and lend to them without expecting to get anything back. Then your reward will be great, and you will be children of the Most High, because he is kind to the ungrateful and wicked.* (Luke 6:27-35 NIV)

PRAYER TO ENCOUNTER YOUR FATHER

Hmmm, what IS the best way to make peace with a difficult person? I will seriously consider this question as I come into Your presence, Lord. I know You will give me the right answer.

THE GOLDEN RULE

In yesterday's cited passage, Jesus reveals the path of blessing and intimacy:

1. "Love your enemies," and you take on the spirit of Christ!
2. "Do good to those who hate you," and you may make them your friend!
3. "Bless those who curse you," and you inherit a blessing!
4. "Pray for those who mistreat you," and you begin to see them through the loving eyes of the Father!

By following these four principles, you begin to enter more deeply into Father's presence. Jesus walked out these principles with the one who hurt Him most—Judas. He knew what was in Judas' heart from the beginning, yet Jesus continued to serve and minister to him for three years. He allowed Judas to minister beside Him. He washed Judas's feet right before the betrayal. He broke bread with him and lived faithful to the covenant of loyalty with Judas in spite of his actions toward Him. He never stopped receiving and valuing Judas. Where would we be if Jesus had not received Judas as a blessing and as the one who would move Him toward the cross? Jesus' whole life demonstrated how we are to relate to other people. When He was mistreated and rejected, even when He was spat upon and when people attempted to kill Him, He responded with an attitude of grace and honor. His modeling sets the standard for us to live by in our relationships with other people.

Do to others as you would have them do to you. (Luke 6:31 NIV)

PRAYER TO ENCOUNTER YOUR FATHER

"Do unto others as you would have them do to you" has become almost cliché, Father. With Your Holy Spirit living in me, I can put this principle into daily practice. Help me to make this happen.

YOU GET WHAT YOU GIVE

It helps me to look at it this way: It is not a matter of what I want to give to someone who hurts me. It is a matter of what I want to receive in the future from other relationships. Do I want to receive a hardened, wounded heart that separates me from intimacy with God and leads me into resentments, pride, and walls of self-protection? Or do I want to enter into God's rest and walk in the joy of a lifestyle of forgiveness that produces a meek and gentle spirit? When I choose my response to wounding situations, I also choose what I will receive in the future from others.

The Bible is full of warnings that the standard by which we judge others will be the standard by which we ourselves will be judged. When I lived by the love of law, I had no revelation of Father's love; thus all my favorite Scriptures were about judgment, righteousness, holiness, and discipline. I breezed right past those on grace and mercy. After a year or two in ministry, I began to see many of the things that were wrong with the worldwide Church and its leaders. Trisha and I established Shiloh Place Ministries to straighten out the lives of Christian leaders. But my heart attitude was wrong. I was not walking in love, but law; not grace, but judgment—and what you give is what you will get!

You intended to harm me, but God intended it for good to accomplish what is now being done, the saving of many lives. (Genesis 50:20 NIV)

PRAYER TO ENCOUNTER YOUR FATHER

While walking with You in the coolness of the morning (or evening), Father, are You pleased with me? Or am I walking ahead in law or behind in judgment, rather than with You in love and grace? Show me where I am with You so that I can position my heart for change.

APRIL 23

LIVE PEACEABLY

I developed into a person who valued being right over relationship. I began valuing the people who seemed to have the same spirit as me and promoted my ministry. Those who did not promote my ministry or me, I did not feel comfortable around them—and they certainly did not seem comfortable around me. Please understand that all during these years I was a man of integrity and truth, the person teaching seminars on bitterness, forgiveness, marriage enrichment, and healing the wounded heart. I did not know I was in bondage until I was free from it.

Outwardly, I had a smile on my face and honored other Christian leaders. But inwardly, I was competitive and sat among groups of ministers, judging their faults and weaknesses and wondering why I was not as favored as they appeared to be. So the law of sowing and reaping, giving and receiving continued in its effect—and you usually reap a lot more than you sow! I began receiving from others what I was giving to others in my thought life and conversations with my wife. The rigid scrutiny I gave others, others began to give me, and there were many faults they could focus upon, though I could see few within myself. There is nothing easier than self-deception.

> *Make every effort to live in peace with everyone and to be holy; without holiness no one will see the Lord. See to it that no one falls short of the grace of God and that no bitter root grows up to cause trouble and defile many.*
> (Hebrews 12:14-15 NIV)

PRAYER TO ENCOUNTER YOUR FATHER

Father, I totally welcome You to dig up any bitter roots that may be growing up inside me that will cause trouble and defile others. I ask You to help me understand the root issue that would cause me to judge another's value. Hurry!

THE PRICE IS RIGHT

Most people don't realize the consequences of judging others by a higher standard than they judge themselves. When you practice a lifestyle of the need to be right and the love of law, you begin walking down a path of self-defilement that will eventually lead to isolation and an inability to maintain healthy, intimate relationships. The following six steps may seem gradual, so it is important to be aware of them when you are beginning to stray from living by the law of love and grace. For preventive measure, allow me to share the pattern that I once followed.

1. *Negative attitudes.* The first price I paid when I chose being right over having relationship was to foster a negative attitude toward those who did not think and act like me. I began to focus more on the faults of others than imparting to them God's grace and unconditional love. Eventually, my whole outlook on life and Christianity became critical and cynical—I had taken the first step to defiling myself. Others didn't defile me. I chose that route myself with my accusatory thought life. What patterns do you notice in your own thought life? Are you constantly exasperated by the perceived shortcomings of other people? Do you notice yourself becoming more critical of your pastor, other ministers, your boss, coworkers, friends, or family members in your thoughts? Do you consider yourself "better" than most people you meet?

Do not judge, or you too will be judged. (Matthew 7:1 NIV)

PRAYER TO ENCOUNTER YOUR FATHER

Father, I ask You to help me understand what You are doing in the lives of the people I am in relationship with. Help me not to judge them according to my negative thinking. Help me to be sensitive in their situational needs and I bring all of my negative thoughts to the cross and ask You to forgive me and cause me to hear what You think so I can be a source of encouragement to all.

THE PRICE IS RIGHT
(CONTINUED)

2. *Impure motives.* Once I spent a lot of time replaying in my thought life how others seemed more favored than I was, how others did not have the revelation that I had, how this person had done that to me and that person hadn't done this for me, it began to build an attitude (a habit structure of thinking) that unconsciously affected the motivations of my heart. My primary motive was no longer to help others and spread God's Kingdom of love on the earth; I became motivated out of my own self-righteousness; the good works and hyper-religious activity helped me prove to myself that I had greater maturity and revelation than others. This all overflowed into my motives with family. I came home wanting everyone to meet my needs instead of living to make Father's love known to them.

What is behind the motivation for your service to others? Do you take an unhealthy pride in your accomplishments in the ministry or in charitable organizations? Do you look down at other people who do not perform as many good deeds as you do? Is your service leaving you with an angry edge at home?

Pride goes before destruction, a haughty spirit before a fall. (Proverbs 16:18 NIV)

PRAYER TO ENCOUNTER YOUR FATHER
I know, Father, what pride can do to people. I know what it did to Your angel who was banished from Heaven. Please help me keep my pride in check, Lord God. I ask You for a heart of humility.

THE PRICE IS RIGHT
(CONTINUED)

3. *Defilement of speech.* The attitudes of my heart soon began to affect my conversations about others. *"For the mouth speaks what the heart is full of"* (Matthew 12:34 NIV). I knew better than to criticize or gossip about others outwardly, but beneath my words was often a condescending undertone. Subtly demeaning or devaluing other's beliefs or gifting was my way of proving my own self-righteousness and making me look good. Do you use a tone of superiority or condescending looks or words toward others? Do you find yourself demeaning other people when they happen to come up in a conversation? Are your words critical, or do you defend and help to point out the good in the person?

4. *Divisive actions.* Once I could no longer speak words of honor about a person, it was not long before my actions unknowingly began to follow the same destructive path. It became those who think like me against those who don't. I began drawing people to my side with subtle innuendoes that others were not as mature or had as much understanding as I did. I was not aware that I was creating an environment of distrust, rivalry, and strife among the people around me. When you encounter someone who does not live up to your expectations, how do you treat them? Do you create an atmosphere of trust, or do conversations develop that help you convince others how much wiser or right you are than they are?

> *Life and death are in the power of the tongue.* (Proverbs 18:21)

> *For they loved human praise more than praise from God.* (John 12:43 NIV)

PRAYER TO ENCOUNTER YOUR FATHER

Father I ask You for Your Holy Spirit to give me an early warning sign when I began to think negative thoughts so they don't lead into negative words spoken over someone.

THE PRICE IS RIGHT
(CONTINUED)

5. *Damage to relationships.* The negative attitudes I developed toward others were taken home in my relationships with my wife and children. I had to be right, and it left my wife and children with a tremendous fear of failure and rejection around me. How are your relationships with your family members, friends, and other people? Are you developing vibrant, caring relationships based on intimacy, honor, and trust, or are those closest to you obeying you out of fear? Are you expressing your love to those around you in ways that they can understand?

6. *Isolation.* Another price I paid—many people just didn't enjoy being around me. I was too intense and driven to be right. I was not able to be home for my family even when I was home. It was difficult for some people to receive me or my conversations because I lived in such a state of agitated resistance against everyone and everything. Only those very secure in God's love or those who could maintain such a rigid standard of excellence befriended me. How many true friends do you really have? When they do reject you, do you shrug it off, telling yourself that they are the ones who are wrong? Are your spouse and family members really present in their relationship with you, or is emotional distance beginning to take its toll?

Search me, God, and know my heart test me and know my anxious thoughts. See if there is any offensive way in me. Psalm 139:23-24 (NIV)

PRAYER TO ENCOUNTER YOUR FATHER
Father, Your Word says that stubborn pride will be broken down by You. I know that You keep Your promises so I ask You to forgive me of pride and I ask for a crop failure for all the past times I spoke or thought in a prideful way toward my family, peers and friends.

THE GREATEST PRICE OF ALL

The price for grasping to be right is high, and the consequences can be tragic. Marriages fail, families are destroyed, and relationships are ruined, all because of the deceptive allure of self-justification, self-righteousness, and the need for self-vindication. There is a higher place to which Father wants His children to aspire, a higher place than striving to be right. Placing the law above grace results in a vicious cycle that will only sabotage the very thing that all human beings are longing for—intimacy with God and with others.

While a tragic consequence of always having to be right is isolation and unhealthy relationships with other people, there is an even costlier result of such a lifestyle—the loss of intimate fellowship with the heavenly Father and entering into His rest. Dwelling in Father's embrace requires an attitude of humility, of admitting our failings and shortcomings to God and others, and asking for their forgiveness.

Experiencing Father's embrace goes hand in hand with loving, not judging our neighbors. We begin to enter into the realm of God's grace when we are willing to humble ourselves in His presence and with others, admit our faults, and accept His free gift of unconditional love.

> *"I remind you that it is written, 'He that is within me is greater than he that is in the world.' I command you to bow your knee to the Name of Jesus and leave me."* (1 John 4:4)

PRAYER TO ENCOUNTER YOUR FATHER

Father I ask You to show me through Your early warning system before I speak with the motive of having to be right or to correct someone who does not think like me. I give the Holy Spirit permission to cause me to hold my tongue when I feel I need to be right. Show me what You would say and do in that moment.

APRIL 29

BREAKING FREE

Follow these four principles to begin the process of breaking free from the need to be right:

1. *Choose to forgive each person who has disappointed you.* In a place of solitude, speak each individual name aloud and tell them that you choose to forgive them for the hurt brought to your life. Be specific. Personally, I have many times sought out people gifted in healing prayer to help me walk through the forgiveness process. You can go to the Prayer Ministry page on our Website to find ministries equipped in healing prayer in your area (www.shilohplace.org).

2. *Seek God's forgiveness for violating the law of judging.* Ask God to forgive you for each judgment you placed upon another person, each time you came in agreement with the enemy instead of with God's grace. Renounce each violation of the law of judgment that has been in your thought life. Yes, this may take some time. But it is worth it when you allow the blood of Jesus to cleanse you from all sin (see 1 John 1:7-9).

If we claim to be without sin, we deceive ourselves and the truth is not in us. If we confess our sins, he is faithful and just and will forgive us our sins and purify us from all unrighteousness. (1 John 1:8-9)

PRAYER TO ENCOUNTER YOUR FATHER

Heavenly Father, if I claim to be without sin, I am deceiving myself and the truth is not in me. I confess my sin of the need to be right to You right now. Please forgive me and purify me from my judgements. I choose to forgive those have disappointed me.

BREAKING FREE
(CONTINUED)

3. *You may need to practice the principle of restitution.* If your judgment of others has brought harm to their life, often asking for forgiveness from God is not enough. For you to be healed, you may need to go to them and ask forgiveness from them. Do not mention their fault—only take ownership of your own. Seek mature counsel about the best way and the choice of words to use.

As God was bringing me this revelation, I spent months going to each person, making phone calls and writing letters seeking for their forgiveness for my relating to them for so many years out of my own pain and immaturity. It transformed my life and resulted in a greater ability to make Father's love known to my family and to the world.

4. *Begin renewing your mind daily.* Cast down all thoughts and imaginations that are contrary to God's grace (see 2 Cor. 10:4-5). John Arnott's book, *What Christians Should Know About the Importance of Forgiveness,* helped me see the price I was paying for my choice to live by the law. I began making conscious choices several times each day for my thought life to turn from law to dwelling in grace. When I first started this, 90 percent of the time my thought life was in law. Today, I believe that 90 percent or more of the time I dwell in grace. It has changed what I am reaping in my life, family, and ministry.

Humble yourselves before the Lord, and he will lift you up. (James 4:10 NIV)

PRAYER TO ENCOUNTER YOUR FATHER

Thank You, Father, for sending Your Son to pay the price for my sins. You love me the way I am, not the way others say I should be. I am so very grateful for Your grace and unconditional love. Show me ways to make restitution for judgments that I have made that brought harm to other's lives.

MAY 1
THE LIGHT

I traveled to Slovakia to conduct a pastors' retreat for a friend of mine. While I was there, I had the opportunity to take a tour of a cavern formed deep inside a mountain. My friend insisted that it was a sight I had to see. He neglected to tell me that it was a hike of 990 steps to the bottom depths of the river below! As we progressed deeper into the mountain, our tour guide turned on lights in each cavern chamber we entered so that we would be able to find our way.

Eventually we reached the particular cavern through which an underground river flowed. It was breathtakingly beautiful. Our tour guide told us that this river produced some of the healthiest water in the world. When questioned why this particular river produced such life-giving qualities, the guide responded that it was because of the mineral content in the water that came from rich mineral deposits inside the mountain. She then asked everyone to stand still, and she turned out the lights. For ten seconds, we stood in utter darkness. When she finally turned the lights back on, she explained, "One reason this water is so pure is that nothing—no bacteria, no pollutants—live in the river as long as it flows in this utter darkness. Life is produced only as the river flows out of the mountain into the light!"

But if we walk in the light, as he is in the light, we have fellowship with one another, and the blood of Jesus, his Son, purifies us from all sin. (1 John 1:7 NIV)

PRAYER TO ENCOUNTER YOUR FATHER
Father, help me to identify all of the pollutants in my life. Turn on Your light and reveal the good, bad, and ugly. Then purge the bad and the ugly.

NO DARKNESS AT ALL

Revelation began breaking forth within me as I thought of how many Christians attend powerful conferences and experience deep encounters in the presence of God's love, only to return home and fall back into their habitual patterns of sin and shame. Others receive breakthroughs in counseling or prayer ministry, yet a short time later they can't seem to sustain an intimate and healthy relationship with God or their spouse and family. They end up just as harsh, unyielding, and condescending with their family as they ever were, or they continue to perpetuate the same problematic struggles with intimacy and relationships as before. When the tour guide said that the river produces life when flowing only in the light and not in the darkness, I realized that dwelling in a place where Father's love is constantly renewing and restoring you to intimacy with others can take place only when we are willing to walk in the light of God's love. Fellowship with God is greatly hindered when we choose darkness over light.

Not only is God's nature love, but He is also light; by His very nature God is against any darkness that lies within us. He is not against us. He created us for love; therefore, He is against any darkness that may hinder us from His love producing life and intimacy with Him and others. The very purpose of light is to set us free from anything that hinders deeper intimacy with Him.

This is the message we have heard from him and declare to you: God is light; in him there is no darkness at all. (1 John 1:5)

PRAYER TO ENCOUNTER YOUR FATHER
Father I thank that You are not only love but light and in You there is no darkness of shame and sin. I ask You for greater revelation into the hidden and dark areas of my heart. I bring those areas to Your cross Jesus and ask You to forgive me and heal me of those areas of pain.

LOVE, LIGHT, DARKNESS

Unconditional love is never based on the performance or goodness of the person who is receiving the love. It is based on the nature of the one giving it. There is nothing you can ever do to receive any more love than you have already received from the Father; He has proven His absolute and unconditional love for you by the selfless act of His Son, Jesus Christ, dying at Calvary.

God's love for you is not based on your performance; it is based on who you are in Christ, His beloved son or daughter. All you ever have to do is receive His love. Accepting God's gracious gift and dwelling in intimacy will cost you everything, especially your pride. I like the definition of darkness that Jack Winter taught me: Darkness is a moral state where you hide things, have secrets, and give the enemy ground to traffic in your life.

Darkness is not just a place void of light. Darkness is also the dominion of satan (see Acts 26:18). Anywhere we allow darkness to remain can be an open door for the thief to come and steal, kill, and destroy (see John 10:10). The very thing the enemy wants to take from us is the very thing he lost—intimacy and fellowship with God. Darkness gives the enemy ground to traffic in your life and slowly drain away a sense of intimacy, acceptance, and love.

> *The thief comes only to steal and kill and destroy; I have come that they may have life, and have it to the full.* (John 10:10 NIV)

PRAYER TO ENCOUNTER YOUR FATHER

Father, most people are afraid of the dark. I am afraid of being without Your light. If pride gets in the way, shove it aside so I can come to You, Lord, the Light of Life. Make me more aware and sensitive to the enemies plot to try and steal from the changes I desire to make in my life.

FOUR AREAS OF DARKNESS

Darkness in us can be: 1) Hidden and unconfessed sin; 2) Someone else's darkness invading our light; 3) Our masks, cover-ups, walls, and pretenses; 4) The shame of past immoral sins. We will look at these potential areas of darkness individually in the next few days.

1. *Hidden and unconfessed sin.* Because I was so afraid of what others would think if they really knew me, I had kept unconfessed sin in my heart, areas of my thought life that I would not allow my wife or children to see. I'm not speaking of outward immoral sins, but the motives that drove me in my Christian walk—the attitudes of pride, competition, jealousy, and envy—the aggressive striving to be somebody and to be seen and known. The thoughts and intentions of my heart that were all wrapped up in self-love. These were the hidden sins of pride and self-love that I struggled with most. I had a prayer partner I talked many things over with, but I was a closed book at home to my family. My darkness gave the enemy ground to traffic in every area that I chose darkness over light, and thus made it difficult for me to dwell in Father's loving embrace. Light is an armor that protects you from temptation and burns away the flesh and its lusts. Only in darkness can pride defile us.

> *The night is almost gone, and the day is near, therefore let us lay aside the deeds of darkness and put on the armor of light. Let us behave properly as in the day, not in carousing and drunkenness, not in sexual promiscuity and sensuality, not in strife and jealousy. But put on the Lord Jesus Christ, and make no provision for the flesh in regard to its lusts.* (Romans 13:12-14)

PRAYER TO ENCOUNTER YOUR FATHER

Daily, Father, I will choose to put on my armor of light to ward off the deeds of darkness. No longer will I face the enemy without my armor. Thank You for Your Word that gives me direction.

WOUNDS FROM OTHERS

2. *Someone else's darkness invading our light.* Darkness also can enter in as a result of wounding that we have received from others. It is not always a result of our own wrong moral choice; darkness can also be the result of our reactions to those who have disappointed or hurt us. Where unconditional love is, we often feel secure enough to walk in the light, but when we feel love becomes conditional, get ready to be blindsided. Unresolved conflict in relationships can be an open door to darkness. We are usually the ones who think we are right in the situation, so we think that our rightness justifies our negative attitude or closed spirit.

I was neglecting my wife, but I couldn't see it. It was an area of darkness in my life that was affecting my spouse and family. My darkness invaded Trisha's light, and her darkness was about to invade me. Our darkness blinded us to the motives of our own hearts, and we began to lose sensitivity to God's voice.

Have you ever noticed how often God uses your spouse to reveal the unyielded areas of your heart? Conflict reveals unresolved issues of pride, independence, and self-love. This happens not only in family relationships; let unforgiveness and unresolved conflict remain in any of your relationships, and darkness slowly begins to creep back in, and you easily lose the sense of dwelling in Father God's embrace.

> *Anyone who claims to be in the light but hates a brother or sister is still in the darkness. Anyone who loves their brother and sister lives in the light, and there is nothing in them to make them stumble. But anyone who hates a brother or sister is in the darkness and walks around in the darkness. They do not know where they are going, because the darkness has blinded them.* (1 John 2:9-11 NIV)

PRAYER TO ENCOUNTER YOUR FATHER

Father, am I blinded by the darkness hidden somewhere inside? Use a spotlight to reveal it to me, as I may be oblivious to what is going on. I trust You to show me.

MAY 6
LIGHT LIFE, DARKNESS DEATH

3. *Our masks, cover-ups, walls, and pretenses.* One of the greatest hindrances to intimacy is when we let darkness into our lives by being unwilling to allow ourselves to be known by God or by others. Light is silent, brings warmth, and is a necessity for life. But darkness is cold and drives us to hide behind walls of self-protection, where we are unreal, or to pretend to be more spiritually mature than we really are.

Hiding the truth about ourselves from others, pretending to be better than we really are and wearing religious masks—these are the supreme sins that ultimately caused the Pharisees to crucify Jesus. The first sin disciplined in the Book of Acts was a sin of deception and cover-up. Ananias and Sapphira pretended to be more spiritual, more sacrificial than they really were, and they died because of it (see Acts 5:1-11).

Many people think they will be rejected if others know the truth about them. That may be true for some, but there are also many more who will value your open heart. They will feel secure in your presence and know they can trust you because you are hiding nothing. Only in walking in the light do we experience the cleansing power of God's love that produces the lasting fruit of a transformed life. Bondages begin to be broken that may have hindered the flow of intimacy and love for a lifetime.

> *…Why is it that you have conceived this deed in your heart? You have not lied to men but to God.* (Acts 5:4)

PRAYER TO ENCOUNTER YOUR FATHER
I pray to be open and transparent regarding my life to You and everyone. The Ananias and Sapphira story has always stuck in my mind—and I don't want to repeat their mistake of lying to You.

THE SHAME OF SIN

4. *The shame of past immoral sins.* Once you step out of the light of God's love, whether through your own sin or from the mistreatment of someone else, you feel the need to bond to someone or something else because you were created for love and intimacy. Many times this involves immoral sexual activity. We must bond to something, but when inappropriate sexual behavior or impure lustful passions become the source of our search, we step out of the light into darkness. Sexual sin is a counterfeit affection that many of us have used as a substitute for the lack of intimacy with God and others, and it can leave us clothed with a garment of shame. So many are seeking love in all the wrong places. Even if you fill a room with Spirit-filled believers, there will still be those silent cries being made all over the room: Somebody, love me. Somebody, give me the comfort and affirmation I need.

Somehow those people end up attracted to each other like magnets. Inside they are crying to be loved because the darkness in them stirs up the passions of the flesh. God wants us to flee from all sexual immorality, not because He is trying to deprive us of our fun, but because He knows the pain, despair, and shame that can be the end result of such a lifestyle.

> *Flee immorality. Every other sin that a man commits is outside the body, but the immoral man sins against his own body. Or do you not know that your body is a temple of the Holy Spirit who is in you, whom you have from God, and that you are not your own? For you have been bought with a price: therefore glorify God in your body.* (1 Corinthians 6:18-20)

PRAYER TO ENCOUNTER YOUR FATHER

Shame seems to be irrelevant in these promiscuous times, Father God. But deep inside every person knows right and wrong and feels ashamed when Your commands are broken. I choose to flee immorality quickly.

MAY 8

SEXUAL SIN

Sexual sins can be devastating to your entire personhood, your spouse, and your family! But even after you have asked for forgiveness and placed the sin under the blood of Jesus, there can still be a residual sense of shame. Every other sin takes place outside of the body, but because sexual sin is a sin against the body itself, the remnants of it can stick to you. You may feel the sense of shame, even in your physical body. Sexual sin violates the first and greatest commandment to love the Lord our God with all our heart, with all our soul, and with all our mind.

Pornography gives a false sense of intimacy; it is a seeking of comfort in the flesh because darkness has hindered you from walking in intimacy with your spouse and with God. These sexual bondages are often the most difficult to break because you feel too unclean to receive God's love. In an attempt to regain that lost sense of love, you may fall further into the sexual sin. When you repent of these sins, Father will forgive you and wash you in the blood of Jesus, but the feelings of shame and uncleanness may remain if you are too ashamed for these sins to ever be known or brought into the light.

For this is the will of God, your sanctification; that is, that you abstain from sexual immorality. (1 Thessalonians 4:3)

PRAYER TO ENCOUNTER YOUR FATHER
Father, wash me with the blood of Your Son, Jesus in the areas where I have given in to immorality. I choose to stop shaming myself and to always seek You for clean and beautiful intimacy that I was created to experience. Embrace me now.

THE CONSEQUENCES OF DARKNESS

The blood does not cover what we leave hidden in darkness and refuse to uncover. We can confess our sin to God, and He forgives us the first time we ask, but we can still carry the shame of our sin because of guilt and the fear of anyone ever finding out about it. This has the power to steal years of intimacy from our life and relationships.

My wife and I ministered to woman who for more than fifteen years of marriage could not fulfill her husband's sexual needs because of the shame she carried. She told how they were both Christians and virgins. But one night she got mad at her dad and went to a bar and unwillingly had sex with a man. She asked God to forgive her, and He did. But she was too ashamed to tell anyone, especially her future husband. She ended up living in darkness. A few weeks later she learned that she was pregnant. Out of desperation she had an abortion. She asked God every hour of every day to forgive her, and He did. But because she chose to hide everything, the enemy had grounds to traffic in her life with accusation, self-condemnation, and shame. The wedding day came. The shame kept her from the wonderful joy that God had intended for that night. She was totally forgiven—but the power of darkness stole the intimacy and love for which God created them.

> *But if we walk in the Light as He Himself is in the Light, we have fellowship with one another, and the blood of Jesus His Son cleanses us from all sin.* (1 John 1:7)

PRAYER TO ENCOUNTER YOUR FATHER

When I ask for forgiveness, I will also ask for You to remove my shame. Shame can hang around my neck for way too long. I will believe and have faith that when You forgive me, You will also take away my shame.

MAY 10

CHOOSING LIGHT OVER DARKNESS

Unexposed areas of darkness can be one of the greatest hindrances to experiencing Father God's embrace. When we walk into a dark room, we do not cast out the dark, we turn on the light. The light effortlessly dispels the darkness! For intimacy to flow freely in our relationships we need to choose a life of openness and transparency. We need to be honest with our inward darkness before we are free to experience and maintain a life of true intimacy with God and with others. *"You desire truth in the innermost being…"* (Psalm 51:6).

If there is an area of darkness in your life in which you may have received forgiveness but have not sensed the deep cleansing of the shame that you feel, you may want to find a trusted prayer partner to pray with you. *"Confess your sins to each other and pray for each other so that you may be healed. The prayer of a righteous person is powerful and effective"* (James 5:16 NIV). Or you may want to begin by praying this aloud yourself. Do not just pray it word for word, be very detailed and specific about each area of concern. Then pray the following verse over each area and proclaim forgiveness and healing.

> *How much more, then, will the blood of Christ, who through the eternal Spirit offered himself unblemished to God, cleanse our consciences from acts that lead to death, so that we may serve the living God?* (Hebrews 9:14 NIV)

> *If we confess our sins, he is faithful and just and will forgive us our sins and purify us from all unrighteousness.* (1 John 1:9 NIV)

PRAYER TO ENCOUNTER YOUR FATHER

Father, I come to You in Jesus' name. I thank You that the blood of Jesus forgives me and cleanses me from all sin and unrighteousness. I renounce the hidden works of darkness over my life. I want to experience Your liberty in all areas of my lustful flesh man. I believe as Your child this is possible.

FATHER, I GIVE YOU...

Father, I give You my eyes. You know every way I have opened the door to darkness through the eye-gate—unclean things that I have looked upon, unclean pictures, pornography, lusts of the eyes, scenes of the past that have released darkness in me. I renounce those sins of darkness and ask You to forgive me.

Father, I give You my ears. You know every unclean thing that I have listened to and that has defiled me through the ear-gate. Forgive me for listening to gossip and evil spoken of others. I renounce the darkness and ask You to cleanse me.

Father, I give You my mouth and my tongue. You know how I have used my mouth in unclean ways—unclean speech, gossip, speaking evil of others. Wash my mouth clean in the name of Jesus.

Father, You know how I have used my hands in ways that have brought pain to others. I ask You to forgive me for sinning with my hands.

Father, I give You my mind, thoughts, and imaginations. Father, I give You my body, that which is uniquely male or female. I ask You to cleanse my body with the washing of the water of the Word from all defilement and uncleanness.

Therefore, I urge you, brothers and sisters, in view of God's mercy, to offer your bodies as a living sacrifice, holy and pleasing to God—this is your true and proper worship. (Romans 12:1 NIV)

PRAYER TO ENCOUNTER YOUR FATHER

I choose You to be my Father and I choose to be Your child. I need Your fatherly love and affection to come to me and penetrate my character and personality.

TWO PATHS INTO
FATHER GOD'S LOVE

My journey into Father's love began something like the "cliff diver." You've seen those guys on television diving off the cliffs in Acapulco or bungee-jumping off bridges. Some of these guys are not playing with a full deck. Others have no fear. Some have a hidden death wish. I think I fit into the death wish category. I've experienced so much pain in my life that I have become a specialist in giving that pain to others.

I go for seasons living in "numb-numbville," blind to the pain my intensity causes in others. Then out of nowhere I get in touch with my hidden core pain, and all this emotional release occurs. My pain, which is plain to see by others, is all over me, and I have no choice but to jump. My death wish is not physical, but a heartfelt grief over the fleshly things in my life that bring pain to others, and then a cry to put to death the self-love with which I struggle. Then I get just crazy enough to jump off anything into the arms of my loving Father.

Trisha, my wife, is a "wader." She stands by the shore at the beach and waits for the tide to slowly rise. She watches and waits for the sea to wash around her feet. It is safer that way. She is not as likely to drown, while I come pretty close at times.

These are the ones I look on with favor: those who are humble and contrite in spirit, and who tremble at my word. (Isaiah 66:2 NIV)

PRAYER TO ENCOUNTER YOUR FATHER

Sometimes I'm a cliff diver and other times a wader, Father. Please let me know which one You prefer—I want to be in Your will for my life, the safest and most rewarding place to be!

WALKING IN THE SPIRIT

Walking in the Spirit is a daily process that takes place moment-by-moment, step-by-step. It is determined by every decision I make, whether I choose to focus on the things in Father's heart and live in peace, or whether I choose to follow self-love and live in fear and insecurity.

There are days when I choose to walk in the Spirit, and they are so rich and full of a sense of peace and joy. These are the days God's nature rubs off on me and I live to give His love away to others. I love the expressions I see on the faces of my wife and children when I walk in the Spirit of God's love. It is what makes life worth living. By the end of the day, I am left with an overwhelming sense of the abiding presence of Father's love, not just flowing vertically from the Father to me, but also flowing horizontally as I purpose in my heart to make His love known to my family first, and then to others and the nations. What an adventure! It is more fulfilling than in my younger days at sea when I caught groupers up to 400 pounds or filled my boat with 9,000 pounds of fish in one day on a hook and line, making $4,000.

> For what the law was powerless to do because it was weakened by the flesh, God did by sending his own Son in the likeness of sinful flesh to be a sin offering. And so he condemned sin in the flesh, in order that the righteous requirement of the law might be fully met in us, who do not live according to the flesh but according to the Spirit. (Romans 8:3-4 NIV)

PRAYER TO ENCOUNTER YOUR FATHER

Father, I choose to focus on the things in Your heart and live in peace—I choose NOT to follow self-love and live in fear and insecurity. I choose to walk in the Spirit as You guide me each day. Thank You for giving me the choice.

MAY 14

ABIDING

Oh the days that I am wrapped up in my own need and self-love. Yes, I still have those days. And each one I have serves as motivation to walk in the Spirit tomorrow, because the days of my flesh are filled with aggressive striving, anxiety, and hyper-religious activity as I seek to find acceptance in the things I do. By the end of the day I see my family's countenance fade to that of insecurity and fear in my presence. I lie in bed at night seeking for Father God's forgiveness and often rise the next morning asking others to forgive me. This is what brings me back into a walk in the Spirit—acknowledgment of each sin against love and choosing not to live in guilt and shame, but to step back into the center of Father's love.

This is a key to abiding daily in God's love. It is not just in our past dramatic experiences. It cannot be a walk that is based on emotions, on running to a revival meeting seeking a new soul-stirring experience. It is simply dealing with the issues in your life moment-by-moment, not waiting for a crisis to take place to seek God's face, but living with Him daily in all the matters that come up, no matter how big or small.

For if you live according to the flesh, you will die; but if by the Spirit you put to death the misdeeds of the body, you will live. (Romans 8:13)

PRAYER TO ENCOUNTER YOUR FATHER

Father forgive me for each sin I have committed in misrepresenting You to my family first. I can tell the days when I'm walking in Your Spirit, God—and so can everyone around me. When filled with Your presence, I float above the chaos and nit-picking and this is how I want to live my life in You and around others.

ABIDING
(CONTINUED)

The enemy of our souls does not want us to abide in God's presence. It is in that place of humility and love that we do great damage to his domain. He has three basic tactics that he uses to prevent us from abiding in love: decoy, despoil, and destroy. Satan seeks to decoy or distract us from focusing on our mission to make Father's love known to others. He wants to despoil our inheritance that we receive in Father's love, and he will try to destroy our sense of the abiding presence of the Father.

In my earlier years as a Christian, one of the enemy's primary decoys that he used on me was a dramatic experience that either I had in the past or that someone told me about. During those years, I often hit rock bottom, and God had to take dramatic measures to rescue me and save me from myself. Of course, I never forgot those feelings of overwhelming joy and peace that came when I experienced great breakthroughs. The problem was that I started spending much of my time trying to regain that feeling or waiting for the next breakthrough before I would walk in humility and love at home.

The Spirit himself testifies with our spirit that we are God's children. (Romans 8:16)

PRAYER TO ENCOUNTER YOUR FATHER
Father, have I become dependent on the next great dramatic experience from You? Have I neglected the everyday miracles You reveal to me? I'm open to experiencing them! Help me with this.

ABIDING
(CONTINUED)

Satan's second tactic was to despoil me of my inheritance. Even though I was a child of the Father of creation, the accuser would constantly throw self-judgment at me each time I misrepresented Father God's love to my family through being hard, accusatory, or insensitive. I would be consumed with shame, guilt, and self-condemnation. Instead of humbling myself and acknowledging my sin against love and asking my family to forgive me, I had to wait until I could receive ministry from someone else to renounce the shame and self-condemnation.

The enemy's third tactic was to destroy my sense of Father's abiding presence by trying to prevent me from keeping short accounts with God. When we fall into sin, we immediately recognize it and confess it. Most of us prefer to walk with our "respectable Christian sins" rather than walk in the Spirit. But a daily walk with God means guarding our hearts and thoughts and taking care of any sins against love moment-by-moment as they arise, not waiting until the next church service to repent. If we have misrepresented Father's love to another person during a time when we are walking in the flesh, a return to the Spirit is very simple. Go to the one you have hurt, acknowledge your sin, ask for forgiveness, and ask God to forgive you (James 5:16). You are then cleansed of your sin and restored into Father's love. You simply enter in by humility and faith.

> *Let your ear be attentive and your eyes open to hear the prayer your servant is praying before you day and night for your servants, the people of Israel. I confess the sins we Israelites, including myself and my father's family, have committed against you.* (Nehemiah 1:6 NIV)

PRAYER TO ENCOUNTER YOUR FATHER

I am entering Your presence with humility and in faith, Father. I ask You to receive me as You would receive any wayward child. I thank You for loving me, Father and I do repent of my sins and sinful nature.

HE DELIGHTS IN PLAIN PEOPLE

The Christian walk is a walk of humility. It is our way to healthy relationships. Humility is the way to dwelling in the abiding presence of Father's love. The number one hindrance to an intimate walk with God, one in which we truly know and are truly known by Him, is the absence of humility. When we are more concerned with what other people think than with what God thinks of us—that is the absence of humility. When we justify our behavior, shift blame, accuse, find fault, criticize, or seek to vindicate ourselves, when we would rather be right than have relationship, when we do not confess our sins and our failures to others, when we do not acknowledge our sins against love—that is the absence of humility. When we do not daily admit our desperate need for God—that is the absence of humility.

Humility involves letting go of our pride and will, and becoming like Jesus in the Garden of Gethsemane (Luke 22:42 NKJV). God is opposed to anything within us that lacks humility, anything not humbled in our lives. Any area in which we lack humility will not have His life and grace flowing through it. A humble willingness to be known as we really are reveals a heart of sincere repentance and hunger for God. Anything other than that is usually rooted in the sin of pride, a sin against love.

> …But all of you, leaders and followers alike, are to be down to earth with each other, for—God has had it with the proud, but takes delight in just plain people. (1 Peter 5:5 MSG)

PRAYER TO ENCOUNTER YOUR FATHER

When prideful sin is up against genuine love, Father, I trust You to push me toward love and away from sin. I ask You to also forgive me for a lack of hunger to be more like You. I am so grateful that according to Your word in Galatians 5:17 You have intense cravings for relationship with me. How awesome is that Father?!

LEAVE ME ALONE

Before I had a revelation of God's light and before I was living my life to receive His love and give it to the next person I meet, my excuses and self-justification for much of my "respectable Christian sins" and negative attitudes went something like this:

"I've got to keep my walls up, or somebody will hurt me again." No, that's called the sin of independence.

"Well, if I am real, open, or transparent, people will begin to reject me. They won't want to get to know the real me." No, that's called the sin of pride.

"I'm just so tired. When I get home from work, I'm worn out. I have just given too much of myself away to others; that's why I have been impatient and unloving." No, anything unloving is a sin against love.

"You don't know what I've been going through at work. I am stressed out, and I just don't feel like talking after I get home." No, that's the sin of separation.

For many years I had all these little pet excuses for the barriers that I put up, for why I didn't walk in God's love, grace, and goodness. "I'm withdrawing from you because I don't feel safe in your presence." That was my sin of isolation and self-love. Sometimes transparency and brokenness is hard. It usually requires self-sacrifice.

> *Didn't we say to you in Egypt, "Leave us alone; let us serve the Egyptians?"* (Exodus 14:12 NIV)

> *"Loners who care only for themselves spit on the common good."* Proverbs 18:1 (MSG)

PRAYER TO ENCOUNTER YOUR FATHER
Father sometimes I do feel better when I'm by myself, not being bothered by anyone yacking in my ear. Help me correct this self-absorbed attitude. Make me aware of my daily assignments to love that one person that needs to know how much they are loved today.

THREE KEYS

Blame-shifting and justifying has been a habit structure of thinking in me since my youth as I tried to avoid admitting fault and feeling broken or rejected. The following are three keys that helped me break the power of these stronghold and ungodly beliefs.

1. I had convenient names and excuses for my sins. When I chose to begin calling sin for what it was, that was my first step toward true repentance. I chose to believe that anything that steals the peace of God from my heart or misrepresents Father's love to another living thing is sin.

2. I used to seek ways to cover up my sin deliberately. I attempted to make myself look better than others by pointing out their faults, the speck in their eye, rather than dealing with the log in my own. To be free, I began to recognize that anything I hide from others in order to make me look good is darkness

3. I deceived myself. For someone with my history of pride and self-justification, I do not think there is anything much easier than self-deception. Once I reject the first two points listed, eventually I am unable to recognize sin in my own life at all. First John 1:8 tells us that "if we say that we have no sin, we are deceiving ourselves." To protect myself from me, I gave my family and several respected people in the Lord permission to speak the truth to me.

And you will know the truth, and the truth will make you free. (John 8:32)

PRAYER TO ENCOUNTER YOUR FATHER

I plan to use these three keys to unlock myself and open wide the doors and windows to my thoughts, actions, and intents. I ask You to enlighten me when I try to understand myself when I am acting out one of those keys of blame shifting. I welcome You!

Transparent Witnessing

It is not enough to get my sins right with only God so that I can have intimacy with Him and at home. What God is doing in me also belongs to the people with whom I work, the one I sit next to on the plane, and those I come in contact with in the nations of the earth. Genuine repentance in my heart will be walked out in my daily life by my past defeats becoming God's victories in someone else's life. Abiding continually in Father's love means that I am not only receiving the blessings and benefits of His household, but I am also ready at all times to witness of God's personal dealings with me and my struggles.

Three things happen when I am real, open, and transparent about how God has dealt with me and the sin in my life.

First, I become more sensitive to the shame that a particular sin brings. Confessing to others a past area of sin in my life becomes a catalyst to prevent me from ever committing that sin again. God began bringing a level of freedom to me, and as I began to share how God had helped me overcome a particular sin, I realized that I never wanted to fall into that sin again. I came to a place of humility in that area and understood how great the grace of God was that covered my sin.

Confess your faults one to another, and pray one for another, that ye may be healed. The effectual fervent prayer of a righteous man availeth much. (James 5:16)

Prayer to Encounter Your Father

Father God, thank You for Your great grace. I can't overcome these things on my own but as I confess my faults to others Your ability seems to overcome my weakness as I choose to become vulnerable to You. I owe You my life! I owe me to others You cause me to love.

Transparent Witnessing
(Continued)

Second, transparent witnessing released a deeper cleansing and freedom from sins in my life. As long as I kept my sins hidden, only confessing them to God, I didn't become sensitive to them; they could easily sneak up on me before I knew it. As my tears of heartfelt gratitude took me into deeper cleansing, I also moved into a deeper experience in God's love and in the love of my wife.

Third benefit that takes place as I share an area of past bondage or where I habitually sinned against love is that other people begin to recognize the sin in their own lives and come under deep personal conviction. As I have shared my journey in this devotional, how often have you been convicted of sins against love in your own life? The honesty and openness of another believer who is admitting past sins and testifying of Father God's love delivering and restoring him will do more to bring someone into acknowledgment of their sin and into repentance than 100 hellfire-and-brimstone sermons ever will.

Transparent witnessing must be done with discretion, of course; you should share only those areas where you are an overcomer. An overcomer is one who overcomes more than he or she is overcome—that is, 51 percent or more of the time you have victory in that area. Be sensitive and led by the Holy Spirit for the proper time, place, and people to share your heart.

Whoever conceals their sins does not prosper, but the one who confesses and renounces them finds mercy. (Proverbs 28:13)

For of His fullness we have all received, and grace upon grace. (John 1:16)

Prayer to Encounter Your Father

May my testimony and the cleansing You have done in my life be life-giving to those with whom I share it. Give me the courage, Father, to talk about my mistakes and Your grace.

TEN STEPS TO REVIVAL

True revival is not a series of meetings; true revival takes place in the hearts of the people when they begin to receive a true conviction of their sin and cry out to God for His forgiveness, mercy, and grace. This results in His children seeking His face, craving for intimacy to be restored with God and man, and committing to a daily walk in the Spirit. The path to revival begins with just that—children of God learning to abide in the presence of Father's love and then willing to give it away to the next person they meet. Revival usually follows this type of progression:

1. You begin to become more and more sensitive to the small, daily sins that gradually steal your ability to walk in love, joy, peace, and the sense of God's presence.

2. You begin to recognize that every misrepresentation of God's love to another individual is an area of sin and darkness in your life.

3. You start confessing your sin as soon as you recognize it instead of hiding it, justifying it, or attempting to cover it up.

4. You experience forgiveness and cleansing through the blood of Jesus Christ.

5. You feel clean and free, and gratitude fills your heart for what God has done for you.

Will You not Yourself revive us again, that Your people may rejoice in You?
(Psalm 85:6)

PRAYER TO ENCOUNTER YOUR FATHER

Revive me, Father with the fire of Your Holy Spirit stirring things up within my heart, setting things into motion in my life causing me to change and become like Your Image!

Ten Steps to Revival
(Continued)

6. You experience an overwhelming sense of God's abiding presence, and you begin walking daily in the Spirit. You don't have to chase after a dramatic experience, for by faith, each day you have a sense that you are drawing nearer to the Father.

7. You become so full of God's love and the joy of His presence that you can't wait to tell others. You become an honest, open, transparent witness for what God has done for you.

8. Through your transparent witnessing, others become convicted of their own sin and begin to desire an intimate relationship with God as well.

9. They confess their sins, repent, and receive God's forgiveness and cleansing; they then become transparent witnesses themselves.

10. True revival is released within your family, the church, the city, the nation, and the world.

If you need a renewed sense of Father's presence in your life and wish to recommit yourself to a daily walk with Him, then pray this prayer: *Heavenly Father, I ask You to forgive me of my sins against love. I long to experience life with You on a daily basis, not just in times of crisis. I confess that at times I have placed more importance on the dramatic experiences than I have on daily abiding in Your love and giving it away to others.*

One day spent in your house, this beautiful place of worship, beats thousands spent on Greek island beaches. (Psalm 84:10 The Message)

Prayer to Encounter Your Father
I desire to live as Your child in Your house, allowing Your character to rub off on me. I am willing to become a transparent witness to others of Your goodness and mercy. Stir up these desires in my heart to be a part of revival: setting things into motion.

MAY 24

BRAZIL NUTS

Trisha and I participated in a mission trip on a medical boat that ventured up the Amazon River. People rowed out in their canoes to meet us, and we helped provide dental and medical services on the 65-foot boat. The Brazilians on the river are a generous people; they wouldn't take anything for free. Every person who received our services left a gift: fruit, vegetables, and one person left something that looked like coconuts without the husks. They were Brazil nut shells that grow in huge trees. The natives often build their villages under the shady trees. But when the nuts ripen, they fall off the limbs from 100 feet in the air without warning and cause all sorts of damage. Yet when we ate the Brazil nuts out of the shell, it was like eating candy. They were so moist and sweet.

Over the years, I've thought many times about how much I have been like the Brazil nut. In Christ I am a new creation whose spirit is made new in God's image. At the core of my being (my spirit) I was created for people to taste God's love flowing through me. But outside I was as hard as a Brazil nut. Those who dwelt under my roof were, without warning, in danger of being crushed by my intensity and harsh legalism. They would be left bruised and wounded by my hardened outer shell (my soul).

> *Therefore, if anyone is in Christ, the new creation has come: The old has gone, the new is here!* (2 Corinthians 5:17)

PRAYER TO ENCOUNTER YOUR FATHER

I've heard it said that some people are "hard nuts to crack." Some probably said that about me. As I turn more and more of my old self hardness over to You, Father, may people see my new moist, sweet self.

THE REAL YOU

We were created in the image of God: Father, Son, and Holy Spirit. Each of us is a triune being, made up of a body, a soul, and a spirit. Like the Brazil nut, each person is made up of an inner part and an outer shell. The hard, outer shell is the soul and can be wounded and bruised or wound others. But the inner core is our spirit, where God desires to dwell and cultivate the fruit of His Spirit. At the point of salvation, God fills us with His love and takes up residence within our spirit. We become new creations. Our spirits have become renewed in Christ, but outwardly our soul clothes the spirit and we need to still address the pain and the wounds that remain in our outer shell—the mind, will, emotions, and personality.

Your inner self is clothed with the outer realm of your soul—your thoughts, emotions, and will—which often disagrees with what your spirit tells you. It is this part of you that comprises your personality. Think of the Brazil nut—moist and sweet fruit inside (your spirit) with a hardened and dangerous exterior (your soul). We have two voices speaking to us all the time—one gentle and loving and full of rest as it seeks to meet others' needs, and the other aggressive and driven to get its own needs met.

> *Now may the God of peace Himself sanctify you entirely; and may your spirit and soul and body be preserved complete, without blame at the coming of our Lord Jesus Christ.* (1 Thessalonians 5:23)

PRAYER TO ENCOUNTER YOUR FATHER

Thank You, Father, for designing us in Your image. I pray that my spirit will mimic Your Holy Spirit as I become the person You created me to be.

YOUR INNER SELF

All of us were created to be a reflection of Father's love, and God is at work transforming us into His image. His seed—His DNA, His genetic code—lies within us, and everything inside of us is being conformed to the image of love. When God took up residence in your heart when you were born again, He elevated your spirit to its rightful status. You were created to rule over all of God's handiwork; you have been crowned with His glory and majesty; your spirit was made to rule over all things—and that includes your own soulish realm.

When I came to truly believe that I was created in God's image—when I truly knew what His nature was like and that He was a loving Father and not an angry God—that is when I started becoming like Him. I began walking in a lifestyle of love, being renewed in His love a little more each day. Then my spirit slowly began to take prominence over my thoughts, emotions, or desires that were not in agreement with God's unconditional love.

God created both males and females in His image of love. In the spirit realm there are no gender differences. I can no longer justify being macho or unable to express healthy emotions and affection, because I know that I was created in God's image and there is nothing more natural for me than intimacy and expressed love.

> *There is neither Jew nor Greek, there is neither slave nor free man, there is neither male nor female; for you are all one in Christ Jesus.* (Galatians 3:28)

PRAYER TO ENCOUNTER YOUR FATHER

How am I trying to justify my lack of compassion and intimacy? Am I guilty of trying to live superficially rather than deeply in love? Show me Your answers, Father.

THERE IS LIBERTY

The common belief that men shouldn't cry or show any emotions is a lie. I have the ability to be what God created me to be—a spirit being who can walk in the tender, feminine side of God's image, just as women can foster His masculine side. There are no males or females in the spiritual realm; I am created by the Father of creation in His image, created for God to flow through, created to do good things, created for love to flow freely through me. Every day I am being transformed a little more into a man who was created so that people could experience God's love through me.

When I get up each morning, my first thoughts are usually all wrapped up in what others can do for me today or what others have not been doing for me (outer self thinking). If I stay in that mode of thinking, I will surely hurt someone that day. But after a few minutes of sitting in my study listening to some gentle music about Father's love, I come back into reality. This day is not about me, myself, and I. That is my soul speaking. This is the day the Lord has made, and I am going to rejoice that I can spend the day living out of my spirit and give Father's love away to the next person I meet.

And we all, who with unveiled faces contemplate the Lord's glory, are being transformed into his image with ever-increasing glory, which comes from the Lord, who is the Spirit. (2 Corinthians 3:18 NIV)

PRAYER TO ENCOUNTER YOUR FATHER

This IS the day You have made, Father. And I am going to soak up every moment by loving every person that comes across my path. Whether with a sincere smile, hearty handshake, or a personal conversation, may I imitate You as Your love is released through me!

MAY 28

ALREADY RECEIVED

This is the revelation that changed my life: If I have accepted Christ and old things have passed away in my life and all things are made new in my spirit…if I am a spirit being…if I was created in God's image…if I was made for love… then how can I ever become any more spiritual than I am right now? *In my spirit, I have already received everything God has for me.* I am never going to become more spiritually mature or perfect in Christ than I am right now in my spiritual self. My spirit is God's home. His unconditional love dwells in me. I have already received all of God's love that I am ever going to receive.

God's grace and mercy live at home in me. The fruit of the Spirit is at home in me. The power of God that created the universe lives inside me. His Spirit now lives in my spirit, and in Him there is no darkness at all. His love thinks no evil, and that love is resident in my spirit. Think about it; how can anything I do improve on that! There may be experiences I have when God's presence and love powerfully come upon me and break forth in my soul, but otherwise, it is more about His love breaking forth out through my soul to others than me trying to be good enough to earn more of it.

Love thinks no evil. (1 Corinthians 13:4)

But whenever a person turns to the Lord, the veil is taken away.
(2 Corinthians 3:16)

PRAYER TO ENCOUNTER YOUR FATHER

Oh that I can wrap my head around that beautiful truth! I can hardly believe that I have already received all of God's love, that I'm mature and perfect in Christ's love in my spirit man. Oh help me believe, Lord God!

ALREADY RECEIVED
(CONTINUED)

So why is it that for years I continued to struggle with sins against love, unforgiveness, shame, old wounds from the past, guilt, and failure that hindered the release of God's intimacy and love? The problem did not lie in the area of my spirit (inner self). The problem was within my soul (outer self). I am given a choice each day. Nurture the pain, the past failures, and the guilt, and I allow the temporal outer man to influence my daily life. Or I can release my spirit to take dominion over all those things and tell my soul that it has had its day, but now it is God's day. My outer self cannot mature into the love of God if left alone. My outer self can never think a spiritual thought.

On the other hand, there is nothing more natural for my inner self to think, *to whom can I demonstrate the love of the Father today? How can I lay down my pride and self-love and meet the deepest needs for acceptance and affection that my family might have?* There is nothing more natural than for my soulish pride and insecurities to be displaced by Father God's love. There is nothing more natural than for the Spirit's power to be released through me to bring healing and restoration to others. It is what I was created for! It is the most natural thing on earth! It is why God placed me here!

> *For what I am doing, I do not understand; for I am not practicing what I would like to do, but I am doing the very thing I hate.* (Romans 7:15)

PRAYER TO ENCOUNTER YOUR FATHER

Even the apostle Paul had struggles between his inner and outer self. As I focus more and more on You, Father, I pray that my struggles will become fewer and fewer.

When Walking with God Is Hard

When I first became a Christian, I experienced an outpouring of the love of the Father that touched my heart and changed me forever. But as I became involved in the church and began to learn the disciplines of the Christian faith, my soulish root system of performance made my Christianity a heavy trip! I began to work at my salvation by praying, tithing, reading the Word, fasting, and doing everything I knew to be right. I exchanged the unconditional love of God for a lifestyle of my soul performing for love and acceptance. My outer self accumulated more and more guilt, self-righteousness, self-condemnation, and self-judgment, because I could never do it good enough. My Christian walk got pretty exhausting! My outward self did its best to work at my spirituality. I was trying to make my outward self spiritual, and it became religion.

Any time my walk with God gets hard, I know that I am no longer walking in the spirit but have begun living out of my soul. The inner self (spirit) naturally does spiritual things and thinks spiritual thoughts. The outer self (soul) naturally does natural things and thinks natural thoughts. As hard as I tried, I just couldn't make my outer self more prayerful. My mind always wandered during prayer to thinking about playing golf or going fishing, and it left me feeling guilty. That is completely natural for the outer self. I ended up in bondage to the love of law.

Not that we are adequate in ourselves to consider anything as coming from ourselves, but our adequacy is from God. (2 Corinthians 3:5)

Prayer to Encounter Your Father
I feel totally inadequate without You, Father. With You, I feel, act, and know that I am enough—I have Your seal of approval, through Christ.

SELF-IMPOSED LAWS AND RULES

During the fifteen years that I tried to force my outer self to be more spiritual, I ended up developing self-imposed laws and rules in order to feel that I was more spiritual so I could find acceptance in God. It resulted in the following pattern that brought great discomfort and pain to my life. Follow along this progression with me. You may have already lived there for a few years!

1. First, my childhood filter system of performance thought that through my rigid life of prayer, study, and religious discipline and duty I was making myself more acceptable in God's eyes.

2. As soon as I left the way of grace, I could not pray enough, study enough, or do enough to ever feel accepted and loved by God, so I never attained the sense of closeness with God that I longed for.

3. So I worked harder at making my soul spiritual. I tried praying more, fasting more, doing more, being better

4. After several years I got very weary and the Christian walk became so hard.

5. I began to feel guilty and ashamed for not being good enough and for having so many fleshly thoughts.

6. I felt unworthy to be loved by God and that He had His personal favorites—and I was not one.

Serve the Lord with gladness; come before Him with joyful singing. (Psalm 100:2)

PRAYER TO ENCOUNTER YOUR FATHER

Walking with You, Father, should be easy, joyful, and full of gladness. I will try and keep this in mind when it seems the going is getting too tough.

JUNE 1
SELF-IMPOSED LAWS AND RULES
(CONTINUED)

7. So I started making personal promises and vows to get closer to God and work harder at being a good Christian and fulfill all the religious duties I felt were required of me.

8. I seemed helpless to fulfill all the personal promises that I made to myself to be more disciplined, so my level of guilt, frustration, and anxiety kept increasing.

9. I lost a sense of value and self-worth in God's eyes apart from my performance.

10. I started treating my family and others the way I felt about myself.

11. My love became conditional. The disciplines and duties that I had to fulfill to feel loved and accepted by God is what I required from others for them to feel loved and accepted by me.

12. I ended up with most of my relationships unhealthy as I sought to control them in order to get my own needs met. There is no love in law!

13. I and my family ended up in spiritual burnout!

How many laws have you made for yourself and failed to keep? When you fail to keep your self-imposed laws, do you feel guilty and no longer feel close to God? In Christ and in my spirit there is no striving, no drivenness, no anxiety, and no condemnation. When I have no guilt, I draw closer to God because He is already dwelling within me.

Owe no man anything, but to love one another: for he that loveth another hath fulfilled the law. (Romans 13:8)

PRAYER TO ENCOUNTER YOUR FATHER
Living a guilt-free life seems almost impossible. There's always something that makes me feel guilty. Lord, I am going to write down all my self-imposed laws and then burn them up! I ask You today to help me to live Your law which is to love another.

LIGHTENING YOUR LOAD

How can you position your heart to enter into God's rest and your spirit to rise above the outward self? First of all, agree with what the Word of God says about you. You are created in God's image, and God is love. Every fiber of your being has been created for intimacy with God. His unconditional love for you is never based upon your behavior but upon His character of perfect love and grace. God's truth, love, and grace are the only factors of proof of whether God is with you. You were born of the Spirit to be filled with the Spirit, to walk in the Spirit, to talk in the Spirit, to commune with the Spirit, to live as a spirit being, and for your spirit to rule over strongholds. That is a greater reality than your outer self that is fading away.

Second, often you will have to tell your outer self to be quiet! Seek for peace in the inner man, not in the head. Your mind is to serve your spirit. The emotions are to be subordinate to your spirit. As soon as you don't "feel" close to God, tell your emotions to line up with God's Word. Tell your outer self to line up with your spirit self; allow God's truth to be your only reality. Do not go by feelings or emotions. Do not look to feelings of blessing to determine whether you are close to God.

> *Come to Me, all who are weary and heavy-laden, and I will give you rest. Take My yoke upon you and learn from Me, for I am gentle and humble in heart, and you will find rest for your souls. For My yoke is easy and My burden is light.* (Matthew 11:28-30)

PRAYER TO ENCOUNTER YOUR FATHER

My emotions are so powerful, Father. You know that, of course, but I'm always stunned at how my emotions can get in the way of staying in Your embrace. Please help me work on that.

CHOOSE TO DWELL WITH FATHER

Choose to dwell daily in Father's embrace. Your outward self seeks the power of God to deliver you from your circumstances. Your spiritual self seeks the presence of God to fellowship with you and be with you through your circumstances. When I am overwhelmed in my mind or emotions and cannot seem to get in touch with my spirit, that is when I stop everything, go into my study, and put on some quiet, soothing music about Father's love.

Then I lie on the floor before the Father and say to Him, "Dad, I'm over here in my soul and can't seem to find You. Please help me." I don't pray a deep, heavy prayer, but just admit to Him that I need His help and then surrender to His love: "Father, draw me back into my spirit. Draw me back to You. I have moved over into my own thoughts, emotions, insecurities, and fears; and I feel alone and discouraged. I need Your fathering arms to embrace me. Run to me to give me the love and comfort that I need."

Soon, Father God's love and peace come over me, and my focus shifts. I separate the outward from the spiritual, and I step right back into the things of the spirit. Everything changes; my attitudes, desires, and motivations all begin to realign with the Father's heart, and I am free once more to minister His love to my family and others.

God assured us, "I'll never let you down, never walk off and leave you." (Hebrews 13:5-6 MSG)

PRAYER TO ENCOUNTER YOUR FATHER

Father, when I feel alone and discouraged, I will run to Your arms. Your embrace is what keeps me hopeful and gives me the second wind I need to face each new challenge.

JUNE 4
NATIONAL CRISIS

Experiencing Father's unconditional love is all about choosing to accept our mission in life—the purpose for which God created us. He has created us to experience His love and to make it known to our families and the nations. He has chosen this season in Church history to reveal His affectionate Father's heart—indeed, before every major revival there has been social crisis in the land. Then, God brings a fresh outpouring of His grace and begins to meet the needs of the social crisis. Revival results. Today, the social crisis of our nation and the world is fatherlessness. God is revealing His Father's heart to His children because it is difficult being tender, loving parents until we have experienced the affectionate love of a father's and mother's heart. As Father's love meets our need, His love flowing through us can begin to meet the need of the crisis in the nations.

Our children are suffering the consequences of fear, insecurity, and low self-esteem, and they are crying out for their father and mother's embrace. It is no surprise that rebellious attitudes, drug abuse, immoral sexual activity, out-of-wedlock pregnancy, gang activity, and crime rates among teenagers have risen as the deterioration of the American family continues. What we need is a reformation—a radical change within our families that will sweep across America and restore the hearts of husbands and wives to each other and the hearts of parents to their children.

I will make you a great nation and I will bless you. (Genesis 12:2)

PRAYER TO ENCOUNTER YOUR FATHER
My nation is in trouble, Father. Bless the children with Your loving embrace. I pray that Your light will shine through troubled homes and classrooms—bringing hope to every young heart.

GOD'S PROMISE OF RESTORATION

The earth belongs to God. He created the world and gave humankind dominion over it, but since the Fall, satan has had far too much influence in the life of the family. He has done everything he can to destroy the Christian family and disintegrate the fabric of our society. But God promises restoration of everything that has been lost, and that includes the restoration of your family.

In the end times, there will be a great revival in which families from all nations will return to the Lord and receive healing and renewal. God promises that the hearts of the fathers will turn back toward the children, and the hearts of the children will return to their fathers. The Old Testament closes with the following passage that indicates how important the family is to the Father. He will release a supernatural move of the Spirit to convict the hearts of fathers to no longer seek for their identity in the things they do, but return to finding their identities in what God has created them to be—a manifestation of the love of God to their families. This love will then overflow to the nations of the earth—thus the curse of fatherlessness will be broken off the land.

All the ends of the earth will remember and turn to the Lord, and all the families of the nations will worship before You. (Psalm 22:27)

PRAYER TO ENCOUNTER YOUR FATHER
What a great day that will be when the curse of fatherlessness will be broken and families will live together in harmony as You intended in the first place, I ask You Father to show me how to remember that my life is always to example love to my sons first then the world!

JUNE 6
RESTORE THE HEARTS

Wherever a father's heart is turned toward anything other than his children, a curse can be released upon the family. Even Christian households can fall under deception when the priorities of the parents are not in line with God's priorities. In my own household, my heart was more inclined toward deep-sea fishing in the early years, and then later to ministry. I was blinded to the needs of my family, thus we lived under a curse, and the results were obvious: My wife spiraled into a deep depression, and my children were acting out their frustration in unhealthy and angry ways. I was oblivious to it all. My focus was not on what took place at home; my focus was on building a reputation and a ministry so I could change the world.

In Hebrew, the word "restore" means to bring back to the point of departure, to turn from its evil way, to turn around, to return, to come back. When God restores families, He brings them back to where they were before sin entered the world. He is returning our families to that point of departure. God wants to restore our relationships to the depth of love and freedom from fear and shame that Adam and Eve first shared before their sin and cover-ups brought blame-shifting, separation, and a loss of intimacy to the family.

> *Behold, I am going to send you Elijah the prophet before the coming of the great and terrible day of the Lord. He will restore the hearts of the fathers to their children and the hearts of the children to their fathers, so that I will not come and smite the land with a curse.* (Malachi 4:5)

PRAYER TO ENCOUNTER YOUR FATHER
Father, I am asking for restoration of love in all my relationships, especially the love for my spouse and family members—even those I have ignored or deliberately shoved aside over the years.

JUNE 7
RESTORING THE CHRISTIAN FAMILY

How does the restoration of the family begin after we have received a personal revelation of Father's love? How can our marriage be renewed once it has lost its innocence and intimacy? How do we begin to process Father's love within our family relationships? Please know that your situation may not be resolved overnight, but as you yield to the prompting of the Holy Spirit and cry out to God daily for His grace and love to flow through you to others, you should see healing and restoration begin in your family.

First, restoration began when I realized that I had been more sensitive about getting my needs met than meeting the needs of my family. When we experience Father's love and begin to see how we have been neglecting the emotional needs of our spouse and children, we will begin to value intimacy with our family more than position, possessions, power, or the passions of the flesh. The Word makes it very clear that our primary qualification for leadership in the Body of Christ is when our relationship with God is evidenced by our relationship with our family and the degree that we abide in love and intimacy. Ministry to our families is to take precedence over our ministry to the world (see Matt. 22:37-40; 1 John 4:7-18; Eph. 5:25-33; 1 Peter 3:1-7; 1 Tim. 3:4-5; 5:8).

Beloved, let us love one another, for love is from God; and everyone who loves is born of God and knows God. (1 John 4:7)

PRAYER TO ENCOUNTER YOUR FATHER
Father, I am thinking of all the things that could take precedence over You—but with the assistance of the Holy Spirit, I know I can keep those things in the proper order in my life.

RESTORING THE CHRISTIAN FAMILY
(CONTINUED)

Second, the cry of my heart became for God to teach me what it meant to be a husband and father. I had no concept of what a healthy marriage looked like. Having such difficult issues with my father in my youth, I never felt like a son to my father, so how could I be a father until I felt like a son? But I had used the excuse for too long. Now God's love was breaking forth in deeper ways, and that excuse would not hold water. The Father revealed to me, *"My child, you have always been with me, and all that is mine is yours"* (Luke 15:31). God's love, sensitivity, and compassion lie within me and my family is to experience it through me.

Third, I opened my heart for God to flow through me and meet the emotional and spiritual needs of my family. I have difficulty understanding the mind of a woman and it's hard to remember what it was like to be a teenager. So I rely on the Holy Spirit to cause me to be sensitive to my family's needs. Daily I ask, "Father, show me when I do anything that devalues or brings shame to any family member. Show me how to value them in ways that they can understand. Show me how to humble myself to them and express Your affectionate love." Then I seek to do it, no matter how much pride it costs me.

Beloved, if God so loved us, we also ought to love one another. (1 John 4:11)

PRAYER TO ENCOUNTER YOUR FATHER
I will pray this prayer as well, Father. I don't want to do anything to bring shame to any family member—those with whom I live and my extended family as well. May I be a shining role model of Your love and affection.

JUNE 9
Holy Spirit Conviction

Not long after I began to pray that way, my 18-year-old son Micah came into my study to talk to me. I was very busy at the time, but I waved him in. Not much excites Micah more than playing golf, and this day he couldn't wait to show me his new golf shoes that he bought with his own money.

"Look at my shoes, Dad! Aren't they great?" He started telling me about how his golf game was improving, but his voice began to trail off as he saw my response. My back was still turned to him while I worked at my computer. "Uh-huh, that's wonderful," I murmured, and then I heard the door close as he left the room.

My heart dropped. He was sharing the most important part of his life with me, and I couldn't even take the time to turn around and look him in the eye. The conviction of the Holy Spirit weighed heavily upon me, and I jumped up and ran out of my study after him. He had already left, so I called him at the golf course where he worked and apologized. His response, "Dad, I forgive you. You do it all the time."

My heart was grieved as I realized that my son had become so used to my unresponsiveness that Micah didn't even understand that it was wrong. That event began changed me. I became more sensitive to my children every time they walked into the room.

> *Because you are his sons, God sent the Spirit of his Son into our hearts, the Spirit who calls out, "Abba Father." So you are no longer a slave, but God's child; and since you are his child, God has made you also an heir.* (Galatians 4:6-8 NIV)

Prayer to Encounter Your Father
Father, when I am sensitive to Your Holy Spirit, then I will be sensitive to my children and family and others in my life. Today I will listen very carefully for Holy Spirit's nudging. I ask You to forgive me for my children not being the most important thing in my life.

SHIFTING PRIORITIES

A change in our household was able to take place only when I made a conscious determination to relinquish my pride and seek the humility of Christ. My pride had caused me to place my career, my goals, and my ministry ahead of the needs of my family; but when I began to humble myself and realize that I was created for love and to make it known to my family first and the nations second, then the process of restoration began. My relationship with Trisha was not only renewed, but it also became sweeter and more intimate than I had ever believed possible. When our marriage moved into deeper depths of intimacy, the children became more secure in themselves and in the family, and their lives began to blossom. And ironically, the shift in my priorities was not detrimental to our ministry in any way—in fact, the anointing of God has fallen on us in an even stronger sense, and we now have invitations to minister all around the world.

Are you willing to receive the spirit of Christ (humility) in your family? In the power of Father's love, are you willing to empty yourself of all your selfish ambitions and desires and take on the form of a servant in your home? Are you willing to take up the cross daily for your spouse and your children? When you do that, you become an instrument of Father's love, and restoration begins in your family.

But seek first His kingdom and His righteousness, and all these things will be added to you. (Matthew 6:33)

PRAYER TO ENCOUNTER YOUR FATHER
Father, I choose to allow You to empty myself of all my selfish ambitions and desires and choose to be Your servant reflected in my home and workplace and church. First!

SHARE HIS LOVE

God wants to bring each of us to a new understanding of His love. The Father longs to gather His children in His arms; He craves the relationship of love and intimacy with you for which He created you. Your life will never be more fulfilled than when you follow His lifestyle of love, asking Him each day, "Father, help me to experience Your affectionate love and then pass it along to the next person I meet." God desires a revival to sweep the land—a fresh revival of His love to touch every human being. He promises restoration of our hearts, lives, and families when we turn to Him and experience Father God's embrace.

> *And He said to them, "God into all the world and preach the gospel to all creation.* (Mark 16:15)

PRAYER TO ENCOUNTER YOUR FATHER
Yes, Father, please help me to experience Your affectionate love so I can pass it along to every next person I meet!

HE FIRST LOVED US

The verses below imply that true love for God must stand the daily test of my life with others. I have never been more aware how little of Father's love I have really experienced. It can best be measured by my everyday interactions with people and the love, or lack of it, I display. The thing that often holds me back from deeper experiences and revelation in Father God's affectionate embrace is the great struggle I face daily between pride and humility. There are two master powers, two kingdoms, battling within me for the dominating influence of my life—the kingdom of pride and the kingdom of humility.

Once the revelation of Father's sacrificial love becomes true experience to me, I am to embrace more fully humility and the spirit of servanthood with my family and others, even with those difficult people I have in my life. Only then will others truly experience Father's love through me, and only then will I be released to manifest Father's love to the world.

> *God is love. When we take up permanent residence in a life of love, we live in God and God lives in us. This way, love has the run of the house, becomes at home and mature in us, so that we're free of worry on Judgment Day—our standing in the world is identical with Christ's. There is no room in love for fear. Well-formed love banishes fear. Since fear is crippling, a fearful life—fear of death, fear of judgment—is one not yet fully formed in love. We, though, are going to love—love and be loved. First we were loved, now we love. He loved us first.* (1 John 4:17-19 MSG)

PRAYER TO ENCOUNTER YOUR FATHER

I want to live in the kingdom of humility, Father. Open the gates to this kingdom of Yours and bolt shut the gates to the kingdom of pride. I choose to live my life laid down for others.

JUNE 13

SELF-LOVE VERSUS HUMILITY

I have found a pattern I often seem to follow in the dealings of God that I experience in my pursuit to dwell in Father's embrace.

First, my response to being humbled by God's love is not usually good. I tend to run from the things that give me an opportunity to humble myself and to walk in God's love—things like seeking forgiveness and reconciliation from each person with whom I have or have had unresolved issues. I do not apologize so quickly to family when I've misrepresented Father's love or sought my own desires more than theirs. I find it so easy to center conversations around me and the things that bring me pleasure. I do not always find myself seeking to honor and promote others' ministries as I desire to do my own. It is evident that, though I long for humility, I see no value in humiliations. Therefore, I have not yet learned to seek it at any cost. I do not always let my self-love sell out to humility.

Second, I begin to experience a sense of grief as I realize that humility is not a joy and pleasure to me. I begin to realize that I have moved off center of walking in Father's love and moved into aggressively striving for the higher place. Paul found pleasure and glory in his weaknesses and humiliations. He knew humility to be the place of love, blessing, and power.

The whole point of what we're urging is simply love—love uncontaminated by self-interest and counterfeit faith, a life open to God. (1 Timothy 1:5 MSG)

PRAYER TO ENCOUNTER YOUR FATHER
It is true of me too, Father; I don't always allow humility to trump my self-love. Help me in this regard. I know You can find ways to show me how to stay humble. Thank You.

SELF-LOVE VERSUS HUMILITY
(CONTINUED)

Third, I start feeling the pain my family and others feel from the devaluing I bring to them when they know my personal agenda is more important than relationship with them. The grief I feel over my pride (need to be right) and misrepresentations of Father's love slowly begins to lead me into deeper repentance. I start crying out for greater revelation of God's grace within me. It is only my daily surrendering to Father God's love that can expel the self-love with which I still struggle.

Fourth, after fresh revelation, I begin to make new choices to humble myself before my family and others. I now see each act of humility as a source of deeper experience in God's love, blessing, and power. This is what exalts me into Father's presence where His loving nature begins to dispel layers of pride, resulting in deeper humility and acts of service and love to others.

Therefore, I am well content with weaknesses, with insults, with distresses, with persecutions, with difficulties, for Christ's sake; for when I am weak, then I am strong. (2 Corinthians 12:10)

PRAYER TO ENCOUNTER YOUR FATHER

Father, bring me fresh revelation of Your will for my life. May I continuously seek ways to fulfill my destiny—the one You designed for me before I was born.

CHRIST IS THE INSTRUCTOR

These verses release in me a key to conquering pride and experiencing Father God's embrace—I am to humble myself. Every act of humility before others destroys the workings of pride in my heart! Every time I am hurt, disappointed by someone, or humiliated before people, I let this remind me of my desperate need for a deeper revelation of Jesus' love and grace through His humility being released in me. It is not my work to conquer pride. It is my work to humble myself at every opportunity.

Many times I seek to conquer pride in the flesh and not by the Spirit. This leads to patterns of shame and guilt. I get into self-condemnation. I get tired of the heaviness and try to break pride's hold by the letter of the law. "I must be humble! I must repent!" But my flesh is unwilling to submit to humbling myself before others. There is too much "I must" and not enough "I want more of Jesus' humility and love released in my character!" Then aggressive striving and hyper-religious activity increases!

Only humility can expel pride in me. I do not cast out the darkness; I turn on the light, and the light dispels the darkness. Then God will do what He promised: *"for bodily discipline is only of little profit, but godliness is profitable for all things, since it holds promise for the present life and also for the life to come"* (1 Timothy 4:8).

> *Nor are you to be called instructors, for you have one Instructor, the Messiah. The greatest among you will be your servant. For those who exalt themselves will be humbled, and those who humble themselves will be exalted.* (Matthew 23:10-12 NIV)

PRAYER TO ENCOUNTER YOUR FATHER

Father, only with Your help can I destroy the pridefulness in me. You sent the Light of the world to shine Your glory and goodness into the darkness. I grab hold of Your promise.

NO FEAR!

Mariners call it the "Sea of Fear." Drake Passage, the 500 miles of southern-ocean between Cape Horn and the Antarctic Peninsula, is home to some of the most dangerous waters on earth. Water temperatures there are so frigid that if you fall into the water, you will become unconscious from hypothermia in less than five minutes—with death quickly following. It is also the most confusing body of water in the world to navigate. With no continent to block it, the water in Drake Passage swirls continuously in a circulatory motion from west to east. Add in winds that blow in excess of 35 knots for over 200 days a year, and you have an ocean passage that is dangerously unpredictable. Conditions can change from calm to stormy in a heartbeat, and you never know from what angle the waves will come at you. The Sea of Fear has been the watery grave of over 400 boats and ships that have gone down with all hands.

As a licensed fishing boat captain and more than a bit of an adventurer, I get my kicks from traveling into the remotest regions of the earth. That is how I ended up recently as part of an expedition sailing from the southern part of Chile, past Cape Horn and into the Sea of Fear. Believe me, it was quite a ride, guiding a 74-foot sailboat on a 3-day journey through 40- to 50-knot winds with seas up to 30 feet! We then spent a couple of weeks in Antarctica. It was the time of year on the southern continent when the sun never drops below the horizon. For two weeks we saw no darkness.

The light shines in the darkness, and the darkness has not overcome it.
(John 1:5 NIV)

PRAYER TO ENCOUNTER YOUR FATHER
What exciting adventures You provide for Your kids—if they chose to step out in faith. I would like to take advantage of every opportunity You place before me, Lord. Chase fear from me.

CALM IN THE SEA OF FEAR

As we began our return trip through Drake Passage, the captain of the expedition, who has had years of experience sailing in this part of the world, said, "This is the calmest I have ever seen the Sea of Fear." And, indeed, there was very little wind—so little wind, in fact, that we were operating on motor power. At the same time, we had put out every square foot of canvas possible trying to catch any wind we could. We were 150 miles south of Cape Horn in a region of the sea where many boats have gone down due to 10,000 feet of water constantly moving with the current that comes up the continental shelf and kind of explodes into the air. This was perhaps the most treacherous part of the passage.

It was 1:30 in the morning and we were experiencing the first darkness in two weeks, but only for an hour. Then the sun would rise again. Of the eight of us on the expedition, five were in their bunks below, while the captain and I were on duty in the wheelhouse. The night had been rather uneventful with no wind and relatively calm seas; and we were there mainly just to work the sails and perform other routine tasks as needed. The heated wheelhouse was warm and cozy. Outside, however, the temperature was in the 30s, which actually was somewhat warm for that time of year.

Jesus stepped into a boat, crossed over and came to his own town.
(Matthew 9:1)

PRAYER TO ENCOUNTER YOUR FATHER
What's that old saying, Lord, "The calm before the storm"? I've experienced that calm more than once and the storms that followed would have swallowed me up—if not for You, Father. Thank You!

Holding On

Suddenly, with no warning, the wind rose sharply. Icy sleet blew sideways as the wind quickly reached gale force velocity, and in a matter of minutes the temperature dropped to well below freezing. With every square foot of sail out, we immediately faced a dangerous situation. The sudden onset of gale force winds hitting that amount of canvas threatened to tear the mast off and capsize our vessel. The list meter, which tells how far to port or starboard a boat is leaning, and which pegs out at 45 degrees, was locked on the peg as the wind in our sails keeled us over so far to starboard that water was washing up on the decks.

The captain screamed at us, "Out on deck! We've got to take in some canvas or we may lose the mast!"

There was no time to don our arctic gear (masks, suits, and gloves) because every second lost would increase the chance of disaster. But as we ran toward the door, the captain shouted, "Get your harnesses on!"

Suddenly a furious storm came up on the lake, so that the waves swept over the boat. (Matthew 8:24 NIV)

Prayer to Encounter Your Father

Father, how many times have I run out the door without my harness—my common sense? How many times did I allow fear to overwhelm me and prevent me from being successful in my endeavor? Knock some sense into me, Father.

LATCHED TO THE BOAT

The harnesses had a 10-foot length of rope or lifeline that snapped to another rope that ran from the stern of the vessel to the bow. Wearing a harness ensured that we would remain lashed to the boat in the event we were washed overboard, making it possible for us to be hauled in again (provided, of course, that we didn't have a heart attack from going over the side in a storm or that hypothermia didn't claim us first)!

With our harnesses on, we flew out the wheelhouse door and onto the deck. Because we were listing so heavily, the water was about knee-deep at my location, and the only thing that kept me inside on the deck were two steel cables running along the side of the boat.

Even when there is no wind in the Sea of Fear, you can still experience 10-foot swells because of the motion of the water in that area. And when the wind comes up, it turns immediately into 20- and 30-foot seas. As the bow rises up into the heavens, inertia glues you to the deck. But as the boat crests the wave and falls into the trough, the bow drops from under you, suspending you suddenly 1 or 2 feet above the deck until it comes back up to meet you at the start of the next wave. And the whole time you're grabbing hold of anything you can so as not to be washed overboard.

One of the disciples, the one Jesus loved dearly, was reclining against him, his head on his shoulder. (John 13:23 MSG)

PRAYER TO ENCOUNTER YOUR FATHER

Father, I want to be latched to You when the rough seas of life come crashing down around me. Staying close to You—embraced by You—is where I want to be now, and throughout eternity.

JUNE 20
PARALYZED

Meanwhile, I was on my hands and knees crawling out to the starboard side to take in enough canvas to keep the mast from being ripped off. The wind was howling, the sails were snapping, and the freezing spray and blowing ice were numbing me to the bone. Finally, I finished the job as the captain completed his, and he yelled, "Get back in the wheelhouse!"

As soon as the captain and I crawled back into the luxurious warmth of that wheelhouse, I said, "Man, what an adventure! That was awesome! That's the kind of thing I came on this trip for!" Then we looked up through the windshield and discovered that one of the men was still on the bow! He had brought his sail line in, but in doing so had piled all the extra rope on top of the lifeline that attached his harness to the rope leading from bow to stern. Although he seemed to be tangled, he was still able to move, yet he was frozen on the bow. He remained on his knees, gripping the wire railing for all he was worth, and every time the bow dropped, he lifted 1 to 2 feet off the deck, depending on the size of the wave. Icy sleet was blowing sideways, he was without his arctic gear, his hands were frozen and numb, and he seemed paralyzed.

And saying, "Lord, my servant is lying paralyzed at home, fearfully tormented." (Matthew 8:6)

PRAYER TO ENCOUNTER YOUR FATHER
Fear can be so paralyzing, Father. Although You never leave or forsake me, I can forget that vital truth when facing an unknown. Make Your presence more real than my imagined demise.

FEAR? OR FATHER'S EMBRACE?

What would your life be like if you had no fear—only a healthy respect for God? What if you had no fear of people? No fear of what others think about you because you are secure in the love of your heavenly Father and in His kind thoughts toward you? No fear of opening your heart to truly experience the depth of God's love so that you could live and give away that love to the next person you meet? What would your life be like if you had no fear?

What would your marriage be like? What would your family life be like? Your other relationships? What if you were not afraid to trust, to become vulnerable, to reach out and touch others, and to let them touch you? Fear paralyzes us. Like the man frozen on the bow of that sailboat, mere yards from the safety of the wheelhouse, fear can stop us from making choices that will bring us warmth, security, and abundant life full of love, peace, and tenderness.

Fear the Lord your God, serve him only and take your oaths in his name.
(Deuteronomy 6:13 NIV)

PRAYER TO ENCOUNTER YOUR FATHER

Fear be gone! If only it were that easy. Heavenly Father, as I rid myself of fear, please fill the void of those places with Your love. I want to experience life in Your embrace.

WHAT IF?

What would your church be like if you had no fear? What if everyone in your local body of believers was set free of the fear of trusting, the fear of rejection or abandonment, and the fear of opening their hearts to love and intimacy? Fear disables us. We can know all about the things of God and yet our fear of trusting and of intimacy can hold us back from receiving the benefits of what Jesus died for—to bring restoration and healing in our families and our relationships. So many of us Christians do all the right Christian things, yet fear continues to hold us back from casting ourselves fully into our loving Father's embrace.

Do you rise up every morning feeling like a son or daughter secure and confident in your Father's love, and living to give that love to others? Or do you get up every day feeling like a slave, struggling constantly with fears of failure or rejection, unable to trust, and wondering what you have to do to appease the Master today? Moving from slavery to sonship or daughtership is a matter of reaching the place where you get up in the morning feeling so loved and accepted in your Father's heart that your whole purpose for existence becomes looking for ways to give that love away to the next person you meet.

What would your life be like if you had no fear?

So do not fear, for I am with you; do not be dismayed, for I am your God. I will strengthen you and help you; I will uphold you with my righteous right hand. (Isaiah 41:10 NIV)

PRAYER TO ENCOUNTER YOUR FATHER
I yearn to life a fearless life, Father. I know that courage is not the absence of fear but courage is the choice I make in the face of fear. Show me Your way to conquer fear in my life.

JUNE 23
THE LIFELINE

We either live our life feeling safe, secure, and at rest in Father's heart, experiencing His love and giving it away, or we live our life with apprehension and uncertainty, struggling constantly with the fear of trusting, the fear of rejection, and the fear of opening up our heart to love—the three fears common to all people.

So many of us have hooked our lifeline (sense of security) into "counterfeit affections," that sooner or later will entangle us in unrealized hopes and unfulfilled dreams. Instead of drawing our energy and our source of life and peace from the love of God, we try to find them in these counterfeit affections of performance, the passions of the flesh, power and control issues, possessions, position, people, or places. Somehow we think that unless we have these sources of comfort in our lives, we simply can't go on.

Let's be honest—we all have counterfeit sources of comfort, don't we? Every one of us has people or possessions we turn to or attitudes or behaviors we fall back on when life does not go the way we want it to. Counterfeit affections exert a strong pull, even when we realize they are counterfeit. Sometimes it is easier to hold onto the familiar, and make it our lifeline even if it does not satisfy, than to risk letting go in order to grab hold of something else that will.

Love the Lord, all his faithful people! The Lord preserves those who are true to him, but the proud he pays back in full. (Psalm 31:23 NIV)

PRAYER TO ENCOUNTER YOUR FATHER
Starting today I want to draw my energy and source of life and peace from Your love, Father. I will stop using counterfeit affections of performance as my lifeline and I will pursue Your pursuit of me guiding me to Your manifested presence.

JUNE 24
LETTING GO

When you're out on the bow being tossed by every 20-foot wave and with sleet whipping against your face, it's easy just to grab hold of whatever you can find and say, "I'll just ride it out right here." But unless you let go, unless you relinquish your grip on your false sense of security and comfort, you may never attain the true warmth and security of the wheelhouse—Father's embrace.

For those twenty-one days that we were in Antarctica and traversing Drake Passage, that cramped cabin was home. Whenever we were there, we were warm, safe, and sheltered from the wind and the waves. The problem with us today is that so many Christians have never made their way beyond the sea of fear into a place of safety and security. Isn't the brokenness of so many of our marriages, families, and other relationships evidence enough?

Brothers and sisters, I do not consider myself yet to have taken hold of it. But one thing I do: Forgetting what is behind and straining toward what is ahead. (Philippians 3:13 NIV)

PRAYER TO ENCOUNTER YOUR FATHER
How sad it is, Father, that I spent so many years refusing to leave my brokenness so I could step out in faith to find wholeness and light! I relish my time with You in the warmth and safety of the wheelhouse (that place where I feel Your presence).

TOO GOOD TO BE TRUE

Living life as if we have a home means living to experience God's love on a continuing and ongoing basis and making that love known to others. As Christians, we are sons and daughters of God, yet so many of us live as if we don't have a home. We live, think, and act like fatherless orphans because we have never truly embraced Father God's love on a personal level. The storms, set-backs, and disappointments of life have made us afraid to trust, afraid to let go, afraid to risk becoming vulnerable by believing God when He says, "I love you." Because we do not love ourselves, we feel unlovable and find it difficult if not impossible to believe that anyone else could love us, including God. The thought of Him loving us personally seems too good to be true...and much more than we deserve.

And that's precisely the point: It is much more than we deserve. But it is also true. God Himself said, *"I have loved you with an everlasting love; I have drawn you with lovingkindness"* (Jer. 31:3). Take that verse personally because God means it personally. God never created you to be an orphan with no home. He created you to be a beloved son or daughter who has found a home in His embrace.

> *Neither height nor depth, nor anything else in all creation, will be able to separate us from the love of God that is in Christ Jesus our Lord.* (Romans 8:39 NIV)

PRAYER TO ENCOUNTER YOUR FATHER

I am running home to You, Father! I know how much You love me and I'm overwhelmed with that truth. I that You that even though I don't feel I deserve that love You say I belong if I never do another thing! That You for that unconditional love that I can experience when I position myself for an encounter with You.

HOME SWEET HOME

All of creation is about God wanting to make His home in you and, indeed, in all people. And He will not rest until He accomplishes it. Isaiah 66:1 says, *"This is what the Lord says: 'Heaven is My throne, and the earth is My footstool. Where is the house you will build for Me? Where will My resting place be?'"* Not in a temple or anyplace else that is built by the hand of man. Revelation 21:3 (NIV) provides the answer: *"And I heard a loud voice from the throne saying, 'Look! God's dwelling place is now among the people, and he will dwell with them. They will be his people, and God himself will be with them and be their God.'"*

God is saying, "I will not leave you as an orphan. You have a home with Me." Home is a place of safety and security. It is a place of warmth and love. If you're having a "bad hair day" and everybody is coming against you at school or at work and nobody is speaking anything good about you, home is the place where you can go and hear the voice of your Father say, "No matter what anybody else says, you are the child I love and on whom My favor rests." Home is where you constantly hear the voice of God speaking His affirmation over you, His love over you, and His forgiveness, compassion, and grace over you.

My people will live in peaceful dwelling places, in secure homes, in undisturbed places of rest. (Isaiah 5:10 NIV)

PRAYER TO ENCOUNTER YOUR FATHER

Dear Father, thank You for welcoming me home—no matter the hour of the day or night, no matter in a house, trailer, apartment, or a shelter. You are everywhere—so wherever I feel Your embrace, there is home knowing You are there.

JUNE 27
LIVING LIKE AN ORPHAN

Without this deep experiential knowledge and understanding of Father's love and that you have a home in Him, it becomes so easy to live your life as if you don't have a home, which is a life of fear. And fear produces "numb-numbville." It makes you unable to healthily connect emotionally with God or anyone else with whom you have a relationship. Living like an orphan means struggling constantly with the fear of trusting. It is a life of independence where you believe you are completely on your own. It means living in a state of agitated resistance against people who do not think like you. When you live your life is if you don't have a home, you see every person—even loved ones—as a potential threat or enemy to your independence.

Whether you live your life as if you have a home or live your life as if you don't have a home depends on how you think God feels about you. If you believe that God loves you just as you are, you will live life like a son or daughter of the King. If, however, you believe that God is mad at you and that you always have to try to find out how to appease Him, you will live like an orphan. This is an important distinction because however you think God feels about you is the way you will treat others in your everyday relationships.

I will not leave you as orphans; I will come to you. (John 14:18)

PRAYER TO ENCOUNTER YOUR FATHER
I'm not an orphan, Father. I have You as my everlasting Father, the dad who watches over me constantly and is always in my corner. I thank You for that!

DON'T WORRY, IT'S OKAY

All of creation begins and ends with the Father longing for relationship with you as His beloved child. He created you to live your life as if you have a home. Did you get up this morning and hear the loving voice of your Father say, "Don't worry that you don't have everything together; that's OK. I don't expect you to get it perfect. I love you so much just the way you are. You are the son/daughter I love and in whom I am well pleased"?

Or did you get up thinking, *nobody loves me, Nobody cares about me. I have to have devotions today, and pray enough, and get my three Bible chapters read, and do all the right Christian stuff, just so I can get a crumb from the Master's table today.*

You will treat yourself and others according to the way you think God feels about you. If you know you are loved unconditionally, you will love yourself and others with that same kind of love. But if you feel you have to perform in order to be of value to God, then you will portray the thought to others that they need to perform in order to be of value to you. Either you live your life as if you have a home, or you live your life as if you don't have a home. Fear...or Father's embrace!

And behold, a voice out of the heavens said, "This is My beloved Son, in whom I am well-pleased." (Matthew 3:17)

PRAYER TO ENCOUNTER YOUR FATHER

When my to-do list gets priority over listening for Your voice during the day, Lord, I become fearful and overwhelmed. Focusing on You is ALWAYS the best view of life! I thank You that You created me as Your child fashioned so that I never have to perform for acceptance I was born into it.

JUNE 29

Come Home

I am convinced that in this season of church history more than any other since the days of the apostles, God is calling us to experience a homecoming. He is calling us off the sea of fear into a calm harbor of refuge and safety. It's hard to beat the feeling of exhilaration you get when you move from a place of not knowing whether you will be alive or dead in the next minute into the warmth of that wheelhouse. During that stormy night on Drake Passage, something came alive inside me.

You never know what's going to happen next. But when you choose to confront the sea of fear and cast yourself in faith into the arms of a loving Father, you begin to discover the purpose and meaning of life. God is saying to you, "Live! Live! Live!"

God is saying to all of us: "Come home." And where is home? Anywhere He is. We hear a lot about the Kingdom of God in our churches; to me, the Kingdom of God means seeing God's will and purpose come to pass on earth as they are in Heaven. *"The Word became flesh and made His dwelling among us. We have seen His glory, the glory of the One and Only, who came from the Father, full of grace and truth"* (John 1:14). Jesus came from the bosom of the Father. That word bosom means safe place. And the heart of the Father is where He invites us to return. That is our home. A safe place in His presence. A place of belonging with no fear of failure.

> *But neither exile nor homecoming is the main thing. Cheerfully pleasing God is the main thing, and that's what we aim to do, regardless of our conditions.* (2 Corinthians 5:9 MSG)

PRAYER TO ENCOUNTER YOUR FATHER

I accept Your invitation to return home to You, heavenly Father. I thank You that I belong and can feel safe in Your presence at this very moment. Embrace me.

HEAVEN AND EARTH

Jesus will return to the place from which He came, and He wants us to be with Him: *"My Father's house has many rooms; if that were not so, would I have told you that I am going there to prepare a place for you? And if I go and prepare a place for you, I will come back and take you to be with me that you also may be where I am"* (John 14:2-3 NIV). Jesus is saying to us, "I'm fixing up a special place for you in the family dwelling. My Father's house will not be an empty house. It is your home in His embrace."

Christ, who created all things, came from the bosom of the Father, a place of warmth, safety, and security. He came to make it possible for His home to become our home so that we will know that we are not orphans. Subsequently, when crisis comes, we can be confident that we do not have to face it alone because Father is always there.

No one goes through life without experiencing some degree of shame, disappointment, or betrayal. When these and other crises come, where do you hook your lifeline? That is what creation is all about—God making His home among humankind.

Jesus said…I know where I came from and where I am going. (John 8:14)

PRAYER TO ENCOUNTER YOUR FATHER

It is very hard for me to comprehend that Jesus could leave the ultimate beauty and luxury of Heaven to come to sin-spoiled earth. But I don't have to understand it, Lord, I just have to accept the truth of it. And I do!

JULY 1

A MELTED HEART

When our daughter was 14 years of age, I suddenly went from an agitated dad to a compassionate father—a change that literally melted her heart. I had been so hard to live with that she had reached the point of wishing that whenever I left the house to go on a ministry trip, I simply would not return. She said that prior to my receiving a revelation of God's love, whenever I was home there was no joy in the house; there was only fear—fear of trusting, fear of rejection, and fear of opening her heart to love. Embracing Father's love made all the difference. In a matter of months, my relationship with Sarah changed from an almost total lack of tenderness, affection, and warmth to the place where she became "Daddy's girl."

From the time she was 14 until she was 17, Sarah and I enjoyed the kind of relationship any father and daughter would long for. She would run in the house and yell, "Dad, where are you?" Then she would jump on my lap, give me a kiss, and tell me what an awesome and wonderful dad I was.

One day when she was 17, I was driving her to school and I said, teary-eyed, "Sarah, I just love you so much!" "Daddy," she replied sweetly, "would you quit before my makeup runs?"

It was a very tender moment between us.

Behold, children are a heritage of the Lord: and the fruit of the womb is his reward. (Psalm 127:3-5)

PRAYER TO ENCOUNTER YOUR FATHER

Father I thank You for the bond between my daughter and I thank You that it has been healed. I thank You that we can be very close, but the bond between You and me Father is the ultimate intimate closeness. I'm thrilled to be Your child!

JULY 2
JUST LEAVE ME ALONE

Later that day after school, Sarah came through the back door, slammed it, blew right by her mom without a word, blew right by me without a word, and went straight to her room. Then her bedroom door slammed shut.

I knocked on Sarah's door. "Is everything all right, Sarah?" "Yes!"

"Did I do something wrong?" "No!"

"Well then, why don't you come out and tell us about your day?"

"I don't want to!"

Finally, after several weeks, Sarah began to open up to her mother. She had started trying to stand up for righteousness at school regarding some things that were happening with some other Christian girls. Unfortunately, they responded by trashing her. The same thing happened at church. Now all her friends had pushed her to the outside. I would drive her to school, and she would be desperately trying to hold back the tears, not wanting to go because of the way they were treating her on a daily basis.

Trisha tried to encourage her. "Go talk to your dad. People come from all over the world to hear him. You have free access to him any time. Talk to him."

"I don't want to talk him! I don't want to talk to anybody. I want everybody just to leave me alone!"

When the righteous triumph, there is great glory, but when the wicked rise, [people] *hide themselves.* (Proverbs 28:12)

PRAYER TO ENCOUNTER YOUR FATHER

Standing up for You isn't always easy, Father, especially for young people who depend so much on their peer group. I pray Father that You will supply all the strength and power for all those who are standing for Your righteousness. I ask You to grant them courage to face those that bully them for what they believe. I ask You to align them with like-minded people to strengthen them.

ALL I WANT IS A HUG

One night I stayed up all night praying because my heart was so burdened for her. I knew that if she continued to close her heart off to love, she would most likely find comfort somewhere else. The enemy is very good at sending the wrong people to us just at our time of greatest crisis. Whenever you cut yourself off from those people who love and care about you, get ready for the enemy to entice you with a counterfeit affection. I prayed for Sarah all night: "Please, God, help her find her way home. She's living her life as if she doesn't have a home. Help her find her way back to You."

The next morning she noticed that my eyes were puffy. "Dad, you look terrible!"

"Well, I've been up all night."

"Are you and Mom having problems?"

"No, I've been up all night because my heart is breaking for you."

Sarah shot me the look that said, "Don't go there!" But I still had five more minutes of driving time before we arrived at the school. She was a captive audience. "Sarah," I said, "my heart is breaking because I see that your world is collapsing, and I know that what you need more than anything else is to hear me say, 'No matter what's going on, Sarah, I love you the way you are. And you are beautiful in my eyes.' All I want is a hug."

As a father shows compassion to his children, so the LORD shows compassion to those who fear him. (Psalms 103:13)

PRAYER TO ENCOUNTER YOUR FATHER

Sometimes Father, all I need is a hug to make the world right again. Your embrace is what I long for—what I need right now and always. I ask You to make me aware when my children need a hug from me. Let me example Your compassion creating a safe place for them to come to.

JULY 4
I NEED A FATHER

Later that day, Sarah came home and said, "Dad, I need to talk to you and Mom. I don't know what's the matter with me, but I need to talk. And Dad, I don't need a counselor! I need a father. I don't need any lectures, Dad. I need a hug."

As Trisha and I sat down with Sarah in my study, Sarah said, "Dad, I just don't know. When everything is going right in my life, all I want to do is hug you and be in your presence, but as soon as things aren't going my way, I just want to cut myself off from every other human being. It's like I would rather be alone on a deserted island somewhere and never see another human being again. I can't get hold of God's love. There seems to be a pattern in me where I can find God only when people are saying all the right things about me. But when they are not, I can't find Him, and I don't want to be with you."

As she was sharing her thoughts and feelings, I was thinking, *That's me! When God is answering my prayers and doing everything I want Him to do, how quickly I run to Him! But when I feel like He's not doing what I want Him to do on my timetable, something in me shuts down and I find myself "on the bow" of the boat in the entanglements of the sea of fear.*

I will not leave you comfortless: I will come to you. (John 14:18)

PRAYER TO ENCOUNTER YOUR FATHER
Father I thank You for the chance to comfort my child the way You have always comforted me. I ask You to continue to make me sensitive to the needs of love and comfort my children have as they have to face their worlds. I ask Your Holy Spirit to guard them each day and make them examples of comfort to their friends.

BROKEN TRUST

Then Sarah told the childhood story that affected her deeply. Trisha had brought Sarah to see me, and lowered her over the stern of the boat. When Sarah saw me sitting back in a comfortable chair in the living room of the yacht, my precious 5-year-old daughter came running to me for a hug. She leaped into my lap, knee first…and suddenly I felt the deepest core pain of my life!

My instinctive reaction was self-protection. Although I was rolling on the floor almost nauseous from the pain, my young daughter, while having suffered no physical injury, was experiencing a much deeper pain than I was. She had come running to enjoy her father's embrace only to be tossed onto the sofa as I was writhing in agony. She had risked opening up her heart to me…only to have it slammed shut. How many times have you risked opening your heart for a moment of tenderness, a moment of nurturing, or a moment of warmth, only to receive nothing in return?

As Sarah was screaming and crying, I hugged and kissed her and did everything I could to make it up to her. After about ten minutes, she finally calmed down. Did I intentionally hurt my daughter? Of course not, never. But that was the moment Sarah had stopped opening her heart and receiving me as her father, and she had struggled with that feeling of rejection ever since.

Singing light songs to the heavyhearted is like pouring salt in their wounds.
(Proverbs 25:20 MSG)

PRAYER TO ENCOUNTER YOUR FATHER

Father, I guess we humans never know how are actions and words are affecting others. I pray, Lord, that You will guard and guide my actions and words today and every day so that I am a blessing, through You, to all I meet and greet.

PERFECT LOVE DESTROYS FEAR

We either live our lives as if we have a home and a loving Father's arms to run to when the world is trying to give us what it thinks we deserve, or we live our lives as if we don't have a home. We want to live in Dad's house and enjoy Dad's provisions, but like Sarah, who locked herself in the bedroom and came out only for what Dad could give her—food, credit cards, keys to the car—we fear an intimate relationship.

So, which will it be? Will you live your life like an orphan who has no home, frozen in numb-numbville on the bow in the midst of the sea of fear? Or will you live your life in the warmth of your Father's loving embrace, a perfect love that drives out all fear? (See 1 John 4:18.)

What would your life be like if you had no fear? The choice is yours: Fear… or Father's embrace? I hope you choose no fear!

Well-formed love banishes fear. Since fear is crippling, a fearful life—fear of death, fear of judgment—is one not yet fully formed in love. (1 John 4:18 MSG)

PRAYER TO ENCOUNTER YOUR FATHER

*I **do** choose a no-fear life, Father! I can tell immediately when fear is invading my space and will shove it out of the way and choose Your embrace each day.*

AN ORPHAN HEART

Before we can live a life with no fear, we have to deal with the matter of an orphan heart. We all were born with an orphan heart that rejects parental authority and seeks to independently do everything our own way. The only humans who were not born with an orphan heart were Adam and Eve. Instead, they possessed a spirit of sonship from the very beginning but eventually exchanged it for an orphan heart when they chose to go their own way apart from God. As a result of their fall, their orphan hearts passed down to every succeeding generation, thus becoming the common heritage of all humanity.

So, our quest is not to regain our sonship with the Father; we cannot regain something we never lost if we have received Christ as our savior. Rather, our quest is to enter into the embrace of the unconditional love of Father God and receive a heart of sonship that will displace our orphan heart. It took me many years to learn this truth. I was radically saved and then radically filled with the Holy Spirit, and yet for many years afterward I continued to live with an orphan heart.

When you possess an orphan heart, you never truly feel at home anywhere. You are afraid to trust, afraid of rejection, and afraid to open up your heart to receive love. And unless you are able to receive love, you cannot unconditionally express love, even to your own family.

I will not leave you comfortless: I will come to you. (John 14:18)

PRAYER TO ENCOUNTER YOUR FATHER

Do I possess an orphan heart, Father? Is that why I'm leery about opening my heart to receive love? Show me the truth—for You know all about me. I thank You that I am Your child because I have given Jesus my heart. I want to feel at home in Your presence. Help me to know You as my Father.

JULY 8
STRONGHOLD OF OPPRESSION

You can be born again, go to church every week, tithe, avidly study the Bible, and do all the right Christian "stuff," and still have an orphan heart. Being saved does not automatically mean feeling secure, loved, and accepted as a son or daughter of God; they are two different things. The new birth in Christ makes you a son or daughter of God, but that does not mean that you will enter automatically into the full personal experience of that love relationship with Him as Father.

This is why over and over and over again people come up to me at conferences I teach and confess, "I just can't get it. I've gone to dozens of conferences; I've heard the teachings on the Father's love; I've had countless hours of counseling and prayers for healing and deliverance—and I still can't get free of fear and insecurity in my relationships." For a long time I didn't know what to say to them because I suffered from the same problem—I still had an orphan heart.

Left unchecked, an orphan heart can grow into a stronghold of oppression—a habit structure of thinking or fortress of thought that is so deeply entrenched that only a profound experiential revelation of Father God's love can displace it.

> *For you did not receive the spirit of bondage again to fear, but you received the Spirit of adoption by whom we cry out, "Abba, Father." The Spirit Himself bears witness with our spirit that we are children of God.* (Rom. 8:15-16)

PRAYER TO ENCOUNTER YOUR FATHER

Father, I ask You for wisdom to understand what is going on inside of me that prevents me from being able to believe that I am totally accepted and loved by You the way I am at this moment. I ask You to forgive me for believing that I had to do something to make me better so You would accept me. That produces fear in me Father and I chose to believe You don't want me to be in bondage to fear.

JULY 9

DISPLACING AN ORPHAN HEART

You can't cast out an orphan heart. It is a heart that feels as if it has no home. It must be displaced, and the only way to do that is to introduce the orphan to a loving father. Then the orphan must choose to submit his or her heart to that love. Ideally, this should happen for all of us as children through the examples of a loving mother and father. But there are no perfect mothers and fathers. So what then?

What happens if you run to a parent for love and comfort and affirmation, only to feel hurt or rejected? Left unhealed or unresolved, the wound can set into motion in an orphan heart a twelve-step progression that eventually manifests as a stronghold of oppression powerful enough to handicap people for years emotionally and prevents them from cultivating healthy, loving, and caring relationships. Let's look at these twelve steps:

1. We begin to focus on the faults we see in parental authority. I did not hurt Sarah intentionally; my response to her was an instinctive defensive mechanism. As a result, Sarah closed her heart to me that day. Our true personality is revealed in our family relationships. Even as children, we notice the faults of our parents. We see how they misrepresent Father's love to us and recognize the disappointments, broken promises, and inconsistency in behavior. And these flaws can loom large in our eyes, leading to the next step.

> *When we take up permanent residence in a life of love, we live in God and God lives in us. This way love has the run of the house, becomes at home and mature in us.* (I John 4:17-18 The Message)

PRAYER TO ENCOUNTER YOUR FATHER

I have to admit that over the years I have found fault in the way my parents raised me and related to me. I never felt safe at home and I judged them for not knowing how to love me unless I was doing for them. I ask You Father to forgive me for not allow my life to become a life of love for them or my children.

DISPLACING AN ORPHAN HEART
(CONTINUED)

2. We receive parental faults as disappointment, discouragement, grief, or rejection. Sarah interpreted my momentary instinctive defense response as my personal rejection of her. How often, whether with our children, our spouse, our work colleagues, or our fellow believers at church, do we throw someone aside as a reaction of our own personal defensive mechanism, leaving that person feeling wounded or rejected? We don't mean to do it, but it happens. Parents do not intentionally hurt their children. We do not intentionally misrepresent the love of God. But we can give to others only what has been given to us. How can I ever be a father if I have never felt like a son?

As a child, although I had a father, I always felt more like a slave in his house than a son. There was no nurturing, tenderness, warmth, affection, comfort, or protection. And because I grew up feeling like a servant, that is how I treated my children. I could give to them only what had been given to me. Is it any surprise that they received it as woundedness and rejection? They didn't feel safe trusting me, which brings us to step number three.

Trust in the Lord with all your heart and do not lean on your own understanding. In all your ways acknowledge Him, and He will make your paths straight. (Proverbs 3:5-6)

PRAYER TO ENCOUNTER YOUR FATHER
As You are the only Perfect Parent, please forgive me for wrongs I committed in my family life. I ask You to continue to show me my mistakes so that I can change for the good of my children and spouse.

DISPLACING AN ORPHAN HEART
(CONTINUED)

3. We lose basic trust in parental authority. Once disappointed, rejected, or otherwise wounded by a parent, we close off a part of our heart to keep it from being hurt again. A wall goes up. A certain degree of basic trust is lost. *Trust and basic trust are two different things.* If I walk by you and accidentally step on your foot with my size 15 shoes and say, "Oh, I'm so sorry, please forgive me," you may still trust me as a person. But the next time I walk close by, you will make sure you withdraw your foot so it doesn't get tramped upon. You trust me as a person, but because of your past experience of pain inflicted by me, you fear that the same hurt may happen again. So you withdraw a part of yourself—the part that was injured before because a measure of your basic trust has been lost.

We are not talking about the ability to believe or trust another person, but the capacity to hold your heart open to another person, especially if you believe his or her motives or intentions are questionable. Basic trust is the ability to risk being real and vulnerable, to keep your heart open even when it hurts rather than close off your spirit.

Basic trust is when you can move beyond the weaknesses in others and receive God's healing touch, one moment at a time, and not run away; to retreat into His loving embrace, even when someone close to you may be misrepresenting Father's love to you. It is taking on the Spirit of Christ, a meek and gentle heart, and entering into Father's rest.

Children, obey your parents in the Lord, for this is right. (Ephesians 6:1)

PRAYER TO ENCOUNTER YOUR FATHER

I have a superficial trust for most everyone I know, but I'm not sure about placing my trust in anyone except You, Father. Help me with this flaw.

DISPLACING AN ORPHAN HEART
(CONTINUED)

4. We move into a fear of receiving love, comfort, and admonition from others. Once basic trust is lost, it becomes difficult to receive from others because we are afraid to make ourselves vulnerable. So when the inevitable crisis comes, our response is to just suck it up outwardly and take care of everything ourselves because we don't trust anyone else or believe there will be someone to comfort us. With an orphan heart, you often feel alone, especially in a crowd or during times of crisis.

5. We develop a closed spirit. Once we close our hearts to receiving love, we close our hearts to intimacy (in-to-me-see). We retreat into a closed spirit, isolating our heart from outside influence and from all but the most superficial or unhealthy emotional attachments. Intimacy is lost.

6. We take on an independent, self-reliant attitude. A closed and isolated heart manifests itself with an attitude that says, "If anything is going to get done around here, I'll have to do it myself." Independence and self-reliance are often cherished and valued qualities in our culture. While they may seem to be important and useful in the political or business arenas, they are deadly in relationships, family, and community and can result in restlessness and disease because we are not able to cast all our cares upon Him. Instead, we carry them all ourselves, which leads to the next step.

Even though I walk through the valley of the shadow of death, I fear no evil, for You are with me. (Psalm 23:4)

PRAYER TO ENCOUNTER YOUR FATHER

I can blame Western culture and American society for my independent and self-reliant nature, but when it comes to You, Father, I will chuck all that to be dependent and reliant on You. I chose to walk with You through the fear of opening my heart to You and others, I choose to let my guard down and I ask You to forgive me for my independent nature as I learn to lean into You and Your nature.

DISPLACING AN ORPHAN HEART
(CONTINUED)

7. We start controlling our relationships. With an orphan heart, our independence and isolation are nothing more than issues of control. They may manifest as agitation or apathy. We limit our relationships and conversation to "safe" topics like news, sports, weather, etc. The fear of trusting, fear of rejection, and fear of intimacy prevent us from tackling deeper subjects.

8. Our relationships become superficial. With a closed heart, healthy relationships are very difficult. The three fears listed above unconsciously influence us to keep others at arm's length emotionally. And we rarely realize that we are doing to them the very same thing we fear they will do to us: rejection.

9. We develop an ungodly belief that says no one will be there to meet our need. That is the danger of an independent, self-reliant heart. Not only are we afraid to depend on someone else, but we also feel that no one values us enough to care for us.

10. We begin to live life like spiritual orphans. An orphan heart feels that it does not have a safe and secure place in a father's heart where they feel loved, valued, and affirmed. We have no safe harbor, no refuge, no place of rest. Outside of our identity being in what we do, we really have nowhere to call home. We believe that we will have to argue, wrangle, and fight for anything we want to accomplish in life.

We have come to know and have believed the love which God has for us.
(I John 4:16a NAS)

PRAYER TO ENCOUNTER YOUR FATHER
You are my safe harbor, Lord, I trust You absolutely. I want to call Your embrace my home. I believe that the love which You have for me is a safe haven.

DISPLACING AN ORPHAN HEART
(CONTINUED)

11. We begin chasing after counterfeit affections. Having shut ourselves off from the genuine affections of family and friends, we start looking for counterfeit affections—substitutes for the affections we left behind at home or never had. We were created for love and family; consequently, without them, we will find something to bond to as a replacement, even if it is unhealthy or destructive.

I classify **counterfeit affections** under the **"seven P's"**:

1.passion 2.possession 3.position 4.performance 5.people 6.place and 7.power. Counterfeit affections bring no true fulfillment and easily lead to the twelfth and final step.

12. We begin to daily battle a stronghold of oppression. Having isolated ourselves from cultivating healthy relationships, we become trapped in a cycle of seeking fulfillment in things that can never satisfy. Unable to receive love, acceptance, and admonition either from God or from others, life for us becomes an oppressive mix of tension, agitation, anger, bitterness, restlessness, and frustration that can eventually lead to depression.

Now you can see how a wound can start a progression that eventually manifests as a stronghold of oppression powerful enough to hold you in bondage for years emotionally and prevent you from cultivating healthy, loving, and caring relationships.

The whole point of what we're urging is simply love—love uncontaminated by self-interest and counterfeit faith, a life open to God. (1 Timothy 1:5 MSG)

PRAYER TO ENCOUNTER YOUR FATHER

I am going to need You to help me consider these twelve steps and stop the progression of them in my life and generations to come. I ask You to forgive me for the times that I have sought out those counterfeit affections to replace true intimacy with You.

JULY 15

RESTORING THE FATHER'S HEART

A life of oppression, spawned by an orphan heart, is the common experience of almost every person. Even among Christians, who know the truth of forgiveness of sins and eternal life through faith in Christ, only a small percentage have truly experienced the full embrace of Father's love. Their troubled marriages, families, and relationships are evidence of this fact. Too many Christians are still caught up in the entanglements of the orphan heart. Consequently, few have learned to displace their orphan heart with a heart of sonship.

That number is growing, however. An orphan heart is common in a fallen, sin-ridden, competitive world, but it was never God's desire or plan for us. And He is actively at work to change the situation. In our own generation, we are witnessing the beginnings of the restoration of Father's heart to the hearts of His children, just as foretold in Scripture. The Book of Malachi, the final Book of the Old Testament, closes with a wonderful and powerful promise (see above).

The promise of God is that *"the prophet Elijah"* will come *"before that great and dreadful day"* when Christ comes. We know from Jesus' own words in the Gospels that this promise was fulfilled once in the person of John the Baptist, who came to prepare the way for the coming of the Lord. However, this prophecy also contains a deeper dimension of meaning that relates to the end of the age.

> *See, I will send the prophet Elijah to you before that great and dreadful day of the Lord comes. He will turn the hearts of the parents to their children, and the hearts of the children to their parents; or else I will come and strike the land with total destruction.* (Malachi 4:5-6 NIV)

PRAYER TO ENCOUNTER YOUR FATHER

I praise You, Lord, for restoring Your heart to the hearts of Your children, as written in the Bible, Your Word. Help me to comprehend the meaning of what You have shared with me.

RESTORING THE FATHER'S HEART
(CONTINUED)

Before Christ returns, Elijah will come, this time in the form of an anointing or movement rather than embodied in one person. Why "Elijah"? Elijah was instrumental in overthrowing abusive and controlling authority when he defeated Jezebel's prophets. Later, when Elijah was taken up to Heaven in a chariot of fire, Elisha, his spiritual son who witnessed his ascension, called out, *"My father, my father…"* (2 Kings 2:12). Then in Malachi, *"Elijah"* represents a fathering anointing that will be released on the earth in the end times. Malachi 4:6 bears this out in its description of the effect the release of this anointing will have on the world—to *"turn the hearts of the fathers to their children, and the hearts of the children to their fathers."* Thus, the curse of the orphan heart will be displaced.

Until and unless Elijah comes, the land remains under a curse. And what is that curse? A feeling of fatherlessness. More than at any other time in human history, fatherlessness is the curse of our generation. Today more children than ever before are growing up in fatherless households, and many more are growing up without a father emotionally, even though their biological father is physically present in the home.

> *But also look ahead: I'm sending Elijah the prophet to clear the way for the Big Day of God—the decisive Judgment Day! He will convince parents to look after their children and children to look up to their parents. If they refuse, I'll come and put the **land under a curse**.* (Malachi 4:5-6 MSG)

PRAYER TO ENCOUNTER YOUR FATHER
Father I thank You that I am going to be a part of reviving my family so that they don't experience a curse in their relationships. I need Your Holy Spirit to remind me daily when I try to step back into the strongholds of my past.

BATTLING DEPRESSION

Unfortunately, for many of us, this is not the home life of our experience or memory. As mentioned previously, one study has revealed that, for most Christians, 80 percent of our thinking is negative and in agreement with the enemy, the accuser, who tells us we have no value or are unlovable, and who feeds our orphan heart ungodly beliefs about God's loving nature so that we live as if we don't have a home even though we are children of the King.

An orphan heart can reside over an individual person, over a church, over a city, over a region, or even over a nation. And wherever an orphan heart holds sway, whether individually or corporately, people get up every day feeling like they don't belong. They do not feel accepted. They have little sense of being valued, honored, or loved. Their lives are defined by their perceived need to perform in order to be approved and affirmed.

In these end times, before a major spiritual reformation hits the earth, there will first be a deeper revelation of the heart of the Father that breaks the orphan spirit on the earth today. This is not an automatic product of salvation. Unless our orphan heart is displaced by the revelation of Father's love, even as Christians we can end up battling oppression every day of our lives.

Things will get better and better. Depression days are over. They'll thrive, they'll flourish. The days of contempt will be over. (Jeremiah 30:19 MSG)

PRAYER TO ENCOUNTER YOUR FATHER

So many people these days are taking drugs—legal and illegal—to feel better. Depression affects too many, Father. I ask You Father to help them to understand and forgive their earthly dads for not being there to place value into their hearts thus leaving them with a void and a place for rejection and the orphan heart to find a residence.

JULY 18

DEMONIC OPPRESSION

Derrick Prince was a great Christian evangelist. His evangelistic crusades routinely drew tens of thousands of people to each meeting. Across more than fifty years of ministry, he saw millions of people saved, filled with the Holy Spirit, healed of diseases, and delivered of demonic oppression. Few Christian leaders of the last century established ministries as credible and anointed of the Lord as his. Yet, Prince himself battled demonic oppression every day of his life until he was 80 years of age. He could not find freedom from the oppression that dogged him on a daily basis. It took a powerful personal experiential revelation of Father God's love to set him free once and for all.

Do you feel a sense of oppression, foreboding, and impending disaster? Most mornings do you face another day of pain, another day of fear, another day of people saying all the wrong things about you, another day of not measuring up in the eyes of the people who matter to you the most, another day of wondering whether or not you will survive? How do you go on living like that? How do you go on, knowing that tomorrow you have to get up and do battle with all of it again? Is not the cross of Christ more powerful than the darkness we have to fight our way through every day? This has nothing to do with salvation—but everything to do with experiencing and understanding Father God's love.

This wisdom is not that which comes down from above, but is earthly, natural, demonic. (James 3:15)

PRAYER TO ENCOUNTER YOUR FATHER

Demonic oppression isn't even anything I want to think about, Lord. Because I know You are greater in me than the world is, I will stand on that truth! So Father come and be the Father that my earthly dad could not represent You as.

JULY 19

DAD'S HOUSE

You can experience intimacy, oneness, and a sense of sonship with the Father in this life because of the presence of the Holy Spirit in your life. Jesus is saying, "There's a place for you in Dad's house. That's where I am, and I'm getting your place ready. I will not leave you as an orphan but will come to you, and Father and I will make Our home in you" (see John 14:18-23).

God is love. And feeling secure as sons and daughters in His fatherly embrace is what everything in creation is all about. The Kingdom of Heaven is all about love, joy, and peace, and being free from fear, insecurity, and anxiety. Perfect love is what characterizes Heaven, and God's perfect unconditional fatherly love is available to you each day—no fear, anxiety, anger, bitterness, hurt feelings, or resentment.

There's a place for you in Father's heart right now, where you can live your life hearing His voice saying to you every day, "You are the child I love and in whom I am well pleased." The center of all creation is being at home in Father's heart. His heart is a place of rest from our striving, but few have entered into that place of rest.

I will not leave you as orphans; I will come to you and we will come to them and make our home with them. (John 14:18-23)

PRAYER TO ENCOUNTER YOUR FATHER
When I lay down at night, Father, You know that sometimes I'm just so tired that I can't even rest. I wrestle with sleep because my mind is rehashing the day's troubles. I thank You that I am welcomed me Your heart and I ask for You to give me rest. Thank You.

YOUR MISSION

During my years as a commercial snapper fishing boat captain, I generally fished with a four-man crew. Needless to say, those four men living in close quarters together at sea on a 44-foot boat for seven days often resulted in some very interesting relational dynamics. During one trip, I hired on as a deck hand one of the top captains in the fleet who was presently without a boat. I soon learned that two emotionally immature captains working the same fishing boat go together like oil and water.

He thought that he knew more than me—what rock pile to fish on next, when to move the boat, what bait to use, and so on. You could say he did not take kindly to me as captain nor to my fishing style. Like most captains (me included) he was submitted to no man and to no mission but his own. It was a week of agitation, arguments, competition, and one fistfight. In fact, so much energy was given to our rivalry that we battled fatigue all week, which diminished our harvest of fish. Lesson learned—you can have only one captain on a boat, and no matter how good you think are, if you are going to reap a successful harvest, the crew had better be willing to be subject to the captain's mission, or you will end up wasting time trying to work out each other's differences.

And I saw that all toil and all achievement spring from one person's envy of another. This too is meaningless, a chasing after the wind. (Ecclesiastes 4:4)

PRAYER TO ENCOUNTER YOUR FATHER

Father I see now that I have not always represented Your love to another especially when I was jealous of the others accomplishments. Forgive me for not preferring Your lost son over myself. You're the captain of my boat!

THE FATHER'S MISSION

Whether we are aware of it or not, each of us is on a mission that determines our future harvest in life and relationships. For some of us, our life mission is more clearly defined than it is for others. And the source of our life mission—its point of origin—will determine whether we live life feeling like a spiritual orphan or as if we are a spiritual son or daughter.

So, the basic question each of us has to answer is: Whose mission am I on? We have one of two choices. We will be subject either to the Father of Creation's mission or to the mission of the father of lies, the accuser of the brethren. These are the only possibilities. Even if we think we are subject to our own mission, we are really serving the mission of our enemy, because anything that diverts us from following Father's mission weakens our life and relationships and advances satan's purposes on earth.

Our problem is that too often we don't see ourselves as Father's favored sons and daughters; rather, we feel more like spiritual orphans. God relates to us not on casual terms as servants or even as friends, but intimately as beloved children. All of creation is about Father God longing for a personal intimate relationship with us as His sons and daughters.

I know what I'm doing. I have it all planned out—plans to take care of you, not abandon you, plans to give you the future you hope for. (Jeremiah 29:11)

PRAYER TO ENCOUNTER YOUR FATHER

Father, I trust that You have the best plan for my life. I am open to receiving Your assignment to accomplish Your mission. Fulfill my destiny so that it brings hope for others.

JULY 22
THE FATHER'S MISSION
(CONTINUED)

One inevitable part of this Father–child relationship is discipline. Father God's discipline is evidence that we are His children. Absence of discipline means absence of relationship. This is why the writer says, *"If you are not disciplined… then you are not legitimate, not true sons and daughters at all."*

How are you about receiving discipline? What do you do when someone close to you—your spouse, your prayer partner, a leader of your small group, or your boss, for example—takes you aside and says, "I've been watching the way you relate to others and have observed a pattern in your life that concerns me. Can we talk about it?" Doesn't it give you warm fuzzies to know that someone cares enough about you to risk confronting you? Do you want to say, "Oh, yes, tell me more!" Or does it rub your fur the wrong way?

If someone is trying to bring truth or admonition to your life and you resist it, then you are like an illegitimate child, at least in heart attitude. Inability to receive discipline can be a sign of an orphan heart. Orphan hearts have independent spirts and resist admonition and correction. Whereas, sons and daughters welcome these things, even when they seem unpleasant. They know discipline is a crucial part of the process of nurture and growth to maturity. More importantly, they embrace discipline as proof that they are favored children of a caring Father.

If you are not disciplined—and everyone undergoes discipline—then you are not legitimate, not true sons and daughters at all. (Hebrews 12:8 NIV)

PRAYER TO ENCOUNTER YOUR FATHER

Father I hate it when people try to get me to do things their way because I don't understand that many times experience is the best teacher. When I am disciplined, my fur does in fact get rubbed the wrong way sometimes, so Father I ask You to keep me aware of this attitude and correct it quickly. Help me to welcome correction when it is for development of the plan of Yours in my life.

JULY 23

SPIRITUAL ORPHAN

One time, some of my closest friends and board members at Shiloh Place Ministries sat down with me and said, "Jack, there is a relational pattern in your life that really concerns us." Reluctantly, and a little apprehensively, I replied, "I probably need to hear more." This was significant because for nearly fifty years I didn't want to hear it. My orphan mindset was not open to constructive criticism and correction. After I received the sonship revelation, however, I began welcoming corrective admonition because I knew it would help me learn to think and act like a son.

The "concern" my friends and colleagues shared with me was a heavy one, and my first thought was defensive, *Wait a minute! You do the same thing! And you're teaming up two-to-one on me?* But then I remembered the Scripture from Hebrews that says if I cannot receive discipline—if I struggle against receiving admonition and correction in my life—then I am like an illegitimate child and not a son.

A spiritual orphan is a person who feels that he or she does not have a home or a safe and secure place in a father's heart where he or she feels loved, accepted, protected, affirmed, nurtured, and disciplined. When we are subject to the "Father of spirits," life flows. I like to paraphrase the last part of this verse to say, "Be subject to Father's mission and live."

> *Moreover, we have all had human fathers who disciplined us and we respected them for it. How much more should we submit to the Father of spirits and live!* (Hebrews 12:9 NIV)

PRAYER TO ENCOUNTER YOUR FATHER
Life and death, God—I choose life, which is being subject to Your mission, not mine. I'm determined, with the help of the Holy Spirit, to live in Your embrace.

LIFE AND PEACE

To be subject to our own mission is to be led by our flesh, which leads to death, but to be subject to our Father's mission leads to life and peace. Is your life and relationships at peace? Or is death slowly at work all around you? Your answer to those questions may determine what your life and your relationships—as well as those of your children and grandchildren—may be like in the future. Be subject to your own mission, and barrenness will work its way into your emotions and relationships. Be subject to the Father's mission, and life and peace will begin to flow through you—spirit, soul, and body.

If pursuing our own mission leads to the lack of lasting fruitfulness, while the Father's mission leads to life and peace, then it is important to know what Father's mission is. Simply stated, Father's mission is for you to experience His expressed love and to give it away to the next person you meet. Successful execution of Father's mission is a matter of combining two elements in the proper order and balance—the scriptural mandates many Christians know as the "Great Commandment" and the "Great Commission."

Moreover, we have all had human fathers who disciplined us and we respected them for it. How much more should we submit to the Father of spirits and live! (Hebrews 12:9)

PRAYER TO ENCOUNTER YOUR FATHER

Father, I recognize and appreciate that Your mission is for me to experience Your love and to give that same love to everyone I meet. I want to fulfil Your purposes in my life so that I can live and not die. I will fulfill my mission for You.

THE GREAT COMMISSION

Who could deny that winning souls is seen as a top priority in the Kingdom of God? After all, the Bible says that Jesus came to earth and died on the Cross so that all people could be reconciled to God and that those who are reconciled have been charged with the ministry of reconciling others. When I was attending Bible school, the Great Commission was the emphasis that rose above all others. It was stressed even to the point of implying that unless you were willing to forsake your family and everybody else in order to "go," then the sincerity of your commitment was in question.

As important as the Great Commission is, it is frequently overemphasized to the point of neglecting, and sometimes forgetting, another mission that is even more important—the Great Commandment. One day a religious leader asked Jesus what was the greatest and most important commandment in the law. His reply: *"'Love the Lord your God with all your heart and with all your soul and with all your mind.' This is the first and greatest commandment. And the second is like it: 'Love your neighbor as yourself.' All the Law and the Prophets hang on these two commandments"* (Matthew 22:37-40 NIV).

In effect, Jesus was saying, "When you seek to know God's love and to make it known, you are released from every other obligation in the Word of God."

> *All this is from God, who reconciled us to himself through Christ and gave us the ministry of reconciliation: that God was reconciling the world to himself in Christ, not counting people's sins against them. And he has committed to us the message of reconciliation.* (2 Corinthians 5:18-19 NIV)

PRAYER TO ENCOUNTER YOUR FATHER

Knowing Your love, Father God, is the first and most important aspect of life. Without that knowledge, people just exist rather than live. I ask You Father to help me understand how to live the great commission of loving others more than myself.

NOTHING WITHOUT LOVE

Love is to be the inspiration, the driving force behind everything the Church does, including fulfilling the Great Commission. Jesus left no doubt about the priority of love in the Scripture verses above.

Paul went so far as to say that without love, nothing else we do matters: *"If I speak with human eloquence and angelic ecstasy but don't love, I'm nothing but the creaking of a rusty gate. If I speak God's Word with power, revealing all his mysteries and making everything plain as day, and if I have faith that says to a mountain, 'Jump,' and it jumps, but I don't love, I'm nothing"* (1 Cor. 13:1-3 MSG).

It is in this Great Commandment to love God and to love others where we find the Father's mission. His desire for us is that we receive His love and give it away, thus fulfilling the Great Commission.

A new command I give you: Love one another. As I have loved you, so you must love one another. By this everyone will know that you are my disciples, if you love one another. (John 13:34-35 NIV)

PRAYER TO ENCOUNTER YOUR FATHER

Father, Rather than worrying about fulfilling this law and that requirement, when I focus on spreading God's love to all, unashamed and excitedly, my life is joyful and I can't wait to wake up each morning!

Preach Good News

How do you recognize a person who truly knows and loves God? By how well he or she can preach? By how many people fall down in the Spirit when they pray? Because they have faith to move mountains? By how they relate to others at church on Sunday? By how much Bible they know? No. You recognize a person who knows God by the life of love, compassion, and tenderness he or she shows behind closed doors with family and peers when no one else is looking. A person who loves God is one who seeks the love of God to be made mature and complete in his or her daily relationships. I love the way The Message Bible cites it: *"God is love. When we take up permanent residence in a life of love, we live in God and God lives in us. This way, love has the run of the house, becomes at home and mature in us..."* (1 John 4:17-18 MSG).

What is the key for the world to come to know God's love? *Agape,* a love that seeks the low place of humility, service, honor, and value. And that's where we find God's mission. The Great Commandment is to be fulfilled before the Great Commission.

> *The Spirit of God, the Master, is on me because God anointed me. He sent me to preach good news to the poor, heal the heartbroken, announce freedom to all captives, pardon all prisoners.* (Isaiah 61:1)

Prayer to Encounter Your Father

Father, I know people who are good representatives of Your agape love, Lord. But sadly I know more who are not. Count me in the good rep category. Thank You for all of the changes in my life that have helped me to look more like You.

JULY 28

SELF-MAKING ORPHANS

Consider the examples of the prodigal son and his older brother in Luke 15. Although they were surrounded by the deep compassionate love of their father, each of them had an orphan heart that prevented him from enjoying intimacy with his father. The older son was angry and saw his father as someone to obey, while the younger son saw his father as someone who could give him things. Neither son related to his father on an intimate level.

Lucifer did not start out as an orphan, however. He began in beauty and splendor, surrounded by the glory and love of Father God: *"You were in Eden, the garden of God; every precious stone adorned you: ruby, topaz and emerald, chrysolite, onyx and jasper, sapphire, turquoise and beryl. Your settings and mountings were made of gold; on the day you were created they were prepared. You were anointed as a guardian cherub, for so I ordained you. You were on the holy mount of God; you walked among the fiery stones. You were blameless in your ways from the day you were created till wickedness was found in you"* (Ezek. 28:13-15).

Not only was lucifer continually in the presence of God, he was also the worship leader in Heaven. But that was not enough; he wanted more. And in his greedy attempts to get more, lucifer lost everything.

> *How you have fallen from heaven, morning star, son of the dawn! But you are brought down to the realm of the dead, to the depths of the pit.* (Isaiah 14:12,15 NIV)

PRAYER TO ENCOUNTER YOUR FATHER

Father, I pray for the day I am in Your presence and You welcome me to my heavenly Home, Lord. It's hard for me to fathom how one of Your precious angels would turn on You—the Creator of all beautiful and good. But I also know that at any moment I could also. I need Your Holy Spirit to strengthening me.

JULY 29
SEPARATED FROM GOD

The Kingdom of Heaven is all about perfect love, joy, and peace with no fear, insecurity, or anxiety. Lucifer dwelt there in the beginning and reveled continually in God's perfect love. At some point, however, something in lucifer desired to be subject no longer to God's mission but to be dedicated to his own mission. Anytime we become subject to our own mission, separation goes to work. Lucifer subsequently lost the privilege of dwelling in the Father's house of unconditional love and acceptance. He was separated from his Creator and from his home, as Isaiah says in Isaiah 59:2.

Lucifer became the ultimate spiritual orphan. Separated from his original home, he became resentful toward anyone who enjoyed intimacy with Father God, particularly those human beings God had created in His own image. Because he no longer walked in Father's mission of love, lucifer began to compete for a place of recognition, position, and power.

Jealousy drove lucifer to deceive Adam and Eve. The tool he used to cripple humankind and weaken the nations was orphan thinking. His strategy was to convince them to think the way he did—homeless and cut off from God's love—thereby weakening them to the point where they would give in to temptation and allow shame and fear to replace intimacy.

But your iniquities have separated you from your God; your sins have hidden his face from you, so that he will not hear. (Isaiah 59:2 NIV)

PRAYER TO ENCOUNTER YOUR FATHER
Father, I know how quickly shame and fear can replace intimacy with You. When I know I've sinned, I want to run away from You when I should be running toward You to repent and ask for forgiveness. I thank You for Your grace that continues to help me when I see so that I am never without You.

JULY 30

TAKING THE SHORTCUT

The Father's command was, "Don't eat the fruit from the tree in the middle of the garden." Adam and Eve's desire was, "If we do this our way, we'll more quickly mature and become like God, and He'll appreciate and value us more."

Do you see how orphan thinking confuses the issue? It may sound perfectly logical and reasonable on the surface, but it never leads where we think it will. Instead of leading us closer to God, orphan thinking leads us away from Him— and prevents us from drawing close. I call orphan thinking the "shortcut spirit" because we think that our way will take us where we want to go more quickly than being subject to Father's mission. Adam and Eve wanted to please God; they wanted a place in His heart, and thought that through their human effort they could get there more quickly. However, seeking to do it their way led them far away from Him instead.

There was now no turning back for Adam and Eve. Having disobeyed God, they no longer had the sense of sweet fellowship and sonship they had before. They were now thinking and acting like orphans without a home, which is why they hid when they heard the sound of God walking in the Garden. Look how quickly relationships deteriorate under an orphan spirit.

Adam was not the one deceived; it was the woman who was deceived and became a sinner. (1 Timothy 2:14 NIV)

PRAYER TO ENCOUNTER YOUR FATHER

Father, I realize from the truth found in the Adam and Eve story that there are NO shortcuts when it comes to obeying You, Almighty God. I will obey Your commandments and Your whispers to my heart not because You desire to control me but to lead me into Your plan.

JULY 31

REJECT ORPHAN THINKING

As Christians covered by Jesus' sacrifice, God does not judge us, condemn us, or accuse us (see John 3:16-18; 5:22-24; 12:47-48). He loves us and wants to cover us. Yet Adam blamed Eve for his sin and for their trouble, and she refused to take ownership of her deception, opting instead to pass the buck to the one who deceived her. Thus, Adam and Eve by default chose orphan thinking over being restored into Father's love.

Adam and Eve's sin and ensuing departure from Eden (home) were the source of all subsequent despair on the earth among all people. Fear, anxiety, torment—they all began at this point. Humankind lost all sense of living in a home. Every human born in every subsequent generation was born with orphan hearts and became subject to their own mission; then death, which always involves separation, entered in. The death at work in an orphan heart is separation from God, separation from any sense of having a home, and separation from friends and family because of broken trust.

All of this homelessness, despair, broken trust, separation, and alienation are why these words of Jesus are central to the Gospel: *"I will not leave you as orphans; I will come to you"* (John 14:18). We have a home anytime we want it, whenever we are ready to give up the life of orphan thinking and return to the warm embrace of our Father's love.

> *Whoever believes in him is not condemned, but whoever does not believe stands condemned already because they have not believed in the name of God's one and only Son.* (John 3:18 NIV)

PRAYER TO ENCOUNTER YOUR FATHER

Father, I must remember, that I have a home with You. Not only when I pass from this earthly life into Heaven, but right now I can enjoy my home with You when I seek Your presence and embrace. I choose to believe in Your concepts and in Your example. I can trust You.

CONFLICTING SPIRITS

Today, as in all the ages of human history, two spirits are in constant conflict on earth for our hearts. The first of these is the spirit of sonship, which we can also call the spirit of Isaac, Abraham's heir and the son of promise. People possessed of this spirit live life as if they have a home. Their destiny is sure and secure.

In conflict with the spirit of sonship is the orphan spirit, which causes people to live life as if they don't have a home. This is the spirit of Ishmael, who was Abraham's natural son by Hagar, his wife's handmaid, who was not included in the inheritance promised to Isaac. Isaac grew up blessed and lived in anticipation of his inheritance; Ishmael and his mother were sent away. It was said of Ishmael, *"He will be a wild donkey of a man; his hand will be against everyone and everyone's hand against him, and he will live in hostility toward all his brothers"* (Genesis 16:12 NIV). History bears this out. Ishmael's descendants (the Arab nations) settled near Egypt, far from the land of Canaan, and have lived in almost continual conflict with Isaac's descendants, the nation of Israel.

This describes the orphan spirit—independent; hostile; contentious; with no sense of home, belonging, or of being a son. Quite often, the natural foreshadows the spiritual. In other words, earthly events frequently reflect heavenly realities, revealing what is happening in the spiritual realm (see 1 Cor. 15:46).

The spiritual did not come first, but the natural, and after that the spiritual. (1 Corinthians 15:46 NIV)

PRAYER TO ENCOUNTER YOUR FATHER

Father, This conflict between the natural and the spiritual invades not only the entire world, but also individual nations, cities, communities, churches, families, and every person. Lord, through the Holy Spirit living in me, I know my spirit will overcome my natural inclinations. Thank You!

AUGUST 2

CONFLICTING SPIRITS
(CONTINUED)

Today, in the Arab-Israeli conflict, the orphan heart continues to fight for control and domination of those who possess the spirit of sonship. Although the Arabs, who are descendants of Ishmael, own fifty times as much land as do the Jews, who are Isaac's descendants, they continue to fight to take away what little Israel has.

In the nations of the earth, the orphan heart is waging an all-out war against sonship. Lucifer's orphan thinking has weakened the nations in their understanding of God as a loving, compassionate, and affectionate father. This war is also within the Church, within the business realm, within our families, and within the hearts and minds of individuals. The orphan spirit has gained control of the world system as humankind has become subject to his own mission rather than to the mission of Father God.

The orphan heart is a heart attitude and a mental stronghold that is a temptation for all of us. But it can also become a demonic stronghold over a person, a church, a workplace, a city, or even a nation. If you (or a church) have an orphan heart, as I did for a long time, you feel as though you don't belong. With a heart of sonship, however, you feel loved, valued, honored, and accepted for who you are as God's creation.

> For the mind set on the flesh is death, but the mind set on the Spirit is life and peace, because the mind set on the flesh is hostile toward God; for it does not subject itself to the law of God. It is not even able to do so and those who are in the flesh cannot please God. (Romans 8:6-8 NAS)

PRAYER TO ENCOUNTER YOUR FATHER

Father too many times I hear in the news about the conflict between the enemy nations and Israel. I know You are on the side of Your chosen people, Lord. I am too so help me to keep my mind set on Your Spirit and Your ways. Forgive me when I step back into my flesh nature.

EMBRACING SONSHIP

When we begin to displace our orphan heart by receiving and embracing the heart of sonship, putting the Great Commandment ahead of the Great Commission will become perfectly natural. Much of what passes today for Great Commission ministry and evangelism has been influenced by orphan thinking, resulting in placing the Great Commission ahead of the Great Commandment. The brokenness of so many families of Christian leaders evidence that fact. Our tendency is to live by the love of law instead of by the law of love. Is it any wonder, then, that the church of today, despite having greater resources available than ever before in history, has not turned the world upside down the way the apostles and other early Christians did in the Book of Acts?

If we are more concerned with ministry or our career than with the needs of our family, then whose mission are we subject to? Satan's plan is to weaken the nations, and he does this by weakening families first. If satan cannot stop us from doing good things, he will keep us so busy doing good things for others that we neglect our own children who end up feeling like they don't have a place in our heart, and they too become spiritual orphans.

So that Christ may dwell in your hearts through faith; and that you, being rooted and grounded in love, may be able to comprehend with all the saints what is the breadth and length and height and depth, and to know the love of Christ which surpasses knowledge, that you may be filled up to all the fullness of God. (Ephesians 3:17-19)

PRAYER TO ENCOUNTER YOUR FATHER
Father, please help me keep my priorities in the correct order: You, my family, my work, etc...

AUGUST 4

To Be Like Jesus

In order to come into this Father and children relationship, we have to be led by the Spirit of God, who is a fathering Spirit. He is not a Spirit of slavery leading us into a life of fear again, but the Spirit of sonship. This is a Spirit of intimacy and innocence. Papa or Abba is a Hebrew term of endearment that essentially means the same as "Daddy." It is a term of intimacy, spoken by children who are in the presence of a loving Father whom they love and trust. In Daddy's presence there is no fear, no bondage, no oppression, and no anxiety.

The Holy Spirit gives us the inner assurance that we are children of God. And because we are children of God, we are also heirs of God and co-heirs with Christ. To be led by the Spirit of God means to be subject to Father's mission, and our perfect example is Jesus, our Elder Brother. How did Jesus view His mission? He had only one mission—the mission given Him by His Father: *"I tell you the truth, the Son can do nothing by Himself; He can do only what He sees His Father doing, because whatever the Father does the Son also does"* (John 5:19). And Jesus was completely faithful to Father's mission. The night before He was crucified, He prayed: *"I have brought You glory on earth by completing the work You gave Me to do"* (John 17:4).

> *This resurrection life you received from God is not a timid, grave-tending life. It's adventurously expectant, greeting God with a childlike "What's next, Papa?" God's Spirit touches our spirits and confirms who we really are. We know who he is, and we know who we are: Father and children.*
> (Romans 8:15-16 MSG)

Prayer to Encounter Your Father

Father, I thank You for this amazing adventurous life filled Your plan and Your desire to love all of Your creation. I thank You that You have daily assignments for me each day as I pursue Your dreams for me.

FOCUSED ON GOD

Everything we see in Christ we are heirs to as Christians. The goal of our Christian life is to become like Jesus. But we don't become like Jesus by focusing our lives on Jesus; we become like Jesus by focusing our lives on what Jesus focused His life on. Jesus focused His life on being a Son and revealing the Father and His love so that a world of spiritual orphans could become sons and daughters. The person we become is determined on whom we focus.

The whole mission of creation is about receiving love and bringing us into unity. That is why Jesus commanded us to love each other as a testimony to the world (see John 13:34-35). Father's mission is that the entire world experience His love by the love that flows in and through us as we receive His love and give it to the next person we meet. That is our mission in life. We were created to receive love and give it away. Nothing in life is more natural than walking in the love of our Father and passing that unconditional love on to others.

We will be subject to one of these two missions—the Father's mission or satan's mission—depending on the choices we make. So, choose Father's mission. Follow Jesus' example and focus your life on being a child of God, finding life and peace. Be a gift of love to the next person you meet.

The glory which You have given Me I have given to them, that they may be one, just as We are one; I in them and You in Me, that they may be perfected in unity, so that the world may know that You sent Me, and loved them, even as You have loved Me. (John 17:22-23)

PRAYER TO ENCOUNTER YOUR FATHER

Father, there are so very many distractions in my life that my focus is quickly diverted from You to work deadlines, dinner, taxes, car repairs, sports scores, etc. I'm sorry, please forgive me. I will do my best today and every day to keep my focus on You.

AUGUST 6
SAFE HAVEN

For a seaman looking to escape an impending storm, nothing is more comforting than reaching safe harbor. In Antarctica, safe harbor for a sailing vessel can be hard to find because almost everywhere you go along the Antarctic Peninsula there is nothing but sheer mountainous cliffs, icebergs, and glaciers calving at the water's edge. Weather conditions can change without warning, in an instant turning the most beautiful scenery on earth into the most treacherous and life threatening. A sudden drop in temperature or change in wind direction can turn a safe anchorage into a deadly trap as encroaching pack ice and bergs threaten to crush the hull of any small boat unfortunate enough to get caught there.

One secure anchorage is Port Charcot, a welcome safe harbor during our eight-man sailing expedition to Antarctica where we pulled in shortly before a snowstorm hit. All around us the ice floes froze up causing us to spend two days there among the penguin colonies.

When the ice began to clear, the captain told us that we had a 14- to 16-hour window of good weather to motor another 30 miles farther south to a Ukrainian research station, where we could spend a day or two. Here we were in a safe harbor at Port Charcot, knowing a severe storm was on the horizon, yet something drew us out. We were willing to risk leaving our refuge for "greener pastures," to sail into unknown waters on our quest for adventure.

God, you're such a safe and powerful place to find refuge! You're a proven help in time of trouble—more than enough and always available whenever I need you. (Psalms 46:1 The Passion Translation)

PRAYER TO ENCOUNTER YOUR FATHER
When I know You have provided a safe harbor for me before, during, and after any and every crisis, sometimes I venture out from within Your embrace. Why is that, Lord?

Safe Haven
(Continued)

In the morning, we set out under engine power, and for a couple of hours made pretty good progress. Our 74-foot aluminum sailboat crunched steadily through the seams in the pack ice that was up to one-foot thick. Yet as we continued, the ice kept our speed down to two or three knots, and a few miles from safe harbor at the Ukrainian research station, the pack ice began to thicken to the point that we could see no water in the bay. Eventually, we found ourselves completely surrounded by ice. We couldn't back up because putting the engine in reverse would have sucked ice into the propeller and destroyed it. Our extraordinary and exhilarating journey now threatened to become a fight for our lives.

The captain assured us that we were perfectly safe as long as there was no wind. Under calm conditions, we could handle the pack ice. If the wind kicked up, however, the pressure from the pack ice mixed with icebergs could move in and crush our vessel. Here we were, 600 miles from the nearest civilization, with ice closing in all around us, so we had to climb 50 feet up into the rigging of the mast and try to spot small seams and breaks in the pack ice where we could force our way through. With each minute that passed, the captain's tone became a little more urgent, reinforcing our need to reach the Ukrainian research station before the approaching blizzard hit around 10 o'clock that night.

Whoever dwells in the shelter of the Most High will rest in the shadow of the Almighty. (Psalm 91:1 NIV)

Prayer to Encounter Your Father
What is it about humans, especially men, that makes them seek dangerous adventures? Is this an instinct You instill in us, Lord God? If so I ask You to become my shelter then when I am in the middle of crisis.

AUGUST 8
SAFE HAVEN
(CONTINUED)

Finally, at about 6 o'clock, when we had only a mile to go to reach the research station, we discovered that we were unable to make any more headway. We knew that safe harbor lay just ahead, but because the ice had grown so thick, the captain said we would have to turn around and go back before the wind picked up!

Go back? But we were so close—indeed, almost close enough to see the station on the other side of the island! Just half a mile ahead of us, another sailing vessel was making the turn to starboard that would bring it around to the lee side of the small island where the research station was located—the side that would be ice free. With our own eyes, we could see the other vessel moving into safe harbor, yet we could not get there ourselves!

Because we couldn't back up, we used little seams in the pack ice to turn around. It was a disheartening and agonizingly slow process, but gradually we managed to reverse direction and began motoring north again through the pack ice, slowly pushing aside small bergs that were sitting five and ten feet deep off either side.

You make known to me the path of life; you will fill me with joy in your presence, with eternal pleasures at your right hand. (Psalm 16:11 NIV)

PRAYER TO ENCOUNTER YOUR FATHER
When I'm heading in the wrong direction, Lord, help me realize that the best way is to turn around. When I get off the right path, I will look to You for guidance, as my North Star.

AUGUST 9
SAFE HAVEN
(CONTINUED)

At 10 o'clock at night, still daylight because the sun never sets during the Antarctic summer, the wind grew stronger, reaching 50 knots. Ice, sleet, and snow were blowing sideways, and visibility dropped to less than 100 yards. Although we had broken out of the pack ice, we were now surrounded by giant icebergs—fighting to find our way home into safe harbor.

We were in the middle of a gale trying to run north to reach safety, with only two places within 40 miles where we could even consider tying up our boat. Finally, we pulled into Port Charcot. We could not simply drop anchor, instead we had to tie down by launching a 12-foot rubber Zodiac raft and then run four lines to the shoreline from the bow and stern, both port and starboard—all in the middle of a freezing blizzard.

About the time we tied down the boat, the wind shifted and icebergs anywhere from 10- to 20-feet high began moving into the little cove, threatening to crush our vessel. An iceberg lodged against our hull, and we had to use the motorized Zodiac to drag our vessel out of harm's way. In one moment, what had looked like safe harbor became a deadly trap. But the harbor had looked so secure—so welcome! But it all depended on which way the wind was blowing and how that wind would cause the pack ice to pile up in that cove.

The way of the righteous is smooth; O Upright One, make the path of the righteous level. (Isaiah 26:7)

PRAYER TO ENCOUNTER YOUR FATHER
Many times in my life, Father, the winds seem to be going my way and it's "smooth sailing" but other times the storms rage and there are ice bergs looming on either side, threatening to crush me. Thank You for the good times and remain my safe haven during the rough sailing times.

AUGUST 10
SAFE HAVEN
(CONTINUED)

We fought for two hours to get free of the ice trap, finally making it back out into an open bay. Icebergs were everywhere, the gale was blowing at 50 knots plus, and we wondered where we were going to go. The captain said our only choice was to head for Port Lockroy 20 miles to the north. Our boat was equipped with radar, but the blizzard snow seriously degraded its accuracy. Each man confronted his fears as we battled through raging winds and sleet. Every few minutes someone had to run up onto the forward deck and throw a bucket of water on the windshield because we could hardly see through the Plexiglas that was frozen into a slab of ice.

I can't describe the joy and liberation we felt as we finally entered Port Lockroy, surely one of the most beautiful places on earth! Upon rounding a bend at the head of the channel, suddenly the sun broke out and all around us were mountains up to 5,000 feet high, covered with snow and glaciers in each valley!

Inside Port Lockroy's little bay, it was calm because the mountains were blocking most of the winds. Outside the bay was the fury and danger of the storm, while inside all was peaceful in a little haven of safety that for over one hundred years had saved the lives of many whalers and other mariners.

Though you have made me see troubles, many and bitter, you will restore my life again; from the depths of the earth you will again bring me up. (Psalm 71:20 NIV)

PRAYER TO ENCOUNTER YOUR FATHER
I get excited when I know I've entered into Your embrace where there is peace and safety and comfort, I have to shout, THANK YOU, FATHER, FOR SAVING MY LIFE!

AUGUST 11

BLURRED VISION

A safe haven from the storms of life is what each person searches for, but still so many can't seem to find their way home. We either search for a safe harbor we have never known or seek to return to the safe harbor that once was ours, but have lost our way. At one time, we may have known the eternal safe harbor. We tasted of Christ's forgiveness, salvation, and peace. But through the circumstances of life, the sins of others against us, or our sins against others, we have found ourselves battling a blizzard, in the middle of a whiteout. With our vision blurred, it becomes difficult to hear the comforting and affirming voice of God. We struggle with the consequences of decisions we made, thinking we were pursuing something "better" in life, only to have fallen into a well-laid trap of the enemy that threatens to ice us in and freeze us out.

The ultimate safe harbor is ready and waiting for you. Begin your quest for home again. God's love is reaching out to guide you into that place of safety and security. But that safe harbor is reserved for sons and daughters, not those with orphan hearts. A life of peace, rest, and fruitfulness in Father's embrace is your inheritance, but only those dedicated to Father's mission find it. Orphans subject to their own mission remain outside the safe harbor, buffeted and blown by the wind and the waves, and limited in vision and hopefulness.

> *I am God. I have called you to live right and well. I have taken responsibility for you, kept you safe. I have set you among my people to bind them to me, and provided you as a lighthouse to the nations, to make a start at bringing people into the open, into light.* (Isaiah 42:5-9 MSG)

PRAYER TO ENCOUNTER YOUR FATHER
I will begin my quest for home again today, oh Mighty Captain of my soul! May the beacon of Your lighthouse show me the way.

AUGUST 12
SUBMISSION

In Antarctica, even with all my years at sea as a licensed fishing boat captain, I did not know the way to safe anchorages or how to overcome such violent storms. Therefore, I chose to trust the captain of the expedition who had been there so many times before. I surrendered my independence and my pride as an experienced sea captain and allowed myself to be subject to another captain and to his mission, which was to lead all eight of us to a place of comfort and warmth.

Our quest for safe harbor begins when we acknowledge our need to give up the independence and self-reliance of the orphan heart and humble ourselves willingly to be fathered and mothered by other men and women who have been there before, people who know how to find their way through the storms and the gales of life and who know where to find safe harbor. Safe harbor—the heart and love of the Father, along with all the riches and resources of His Kingdom—is our inheritance when we enter in with a heart of sons and daughters. Whose son are you? Whose daughter are you?

> *As they sailed, he fell asleep. A squall came down on the lake, so that the boat was being swamped, and they were in great danger. The disciples went and woke him, saying, "Master, Master, we're going to drown!" He got up and rebuked the wind and the raging waters; the storm subsided, and all was calm. "Where is your faith?" he asked his disciples. In fear and amazement they asked one another, "Who is this? He commands even the winds and the water, and they obey him."* Luke 8:23-25 New International Version (NIV)

PRAYER TO ENCOUNTER YOUR FATHER

I am Yours Father. You are either in control or You are not. My whole story lies within Your abilities to calm the storm of my crisis and unbelief. I choose to trust You.

AUGUST 13
SPIRITUAL GROWTH

Apostle Paul says in Romans 8:14-18 that either we walk in and are led by the flesh, or we walk in and are led by the Spirit. Walking by the flesh leads to death while walking by the Spirit leads to life and peace. If we are led by the Spirit, we are subject to Father's mission and life will flow. There will be growth and fruitfulness. A sense of unity and a sense of the fruit of the Spirit will begin to grow in us. We will begin to mature in our emotions and relationships. If, on the other hand, we are subject to our own mission, death will flow, and we will find ourselves becoming more independent and isolated in our relationships.

How do you begin movement toward a homecoming in Father's embrace? By focusing your life on being a son or daughter. If subject to your own mission, there is little spiritual growth. You will be surrounded by pack ice, with an inability to move forward in your Christian walk. You might see others making movement through the ice, but you remain frozen, locked in a sea of excuses, blame-shifting, and justifying. Your insecurity with love and relationships stagnates your growth and maturity.

Who moves forward into the Kingdom of God? Those who have a spirit of sonship, a spirit of adoption—not an orphan spirit. Our spirit determines whether or not we will enter into our inheritance—experiencing Kingdom life on earth.

> For those who are led by the Spirit of God are the children of God. The Spirit you received does not make you slaves, so that you live in fear again; rather, the Spirit you received brought about your adoption to sonship And by him we cry, "Abba Father." The Spirit himself testifies with our spirit that we are God's children. Now if we are children, then we are heirs— heirs of God and co-heirs with Christ, if indeed we share in his sufferings in order that we may also share in his glory. (Romans 8:14-18 NIV)

PRAYER TO ENCOUNTER YOUR FATHER
Although I like being treated like a baby, being coddled and tended to, I know I must mature past the milk stage and be fed with the meat of Your Word. I am choosing to believe that I am an heir with Jesus and I will share in His sufferings but I will also share in His glory. Thank You Father.

AUGUST 14
CHILDHOOD DREAMS

My whole childhood dream was to be a fishing boat captain. Growing up in Daytona Beach, Florida, a few blocks from the beach, I didn't want to play tennis the way my father wanted me to; I wanted to captain a fishing boat. I fished every day of the year from the Main Street pier or the Main Street bridge. The house I grew up in, and where my mother lived for fifty-three years, was one block from Boot Hill Saloon, four blocks from the ocean, and three blocks from the oyster beds in the intracoastal waterway. I lived every day fishing, catching trout, snook, bass, drum, whiting, and flounder. My whole dream was to become the best fishing boat captain there was.

But the interesting thing about the fishing business is that it is one of the most difficult professions in the world to get into. Anyone can fish, but being a professional is usually passed down from father to son or father to daughter. Certain businesses and trades are kept secret and passed down as a generational inheritance to the next generation and the next generation. If a fishing boat captain teaches his mate or any other member of his crew all his secrets, that person might become a captain of his own boat and steal the fishing spots. It is a highly secret, competitive business. Few boat captains teach anyone anything except his or her children—it is the children's inheritance.

A good person leaves an inheritance for their children's children. (Proverbs 13:22 NIV)

PRAYER TO ENCOUNTER YOUR FATHER

Father, I don't think about my children's children's inheritance as often as I should. I pray that my legacy is showing them You! In all I do, Father, I pray that my children and grandchildren see my love for You and others is my uppermost priority.

HEIRS

When I was 13 years of age, I began working as the mate on a boat at Ponce Inlet that belonged to one of my dad's best friends. He had three sons and captained a six-passenger sport fishing boat, fishing for mackerel, tuna, mahi-mahi, and billfish. Often his sons were on the boat. And it was the most aggravating thing for me as a mate to be on that boat with the father and his sons. I wanted so much to say, "Captain, please take me up in the wheelhouse. Teach me how to run a boat. Teach me how to find fish. Teach me navigation." I said nothing, and he left me on the deck to cut bait. The sons rarely did anything! They just sat up there with their father while he taught them everything about being a captain. Later, two of them became some of the best.

I was supposed to be on the boat an hour each time before it sailed, and I was always there early because I was determined to have the cleanest and most well-organized boat. I worked harder than anybody else because I had to prove to the captain that I had value. "Teach me, train me, help me grow in the profession! That's my dream!" But I wasn't a son. Those who were the sons would come in with their father at the last minute, and he would pour his life into them. It seemed to me that I did all the work and the sons got all the benefits!

Now if we are children, then we are heirs—heirs of God and co-heirs with Christ, if indeed we share in his sufferings in order that we may also share in his glory. (Romans 8:17 NIV)

PRAYER TO ENCOUNTER YOUR FATHER
As an heir to Your Kingdom, Father God, I accept all of the benefits, and the suffering, that comes with an intimate relationship with You.

AUGUST 16
PROVING A POINT

My dead-end situation working as a mate on boats made me agitated and angry until one day I finally said, "I've had it!" and quit. I felt that nobody was ever going to teach me anything, so I gave up on my dream. I lost myself for a while in the whole hippie and drug culture in Daytona Beach. After a few scrapes with the law, I decided to go back to fishing and visited a family friend in the fishing business who referred me to a captain who needed a good mate.

The captain hired me and put me to work on an old 45-foot boat. While everybody else wanted to work on the other boats because they were newer and finer, I set out to prove myself to the captain. I slaved away on that boat and poured my life into it; any day we weren't at sea, I was there eight or ten hours trying to work my way to the top.

As a slave or servant, we work harder, strive, outperform, and outdo everybody else to prove that we have a right to succeed. But sons and daughters? On their day off, they're usually not working hard trying to prove a point. Why should they? They already own the boat anyway because Dad will one day turn everything over to them. Those with orphan hearts are left to do the dirty work.

And you are heirs of the prophets and of the covenant God made with your fathers. He said to Abraham, "Through your offspring all peoples on earth will be blessed." (Acts 3:25)

PRAYER TO ENCOUNTER YOUR FATHER
I admit working hard to prove to myself and others that I have a right to succeed— under my own steam and ambition. This is a wrong attitude, Father. I am Your heir and have nothing to prove—only to obey Your will for my life.

AUGUST 17
AMBITION

The captain who hired me had spent more than forty years at sea, including service on PT boats during World War II. After the war, he had moved to Ponce Inlet, Florida, and gone into the fishing business, owning and operating the Snow White fleet, which eventually included three vessels. And before long, he had earned a reputation as one of the most respected and prosperous fishing boat captains in the industry.

Now the captain wanted to get out of the business, but there was a problem—he had no children or anyone he could trust to pass on his business, his legacy, and his name. Captain Kline and his wife didn't have children, and considering other people in the professional fishing community was not an option. Drinking and brawling are commonplace, and when I went to work for him, my background was not much different…except I was driven to succeed, to do everything I could to prove that I deserved a place at the top.

Although I was the newest and lowest of the eight mates, I always arrived earlier than any of the others and usually stayed later. My determination paid off quickly. Captain Kline said, "Jack, you appear to be one of the best mates I have ever seen. I've never had a man as conscientious as you." When Captain Kline fired his first mate on the new 70-foot boat, the Snow White III, he promoted me to that position ahead of all the others.

The arrogant cannot stand in your presence. (Psalm 5:5 NIV)

PRAYER TO ENCOUNTER YOUR FATHER
I certainly believe that hard work pays off, and I believe You inspire Your children, Father, to do their best. I also believe that I have to have the right motives, attitude, and focus. So Father I give You permission to change the motives in my heart so that I can example Your love everywhere.

AUGUST 18
DREAMS COME TRUE

The other mates—spiritual orphans like me—were mad, of course, because they all wanted that spot. Orphans are always looking for the high place, the place where they are recognized and affirmed. And because they have no inheritance, they feel the need to scrape, scramble, and fight for everything they want.

Then one day Captain Kline said to me, "Jack, you know I have no son to take over the business, and after forty years at sea, I've had enough. Stick with me, Jack, and I'll teach you everything I know. I'll train you to be a captain and when you're ready, I'll turn the whole business over to you. Just hang with me and all this will be yours."

I could hardly believe what he was telling me. My dream was coming true! I was going to be a fishing boat captain! All I had to do was stay close to Captain Kline for a couple of years until I learned everything he could teach me, and then he would turn everything over to me. I would be the son he had never had and this would be my inheritance.

...Be careful to do according to all that is written in it; for then you will make your way prosperous, and then you will have success. (Joshua 1:8)

PRAYER TO ENCOUNTER YOUR FATHER

When dreams come true—or at least there is a hope of them coming true, my outlook on life is bright and exciting! Yet my self-made dreams can crash and burn at any moment. Father, may Your dreams for me be my dreams for me.

CLOSE TO THE TOP

"Don't worry, Captain Kline," I said. "I'll stick with you." In the mornings, he took me into the engine room and taught me how to listen to every sound, how to notice every flaw, how to determine if a seal needed to be replaced, simply by listening for a certain drip in a particular area of the engine. I came to know those two big, turbo-charged V12 Detroit engines so well that I could have maintained them in my sleep. Within six months, Captain Kline no longer felt the need to personally go down in the engine room. He would simply come aboard and ask me, "Did you check the engines out?" because he trusted me. This was part of my inheritance.

Captain Kline took me into the wheelhouse where only sons entered! He taught me how to operate the boat, how to pilot and steer. He taught me navigation and how to use the fish finder, not only how to locate fish but also how to identify fish by the shapes of their schools. "Here is a rock ledge; notice where the fish are hanging. You're going to have to anchor the boat and allow for the wind and current; don't drop the lines until the boat is sitting right on this little spot." Within a year, I was running his boat.

…Do not turn from it to the right or to the left, so that you may have success wherever you go. (Joshua 1:7)

PRAYER TO ENCOUNTER YOUR FATHER

I have learned to have a teachable spirit, Father. I learned this from You over the years. Thank You for all the wisdom I have gained from others who shared with me their knowledge.

AUGUST 20
LEGACY AND INHERITANCE

This was Captain Kline's legacy…and my inheritance. For two years, I made myself completely available to him. Anything he needed, I was right there. It was easy; anybody could have had a spirit of sonship with someone as tender and gentle as Captain Kline was as a father to me.

Don't get me wrong; Captain Kline was a hard, tough man. He had a drinking problem stemming from his service in the war, where he witnessed much combat, blood, and death. A transfer five days earlier is the only thing that kept him from being killed with the rest of his PT boat crew when a direct hit destroyed the vessel. Like most others in the fishing industry, Captain Kline spent a lot of time in the waterfront bars. He was quite a scrapper and never one to back down from a fight. In fact, he often instigated them. When I began training under him, he often took me into the bars with him where he would seek out the biggest, toughest- looking guy in the place, tap him on the shoulder, and say, "My name is Al Kline, I'm five foot nine, and I can whip your ___ anytime." Then he would push me in front of him! I learned quickly how to think and talk on my feet!

Yet despite his tough demeanor, the captain was always gentle and kind toward me. Never once did he demean, criticize, or tear me down.

Therefore deal kindly with your servant. (1 Samuel 20:8)

PRAYER TO ENCOUNTER YOUR FATHER
Father, I ask for wisdom to be able to disciple those You send me with grace, gentleness and kindness as I pass down a legacy of love to them.

AUGUST 21
GENTLE LOVE

I remember the first time Captain Kline told me to dock the boat. "Jack," he said, "you've got to pull it up, spin it around 180 degrees, line it up between those two pilings, and give it reverse throttle before you drift out of alignment."

Operating a boat at sea is one thing—docking it into a narrow slip against a three-knot current with the wind blowing is another. Add to that the dozens of other boats and an audience of sixty tourists on deck, and you can understand how terrified I was. "I can't do it, Captain Kline. I can't do it!" I was scared to death. Captain Kline walked over, put his hand on my shoulder, looked me straight in the eye, and said, "Don't worry, Jack. I'm right here behind you. You can do this. I believe in you, Jack."

When a father believes in you, you'll try anything. I did exactly what he told me to do, but I wasn't quick enough and drifted out of position before reversing the throttle. As soon as it happened I ducked, expecting the barrage of abusive words and rage over my failure, such as I would have gotten at home. But they never came. Captain Kline just stood there with his hand on my shoulder and said softly, "That's OK, Jack. I'll take care of the pilings. Pull it out and let's try it again."

What do you desire? Shall I come to you with a rod, or with love and a spirit of gentleness? (1 Corinthians 4:21)

PRAYER TO ENCOUNTER YOUR FATHER

Father I want to be as compassionate as a role model as Your representative in Capt Kline was to me for others. Help me to believe in my sons, natural and spiritual in order to grant them grace to try new things testing their abilities in You. May I example courage and challenges so they will find their destinies.

AUGUST 22
I BELIEVE IN YOU

"I can't do it, Captain Kline. I can't do it." I was almost in tears. On the deck below some of the tourists were cursing and screaming, "What's the matter with that idiot kid up there in the wheelhouse?"

"You can do it, Jack," Captain Kline assured me. "In forty years at sea, I've never seen anyone as conscientious as you. I've never seen anyone who learns as quickly as you do. You can do this. You're going to be the best. Pull it on out. I believe in you."

So I pulled the boat out. Captain Kline refused to touch the wheel or the throttle. I moved upstream a little ways and then came back around. I lined the boat up just as before and gave it reverse throttle. This time the boat backed neatly into the slip. I risked failure but succeeded because I had a "father" who believed in me. And I started believing in myself. From that day through the 2,000 days of captaining fishing boats that followed, I never had another docking accident. That doesn't mean I never made any more mistakes. Captain Kline was one of the greatest men I have ever known and I would have done anything for him—anything to please him.

Do not throw away your confidence; it will be richly rewarded. (Hebrews 10:35 NIV)

PRAYER TO ENCOUNTER YOUR FATHER
Although I doubt myself daily, sometimes moment by moment, You have faith in me, Father. I thank You that I don't have to try and please You by obedience but I thank You for Your confidence in the abilities within me.

AUGUST 23
FORGIVENESS

One day, when we had no charters, Captain Kline was two decks below in the engine room changing the fuel filters while I was in the wheelhouse polishing the brass. I pushed the throttle levers out of neutral position into wide open so I could polish the chrome more easily. When I finished polishing the controls, I forgot to return the throttles to neutral.

After Captain Kline replacing the filters, he cranked the engines to test for leaks. I was with him when he pressed the start button. The turbocharged V12 engine roared to life and jumped forward, popping dock lines left and right, and started to take out part of the dock. Captain Kline screamed, "Who put the boat in gear?"

I shot out of the engine room and ran up to the wheelhouse. Frantically, I jerked the throttles into neutral. Captain Kline burst in screaming, "Who put the boat in gear?" At that moment, my orphan heart wanted to blame someone else, but we two were the only ones on board. I hung my head in shame and humiliation. Then, in my greatest moment of failure and embarrassment, Captain Kline started laughing. I looked up in amazement. Smiling, Captain Kline said, "I bet you'll never do that again!"

He didn't yell, ridicule, or condemn me! Instead, he showed me that it was OK to fail every now and then when learning. Captain Kline gave me the gift of honor. That's what a father does.

…That they may receive forgiveness of sins and an inheritance among those who have been sanctified by faith in Me. (Acts 26:18)

PRAYER TO ENCOUNTER YOUR FATHER
I have done many things in life for which I have asked You for forgiveness, Lord. I would like to say I will stop doing stupid things, but we both know that I will no. So I praise and thank You for Your compassion for me in moments of mistakes. I thank that Your grace covers as I learn more about process in living life as Your child.

WORK AS FOR THE LORD

Captain Kline loved me like a son, and I loved him like a father. But that was not enough because I still had an orphan heart. Although I didn't realize it at the time, my relationship with Captain Kline was built around what he was doing for me—he was fulfilling my dream to be a fishing boat captain.

For two years, he poured into me his forty years of knowledge and experience with the sea and with captaining fishing boats. He promised me, "Jack, once you have your 730 days at sea, pass the Coast Guard exam, and get your Captain's license, I'll make you the captain of the boat. Then later, we'll draw up a contract, and you'll be owner of the fleet one day. I'll live off the payments, and the fleet will be yours."

Who wouldn't be faithful and loyal with that type of deal? For two years I never failed to do anything Captain Kline told me to do. I obeyed every command and followed every instruction. I was like a son, and he was like a father to me. But you can't measure sonship—you can't measure true loyalty and faithfulness—simply by outward obedience, because outward obedience can still mask an orphan heart.

But he answered his father, 'Look! All these years I've been slaving for you and never disobeyed your orders. Yet you never gave me even a young goat so I could celebrate with my friends. (Luke 15:29)

PRAYER TO ENCOUNTER YOUR FATHER

When I put my faith and trust in people and exert my effort for their sake, I'm almost always disappointed. But when I put my faith, trust, and effort in You, Father God—I'm never disappointed, I'm rewarded!

True Self

Unconsciously, my relationship with Captain Kline was based upon what he could do for me and not for relationship. Outwardly, it looked as though I was subject to his mission, but in reality I was subject to my own mission. Captain Kline wanted to raise up a son to whom he could leave a legacy. My orphan heart was only interested in fulfilling my dream.

One day, believing that the time was right for me to be captain, I approached Captain Kline. His response was not what I expected. "I'm sorry, Jack, I know what I promised you, but I can't do it yet. My wife has cancer, and her care and treatment are draining every dollar we have. I can't afford it right now. Stay with me through this crisis, Jack, and all this will be yours, just as I promised."

I thought I was ready to captain a fishing boat. Captain Kline had promised it to me, and now I felt that he was breaking his promise. At that moment, I closed my spirit to him and went right down that 12-step progression from an orphan heart to a spirit of oppression. I regarded Captain Kline's response as a personal rejection. He had promised to make me captain but had not followed through. While technically true, that reality was tainted by my orphan's attitude of what was "right' and "fair" to me. There was no room in my heart for what was right and fair for Captain Kline.

Do nothing out of selfish ambition or vain conceit. Rather, in humility value others above yourselves. (Philippians 2:3 NIV)

Prayer to Encounter Your Father

Selfish ambition and vain conceit overwhelms me. Over the years I have wasted too much time attending pity parties for myself. I realize now that I was walking in an orphan mindset expecting rejection when things did not go as I planned. Father help me each day to see what You are doing, to understand Your timing and grace for my life.

AUGUST 26
A CLOSED HEART

As my heart closed to Captain Kline, I bought into other lies: "He doesn't care about you. All he wanted was your service. He's just been stringing you along." Captain Kline did want my service; that much was true. But he had always intended to reward my service with an inheritance. From the perspective of my closed heart, however, I could no longer see it that way. This man who had poured his life and his heart into me for two years; this man who had paid me twice as much as most other mates because he loved me and wanted to make sure I was taken care of; this man who put me on a year-round salary instead of seasonal pay; this man who was my best friend and the first man I had ever really let into my life—and the only thing I could think about was that he had deceived me. I felt he was cheating me out of what was rightfully mine.

Captain Kline tried reasoning with me numerous times, but my orphan heart was so closed to him that I couldn't receive what he was trying to say. I still worked the boat every day, but I refused to go up in the wheelhouse. Orphans rarely look to the future. I felt like I had been denied what was mine, and that was that. Subsequently, my heart was prepared to be deceived by an "angel of light."

> *But if you harbor bitter envy and selfish ambition in your hearts, do not boast about it or deny the truth.* (James 3:14 NIV)

PRAYER TO ENCOUNTER YOUR FATHER
Focusing on my rights and my pain and the injustice done to me opens doors and windows into my mind, spirit, and soul that allows evil to enter and warp all that is good. Protect me, Father, from selfish self.

AUGUST 27
THE ACCUSER

The accuser of believers often comes to us as an angel of light in our moment of crisis. Usually, this angel of light is in the form of another person or opportunity that appears to promise blessing and fulfillment in our life. In my case, it was another boat owner whose captain wasn't making him much money working his boat. He knew that Captain Kline had poured all his knowledge and experience into me, including knowledge of the locations of all his top fishing spots. Each captain possesses his own list of painstakingly acquired fishing spots that he keeps secret from everyone else because they provide him with a competitive edge. Any mate who has acquired (stolen) a fishing location from his captain can walk into any waterfront bar and sell it on the spot for as much as a thousand dollars. That's how important they are.

This boat owner came up to me and said, "I see Captain Kline hasn't made you captain yet. You know, it may be years before he does…if ever. I think he's just taking advantage of you. I tell you what—if you come to work as captain for me, you'll probably double your salary the first year."

For the accuser of our brothers and sisters, who accuses them before our God day and night, has been hurled down. (Revelation 12:10 NIV)

PRAYER TO ENCOUNTER YOUR FATHER
The evil one has had centuries of practice of tempting Your children, Father. I fall into his trap too often. Thankfully—and gratefully—You save me from doing any serious harm. So I ask for You to lead me not into the temptation of the accuser and deliver me from out of any of his traps.

HEARTBROKEN

Even after considering these tempting words from the other boat owner, I was still reluctant to leave Captain Kline after all he had done for me, so I tried to persuade him to follow through on his promise. I was tired of waiting. But he still had to say, "I'm sorry, Jack, but I can't do it right now. Please bear with me. Hang on a little longer, and you'll be captain soon." When I realized that Captain Kline was not going to budge, I said, "In that case, I give you my two weeks' notice."

To this day, I can still see his face, tears welling up in the eyes of this man who had stopped crying in battle while on the PT boats during the war thirty-five years earlier. I remember how he set his shoulders and went into the fighting stance that he had adopted in the bars when he was getting ready to pick a fight. Struggling to hold back the tears, Captain Kline said, "No, Jack. Either stay with me or get off my boat right now."

"What will you do without a first mate? You've got sixty people coming on board today. None of your other mates even know what they're doing."

"I'd rather have them than you. Get off my boat." His heart was breaking.

God's angry displeasure erupts as acts of human mistrust and wrongdoing and lying accumulate, as people try to put a shroud over truth. (Romans 1:18 MSG)

PRAYER TO ENCOUNTER YOUR FATHER
I've been heartbroken, Father, and I've caused other hearts to be broken. Forgive my selfish and self-absorbed attitude and mindset. I sincerely repent.

TOP HOOK

So I walked off his boat and over to the other boat owner. "I accept your offer," and he made me captain that very same day. I didn't think about how much it hurt Captain Kline because I felt I was right and he was wrong. Orphans blame, shift, and justify their actions, no matter how hurtful. Out of a selfish and distorted sense of being "right," I rationalized away all the hurt and pain I brought by demeaning, criticizing, and questioning his motives.

As a newly appointed captain, the very first week I came home "top hook"—I had out-fished everyone else. This was a big deal, and it came with a price—I had to buy all the pints in the pub, but it was worth it. Being "top hook" meant I was now one of the best. My dream to be a top fishing boat captain had come to pass.

Week after week I came in as top hook. No one as young and as inexperienced as I was had become so successful so quickly. Some might say, "Well, Jack, you got your inheritance." Did I? But at what cost to my character and relationships? I found all those fish at the locations I had learned from Captain Kline. Like the prodigal son who valued his father only for what his father could do for him, I valued Captain Kline for what he could do for me.

Scoff at every scoffer and let them be ashamed at every defeat. But let all who passionately seek you erupt with excitement and joy over what you have done. (Psalm 40:15-16 The Passion Translation)

PRAYER TO ENCOUNTER YOUR FATHER

Oh the shame of feeding my wants over other people's needs. How many times have I shunned someone's legitimate desires to pursue my illegitimate lusts? Forgive me, Father. But I thank You that You have the end result in mind as You show me my wounded ways toward others and my selfish desires. Thank You that You work everything for my good and the good of others.

AUGUST 30
VAIN GLORY

I could walk into any of the waterfront bars and bask in the adulation of being one of the best in the business. I had usurped Captain Kline's position, and now he sat alone in a corner of the bar, his head bowed over his beer, while his "bastard" son rose to glory. I became known as one of the top commercial snapper/grouper fisherman on the southeast coast of the United States, but what a high price I paid.

My orphan heart did not value relationships above inheritance. I did not feel compassion or empathy. My life was completely self-centered, self-consuming, and self-referential. I burned out many of Captain Kline's fishing spots—and while I was enjoying my rapid rise to success, he was declining because of a broken heart. My defection cost him dearly.

Captain Kline wouldn't even speak to me. When he looked at me, I could see etched into his face the pain of my betrayal and his broken heart. But in my orphan heart, I could not think of what I had done as betrayal. Still, I always felt grateful to him, and I remembered that I had once told him, "You're the first man who ever believed in me. You've given me something that no one has ever been willing to give me, and if I ever have a son, Captain Kline, I'll name him after you."

Be careful not to practice your righteousness in front of others to be seen by them. If you do, you will have no reward from your Father in heaven. (Matthew 6:1 NIV)

PRAYER TO ENCOUNTER YOUR FATHER
Vain glory—I have enjoyed it from time to time. I pray, Father, that as the years progress I will seek it less and less, and Your favor more and more.

HUMBLE HEARTS, HARD HEARTS

So a year after I left Captain Kline, we named our firstborn son, Micah Kline Frost. With no children of his own, I wanted to honor the man who had done so much for me. A few days after I sent Captain Kline a copy of the birth announcement, the phone rang. "Jack," Captain Kline said in a voice choking up with tears, "I just got the birth announcement. Would you go to breakfast with me tomorrow?" "I'd love to, Captain Kline."

The next morning we met at the usual gathering place where all the fishermen meet. "Jack," Captain Kline said, his eyes glistening with tears, "thank you for keeping my family name going another generation." I replied, "I'm going to do everything I can to keep your name in the Frost family line because I don't know who or where I would be without you."

Then he said, "Jack, would you forgive me for the way I've treated you the last year and for not rejoicing with you over your success?" "I forgive you," I said. But it was twenty more years before I asked him to forgive me. It took me that long to understand how I had wronged him. Orphan hearts rarely feel the pain they cause others. They are unaware of the arrows they shoot into other people's hearts. All they know is how "right" they are, and if someone else is hurting, that's their problem; they shouldn't have acted the way they did.

Do not judge, and you will not be judged. Do not condemn, and you will not be condemned. Forgive, and you will be forgiven. (Luke 6:37 NIV)

PRAYER TO ENCOUNTER YOUR FATHER
Father, bring to my attention anyone in the past I have hurt so I can ask for forgiveness. Please continue to show me areas of my orphan heart so that You can heal the areas of my pain.

SEPTEMBER 1
GODLY WISDOM

I thought I had received my inheritance when I left Captain Kline and went to work for a man who had never invested a day of his life or an ounce of himself into me. What I didn't realize was that a few years later, I would be radically born again, and a few years after that, I would leave the sea and go to Bible school. I went from making $50,000 a year fishing, to nothing.

After I stopped making a living at sea and went to Bible school, the boat owner I made tens of thousands of dollars a year for, never sent me a dollar in support. But Captain Kline has never stopped supporting our family. Through our friendship, his wife came to the Lord before she died, as well as Captain Kline. He would ask, "Have you ever heard of Jack Frost?" "Yeah, isn't he the guy who caught more snapper and grouper than anybody else? He was one of the best there ever was." Then, beaming with pride, Captain Kline said, "I taught him everything he knows."

If any of you lacks wisdom, you should ask God, who gives generously to all without finding fault, and it will be given to you. (James 1:5 NIV)

PRAYER TO ENCOUNTER YOUR FATHER
I can gain much from knowledgeable people, but I can gain much more from You, Father. So I ask You for wisdom to understand Your kids.

SEPTEMBER 2
JESUS CAN

The fishermen would ask, "Didn't Frost leave the sea and go to preaching?" "Yes," Captain Kline replied. "Let me tell you a story." Then he told them of the drug-addicted, pornography-addicted alcoholic (like so many of them) who one day decided to go to sea alone for three days. "While out there, he cried out, 'Jesus, if You're real, prove it.' And from that time on, Jack was set free from drugs, porn, and alcohol. What Jesus did in Jack's life, He can do for you."

Without a heart of sonship, there is no legitimate inheritance. Captain Kline had an inheritance prepared for me, and he poured himself into making me ready for it. But in the end, I didn't receive it legally—I was an orphan at heart, not a son. Only children receive an inheritance. For two years, Captain Kline lived to meet my needs, and as long as he gave me what I wanted, I was right there: "How can I help you, Captain Kline? What can I do for you?"

But the moment Captain Kline had a need, that's when my true spirit was revealed in me. I closed my heart to him and abandoned him in the midst of his wife's illness and financial problems. I valued what he could do for me more than I valued relationship; I was not submitted to the father's mission.

And do not be conformed to this world, but be transformed by the renewing of your mind, so that you may prove what the will of God is, that which is good and acceptable and perfect. (Romans 12:2)

PRAYER TO ENCOUNTER YOUR FATHER
I need to be transformed by renewing my mind in Your Word, the Bible. Your will is revealed in Your Book, and I want my life to conform to it. Show me Your way.

Short-Term Satisfaction

If I had stayed with Captain Kline and waited for my inheritance, the income I would have received as captain and eventual owner of the fleet would have paid for my Bible school education and sustained my family for years to come. Instead, five years later, I wasn't making $50,000 a year anymore and I was in Bible school—with no income for two years and a growing family. Because I was not subject to the father's mission, I chose short-term increase over the glory that would have come if I had waited for my inheritance. We ended up enduring fifteen years of poverty in Bible school and in ministry during which time I could barely feed my family. I gave away a million-dollar inheritance for short-term—and fleeting—satisfaction.

Inheritance comes only after enduring the *"sufferings of this present time."* Part of that suffering is patient obedience—being subject to Father's mission rather than our own. No matter how hard the present seems to be, and regardless of how difficult it seems sometimes to wait, nothing can compare with the glory of the inheritance that will be ours if we are willing to wait for it to come in our Father's good time.

> *For I consider that the sufferings of this present time are not worthy to be compared with the glory that is to be revealed to us.* (Romans 8:18)

Prayer to Encounter Your Father

From now on, Father, I'm choosing to understand Your ways. I am willing to live in patient obedience, Father.

SEPTEMBER 4

SHOW-OFF

The father of a friend of mine bought an antique, wooden, 18-foot speedboat when Peter was a teenager. His dad was prosperous, a member of the yacht club, and wanted to showcase the boat before all his boating buddies. He took the old teak boat to a boatyard and asked them to spare no expense in restoring it to mint condition. It took months of painstaking labor to refinish the wood; install new fittings, chrome, seats, and cushions; remove the old 100-horsepower inboard engine; and install a new 400-horsepower engine.

Upon completion, it looked like a work of art. The father bought a brand-new Jeep and trailer to tow the boat. When all his buddies were eating at the club restaurant, father and son drove to the launch ramp and lowered the priceless antique into the water in front of all his friends.

A number of his cronies pleaded for a ride, but the father reserved the honor for him and his son. The father took off at full throttle and did a few spins back and forth for all to see. Then he came racing back to the dock in front of the restaurant, and at the last second threw the gear in reverse at high rpm's, easing the boat to a stop. However, the force of revving up so much horsepower created a loud thud and water began pouring in from the stern (rear) of the boat.

The higher you lift up yourself in pride the harder you will fall in disgrace.
(Proverbs, 16:18)

PRAYER TO ENCOUNTER YOUR FATHER
Every time I act like a show-off, I end up being embarrassed. A show-off is prideful. I know where that attitude got lucifer—and that's not anywhere I want to be, Father.

FIRST PRIDE, THEN...

Screaming at his son and friends to help bail out the water, he ran to get his new Jeep and trailer before the boat sank. Upon inspecting the boat bottom, they found a huge hole in the keel at the stern. The exterior of the 50-year-old wood was varnished and looked like new, but the wood inside had dry-rotted, giving way to the pressures of the high-powered engine. Humiliated in front of his friends, the father's anger toward the workers at the boatyard exploded with verbal curses and accusation. Enraged, he commanded his son into the Jeep, jumped in, and sped off toward the boatyard to give them a piece of his mind.

Blinded by his temper and embarrassment, he had forgotten to strap the boat down to the trailer, and as he was speeding down the road, the driver in front of him suddenly slammed on his brakes. When the father slammed on his, the boat slid forward off the new trailer, went through the back window of the new Jeep, and left the bow of the boat sitting in the driver's seat. The boat was destroyed, the new boat trailer mangled, and the new Jeep had sustained thousands of dollars' worth of damages.

The moral of the story—if you have not dealt with the dry rot in your life, and God turns up the power, you are in danger of blowing your rear end off!

First pride, then the crash—the bigger the ego, the harder the fall. (Proverbs 16:18 MSG)

PRAYER TO ENCOUNTER YOUR FATHER

Father God, Please forgive me for the pride in my heart and show me how to get the dry rot out of my life....

SEPTEMBER 6
TAKING VERSUS RECEIVING

There is a lot of teaching in some quarters of the church today about claiming or taking your inheritance—that your inheritance from God is your right in Christ, and you just need to reach out and take hold of it. There is truth in this reality, but it is not that simple. "Taking" your inheritance and "receiving" it are two different things that can produce two very different results.

Teaching on our inheritance in Christ is important. Many Christians don't really know who they are or what they have in Christ because no one has ever taught them. Inheritance teaching does address a legitimate and serious need within the Body of Christ, but the "take your inheritance now" emphasis can be easily misleading or misunderstood. An inheritance taken by an orphan heart with orphan thinking is in danger of blowing his rear end off. If we have not embraced healthy accountability relationships, the anointing can quickly empower us and take us places where our character may not be able to keep our boat afloat.

A premature inheritance almost always ends up in waste. Remember what happened to the prodigal son. He took his inheritance early, and as Jesus said in Luke 15:13, quickly *"squandered his estate in loose living."* Why? Because his character was not mature enough to take responsibility for his father's mission. The prodigal son was an orphan at heart, and his orphan thinking was not yet responsible enough to be a wise manager of the inheritance.

> *And summoning the heirs to receive the eternal inheritance that was promised them...* (Hebrews 9:17 MSG)

PRAYER TO ENCOUNTER YOUR FATHER
Father Thank You that it is Your will for us to leave an inheritance to our children's children. I ask that You would increase what You have placed into my hands and give me wisdom to cause it to increase. I ask You to bless the ones that are helping me make those decisions.

SEPTEMBER 7

IMMATURITY

When we insist on taking our inheritance now instead of waiting until we mature, we may end up consuming the blessings of God upon our own lusts. I valued the captainship inheritance more than relationship. My orphan heart was too immature to appreciate fully the value of accountability and covenant relationships. The following are a few characteristics of immaturity and an orphan heart:

1. Immaturity is a slave to circumstances and emotions. Our circumstances determine whether we have a "good hair day" or "bad hair day."

2. Immaturity is a slave to self, seeking to meet personal needs at others' expense.

3. Immaturity seeks the place of comfort, ease, least resistance, and whatever makes us feel valued and affirmed.

4. Immaturity obeys out of a fear of loss or punishment, not because we do not want to grieve the one we love.

5. Immaturity values people for what they can do for us, not for relationship. Thus, we unconsciously use and manipulate people to meet our needs.

6. Immaturity demands its own way or nothing. "If you do not play my way, I am going to take my ball and go home."

7. Immaturity is subject to its own mission. Our thoughts continually gravitate toward me, myself, and I.

8. Immaturity is "obtain-oriented": "How does this benefit me?" Our choices are influenced by what we can gain.

9. Immaturity is self-centered, self-consuming, and self-referential. "Let's talk about you for a while…have you read my book yet?"

So I gave them over to their stubborn hearts to follow their own devices.
(Psalm 81:12 NIV)

PRAYER TO ENCOUNTER YOUR FATHER

Everyone assumes they are mature—including me. And I get offended if someone says otherwise. Maturity is relative in my mind; that is why I need You, Lord, to help me see what I now don't see. I ask You to give me wisdom to judge myself and others rightly so we all can grow in Your knowledge and wisdom to live life.

SEPTEMBER 8

THE APPRENTICE

Even as immature children, then, we are heirs of God and fellow heirs with Christ. This means that the fullness of Christ—everything we see in Him—is our inheritance. It all belongs to us. But that does not mean that we are supposed to get it all right now. In Galatians 4:1-7, Paul describes how a young child is an heir to everything yet does not actually assume ownership until the time set by the father. And until that time, the child can often feel more like a slave than an heir.

In the culture of Paul's day, a son was under the care and authority of tutors until he reached the age of 12, at which time he became apprenticed to his father. For the next 18 years, until the age of 30, the son worked as his father's apprentice, learning from his father everything about the family business or trade. Unlike the hired workers who received regular wages, the son often received no pay during his apprenticeship. Why? Because everything was provided for him by his father. He was still living in his father's house under his father's authority and care. His "pay" was learning from his father all the skills and trade secrets of their profession. Hired hands received wages, but the son was heir to the business. He had to wait, to "suffer" through his time of apprenticeship until he was responsible and mature in his knowledge and understanding of his father's business.

You've been a good apprentice to me, a part of my teaching, my manner of life, direction, faith, steadiness, love, patience, troubles, sufferings. (2 Timothy 3:10 MSG)

PRAYER TO ENCOUNTER YOUR FATHER

I would like to be Your apprentice, Father. Please teach me everything I need to know. I'm ready, willing, and hopefully able to receive Your instruction.

SEPTEMBER 9

THOSE WHO ARE FAITHFUL

Normally, at the age of 30, the son completed his apprenticeship and was ready to receive his inheritance. At that time, if the son had proven himself faithful and remained in patient submission as a son subject to his father's mission, his father would buy or build him a house and establish him in his own business, where he would be set for life. As a child, the inheritance was always his, but first he had to show himself faithful with what his father had put into his hands. Jesus said that those who are faithful with a little will be put in charge of much.

Receiving our inheritance means first "suffering" by being faithful with little as we learn to take responsibility for much and being subject to Father's mission. Then our character is ready to handle God turning up the power. Full entry into our inheritance as heirs with Christ involves suffering with Him for the greater glory to come.

> *His master replied, "Well done, good and faithful servant! You have been faithful with a few things; I will put you in charge of many things. Come and share your master's happiness!"* (Matthew 25:21 NIV)

PRAYER TO ENCOUNTER YOUR FATHER

Oh, Lord, I want to be near You and share in Your happiness. You are my Master and I long to hear You say I am Your good and faithful servant!

OBEDIENCE THROUGH SUFFERING

Before we receive our inheritance in Christ as heirs with Him, we first suffer with Him. Paul said that we are children of God, heirs of God, and heirs with Christ. How did Jesus suffer? Most of us think immediately of His suffering on the Cross, and that is certainly correct. However, only Jesus could die on the Cross for our sins. The only way we can suffer with Him in that way is in the figurative sense of "dying" to self and taking up our cross daily and following Him (see Luke 9:23)—in other words, dealing with the interior dry rot (motives) and not just having an attractive exterior.

We begin to displace being subject to *our* mission and seek to become committed to *His* mission. Paul described it this way: *"I have been crucified with Christ; and it is no longer I who live, but Christ lives in me; and the life which I now live in the flesh I live by faith in the Son of God, who loved me and gave Himself up for me"* (Gal. 2:20). Paul had come to a defining moment in life where he chose to be subject to Father's mission, and no longer his own, even if it was uncomfortable, even deadly, for him to do so.

> ...*We are heirs of God and co-heirs with Christ, if indeed we share in his sufferings in order that we may also share in his glory. I consider that our present sufferings are not worth comparing with the glory that will be revealed in us.* (Romans 8:17-18 NIV)

PRAYER TO ENCOUNTER YOUR FATHER

Even the word "suffering" makes me uncomfortable, Father—but You already know that. I pray that my fear of suffering will be overcome with my loving encounters with You.

HEIRS WITH JESUS

Jesus suffered on the Cross, but there is more involved with His suffering than just the Cross. Through His suffering, Jesus learned obedience—willing submission to the mission of others, especially His Father. The Cross was the ultimate demonstration of His submissive obedience. A companion passage to Romans 8:17-18 is Hebrews 5:7-9:

Even Jesus had to go through *"the sufferings of this present time."* He had to learn the whole walk of sonship because, once His public ministry began, the enemy was going to do everything possible to get Him to think like an orphan. A lot was riding on this. If satan could succeed in deceiving Jesus into orphan thinking, then Jesus never could be our Savior because He would become subject to satan's mission rather than His Father's. None of us then could be saved; none of us could experience the fullness of Father's love or of His gifts in our lives. Before Jesus could become the source of eternal salvation, He had to learn the obedience of a son and walk in a spirit of sonship.

In the same way, our gifts and calling are in danger of blowing our rear end off until we learn obedience from what we suffer as spiritual sons and daughters to someone. Whose son are you? Whose daughter are you? Do you value people for relationship or for what they can do for you?

> *Although He* [Jesus] *was a Son, He learned obedience from the things which He suffered. And having been made perfect, He became to all those who obey Him the source of eternal salvation.* (Hebrews 5:8-9)

PRAYER TO ENCOUNTER YOUR FATHER

Lord God, I am Your child! I am thankful and grateful for the position I hold in Your family. I will focus on what I can do for others, rather than what they can do for me.

SUBMISSION

How did Jesus learn obedience? First, by being in submission to his earthly parents and then to His heavenly Father. In his childhood years, Jesus learned to love, obey, honor, and respect His earthly parents. A major shift began to occur when Jesus visited the Temple in Jerusalem at the age of 12 and culminated with the inauguration of His public ministry eighteen years later at the age of 30. This period coincides with the time Jesus would have been apprenticed to His earthly father, Joseph, in the carpenter shop. His honor and submission to His earthly father was part of the apprenticeship to His heavenly Father and part of being subject to His mission.

Jesus' parents took Him home with them where He *"continued in subjection to them."* Jesus learned obedience *"from the things which He suffered."* We usually think of suffering as experiencing something painful or unpleasant, but the word also means to endure, to tolerate, or to put up with something. By "suffering" His parents' authority until He was 30, Jesus learned obedience. He was an obedient, faithful son to His earthly parents and to His heavenly Father.

> *Then, after three days they found Him in the temple, sitting in the midst of the teachers, both listening to them and asking them questions. …His mother said to Him, "Son, why have You treated us this way? Behold, Your father and I have been anxiously looking for You." And He said to them, "Why is it that you were looking for Me? Did you not know that I had to be in My Father's house?" …And He went down with them and came to Nazareth, and He continued in subjection to them.* (Luke 2:46-52)

PRAYER TO ENCOUNTER YOUR FATHER

I admit that I wasn't always—and am now not always—obedient to my earthy parents. This is unacceptable in Your sight, God, and right now I repent of dishonoring them by not listening to their wisdom in their life experiences. I choose to change my attitude toward them.

SEPTEMBER 13
RECEIVING FATHER'S FAVOR

Whenever we accuse or judge our earthly parents for any reason—abuse, indifference, lack of understanding and empathy, failure to accurately model the love of Father God, or whatever—we reject the spirit of sonship and become subject to our own mission in life. Later in life, this can become the dry rot that can sink our vessel. Jesus knew He couldn't go that route. He knew that the first step to being subject to His heavenly Father was to be subject to His earthly parents. The result was that Jesus *"matured, growing up in both body and spirit, blessed by both God and people."*

Favor with God is preceded by faithful submission (being underneath and dependent) to earthly parental authority. For thirty years, Jesus was subject to His mother and father even though they did not have nearly as much spiritual insight and wisdom as He did. For eighteen years, He labored in the carpenter shop, learning the trade and assisting His father in various carpentry projects to help support the family. He suffered patiently in waiting and working in His father's house in spite of the anointing, gift, and call of Father God on His life. Death to self-centeredness, self-consumption, and to being self-referential begins to occur when we become subject to someone else's mission.

> *So he* [Jesus] *went back to Nazareth with them, and lived obediently with them. His mother held these things dearly, deep within herself. And Jesus matured, growing up in both body and spirit, blessed by both God and people.* (Luke 2:52 MSG)

PRAYER TO ENCOUNTER YOUR FATHER

Father, please help me submit to authority—especially Your ultimate authority. I pray for a crop failure in all the ways I might reap in dishonor that I have sown toward my earthly parents. Help me to see what they have accomplished and grant me insight to the wisdom of the ways You taught them.

SUBJECT TO SPIRITUAL AUTHORITY

Now, at 30 years old, the time appointed by the Father had come, and Jesus was ready to move from servanthood to sonship. The favor of God was upon Him, a fact demonstrated by another significant event in Jesus' life.

John knew he was not worthy to baptize Jesus because to do so would put him in a place of spiritual authority over someone greater than he. In another place, John confessed that he was not worthy even to untie Jesus' sandals (see John 1:27)—a menial task for the lowliest household slave. Yet Jesus insisted that John baptize Him. He continued to subject Himself to the spiritual authority of someone inferior to Him. He submitted to the spiritual authority of John, whom God was using at the time to bring revelation and repentance to Israel. Jesus' submission was part of His spirit of sonship. He would not allow dry rot to enter His soul.

> As soon as Jesus was baptized, he went up out of the water. At that moment heaven was opened, and he saw the Spirit of God descending like a dove and alighting on him. And a voice from heaven said, "This is my Son, whom I love; with him I am well pleased." (Matthew 3:16-17 NIV)

PRAYER TO ENCOUNTER YOUR FATHER

Arrogance creeps into me when I least expect it, Father, and prevents me from submitting to spiritual authority. This should not be so. Help me to recognize pride and arrogance before they keep me from making the right decisions.

EVERYONE HAS SOMETHING TO LEARN

One characteristic of a son or daughter is a teachable spirit, a willingness to receive and learn from others even if they are less skilled or knowledgeable. Virtually everyone has something to teach the person who is willing to learn. Learning is the key to continuing growth throughout life. Those who stop learning stop growing, and those who stop growing start drying up while dry rot sets in.

People sometimes say to me, "Jack, you have an international ministry; you have counseled and helped bring healing and deliverance to thousands around the world. Why do you continue to position yourself frequently to receive ministry? Why do you still sit under others for prophetic prayer ministry and for marriage and family counseling?"

The answer is simple. How can I minister to others what I am not willing to receive myself? I have learned that I cannot effectively breathe life into others that which I am not willing to get underneath in humility and submission and receive for myself.

I shall give thanks to You with uprightness of heart, when I learn Your righteous judgments. (Psalm 119:7)

PRAYER TO ENCOUNTER YOUR FATHER

Opening my mind to learn new facts and insights into Your Kingdom and the world brings exciting new perspectives about people, places, and things. Thank You for every opportunity to learn—and to teach, Father God as You continue to teach me. I ask Your Holy Spirit to cause me to give away through example what I have applied to my life.

HUMBLE SUBJECTION

Humble subjection before God begins with humble subjection before legitimate human authority. A funny thing about love—you can't receive it without humbly submitting to it. Love always involves humility and submission. To paraphrase John, then: How can we have a heart of submission to God, whom we can't see, if we don't have a heart of submission to man, whom we can see?

Jesus understood this connection. He knew that part of His submission to His heavenly Father was to be in submission to His earthly parents and, in the case of His baptism, His cousin John. That's why He told John, *"Permit it at this time; for in this way it is fitting for us to fulfill all righteousness."* Because Jesus was subject and obedient as a son to legitimate earthly authority, He received powerful affirmation of the favor of His heavenly Father. The heavens opened, the Holy Spirit descended like a dove, and a voice from Heaven said, *"This is My beloved Son, in whom I am well-pleased."*

> *Whoever claims to love God yet hates a brother or sister is a liar. For whoever does not love their brother and sister, whom they have seen, cannot love God, whom they have not seen.* (1 John 4:20 NIV)

PRAYER TO ENCOUNTER YOUR FATHER

What a thrill for Jesus and John to "fulfill all righteousness"! I'd love to be able to say that, Father, help me to know when I have not fulfilled Your purposes in me when I step out of the wisdom of my father's house.

Jesus' Dry Season

The process of Jesus' life toward entering His inheritance and becoming the source of eternal salvation illustrates the sequence of the Great Commandment preceding the Great Commission. First, at His baptism, He experienced the expressed love and favor of His Father, and then He was released to ministry. So often today we reverse the process—we seek release into ministry hoping to find God's favor by what we do or achieve. This process characterizes orphan thinking and can easily turn to dry rot.

Assured by the favor of His Father on His life, Jesus had one further test, one further training ground before He was released fully into His ministry—He had to endure a "dry season" in the wilderness. When we first receive the experiential revelation of Father's love, it seems that His love is the only love and affirmation we receive for a season, while many of the support structures that have been comforting us and feeding our need for attention and identity are ripped out from under us.

Dry seasons help us discover whether or not we truly believe that Father's love is really all we need, so the Holy Spirit leads us into a wilderness season. Here the enemy will try his hardest to steal from us our spirit of sonship by enticing us with orphan thinking and counterfeit affections.

Then Jesus was led up by the Spirit into the wilderness to be tempted by the devil. (Matthew 4:1)

Prayer to Encounter Your Father

Father, I've known dry seasons, seasons of temptation, times when I was looking the other way rather than toward You. I know now that only being totally dependent on You will move me through those seasons into Your everlasting land of promises.

LED BY THE SPIRIT

Just as he had done with Adam and Eve, satan tried to create doubt in Jesus' mind about the integrity of God and His Word. He began by appealing to the passions of the flesh and enticed Jesus with the idea of focusing on meeting His own personal needs. After forty days of fasting, Jesus was hungry, so satan suggested that He turn a stone into bread. Jesus responded that there was more to life than food.

Satan's next tactic was to try to coax Jesus into abandoning His Father's mission by promising Him wealth, power, and influence without having to work for them. All Jesus had to do was become subject to satan's mission. Jesus refused, saying that God alone was to be worshiped and served.

Finally, satan appealed to the "shortcut" spirit of the orphan heart by tempting Jesus to take the easy way to winning the acclaim of men. If he would jump from the roof of the Temple, angels would save Him from death and everybody would acknowledge that He was the Son of God. Jesus refused again, saying it was wrong to presume upon God.

Three times Jesus was tempted, and three times He resisted orphan thinking. Through it all, He maintained His identity as a son and remained faithful to His Father's mission. Jesus passed the test of sonship and was ready to be released into His ministry. He was ready to receive His inheritance.

Jesus, full of the Holy Spirit, returned from the Jordan and was led around by the Spirit in the wilderness for forty days, being tempted by the devil. (Luke 4:1-2)

PRAYER TO ENCOUNTER YOUR FATHER

Father, may I pass every test that comes my way, either from satan or from You. I want to know Your plan for me and make it known to the world. This can only accomplished when I'm led by Your Spirit so I ask for You to lead me into all truth.

The Power of the Spirit

Luke 4:14 says that Jesus returned from the wilderness *"in the power of the Spirit"* and began teaching in the synagogues. His time had come; His ministry had begun. One Sabbath, speaking in the synagogue of Nazareth, His home-town, Jesus described His ministry in the words of the prophet Isaiah:

> *The Spirit of the Lord is upon Me, because He anointed Me to preach the gospel to the poor. He has sent Me to proclaim release to the captives, and recovery of sight to the blind, to set free those who are oppressed, to proclaim the favorable year of the Lord* (Luke 4:18-19).

It is important for us to understand the progression in Jesus' life from slavery to sonship and into His inheritance, because our progression is the same. Jesus' heart of sonship is the prototype for every person ever born. Whatever we see in Jesus is ours as well because we are heirs with Him.

> *And Jesus returned to Galilee in the power of the Spirit, and news about Him spread through all the surrounding district.* (Luke 4:14)

Prayer to Encounter Your Father

I would much rather be a child of Yours than a slave to my flesh or worldly endeavors. Thank You, Father.

SEPTEMBER 20
JESUS' LIFE PROGRESSION

Jesus went to the Cross to make it possible for you and me to bear our own crosses and to crucify self-love. Let's summarize this progression in Jesus' life:

1. Jesus submitted to the authority of His earthly parents. For thirty years, He willingly made Himself subject to their mission.

2. Jesus submitted to the spiritual authority of someone who was less than He—John the Baptist.

3. God the Father affirmed Jesus in His sonship after His baptism: *"This is My beloved Son, in whom I am well-pleased"* (Matt. 3:17).

4. Jesus endured and passed the wilderness test, which determined whether or not He would be subject to His Father's mission. In the wilderness, Jesus did not focus on the enemy or His own authority; He focused on being a faithful Son.

5. Through the power of the Holy Spirit, Jesus was equipped and released into His ministry and calling. He walked in the fullness of His heavenly Father's inheritance.

Notice that Jesus received affirmation of His Father's love and favor before He sought to overcome temptation in the wilderness. No one can consistently overcome temptation either in life or in ministry without the revelation of how much Father loves us; sooner or later orphan thinking will wear us down.

People will be lovers of themselves, lovers of money, boastful, proud, abusive, disobedient to their parents, ungrateful, unholy. (2 Timothy 3:2 NIV)

PRAYER TO ENCOUNTER YOUR FATHER
Following the same progression as Jesus did will assure me of safe passage through my wildernesses also so then being equipped to fulfill my calling. How exciting is that! Praising You Father, for my life.

SEPTEMBER 21

DESTINY

Many people in professional ministry succumb to sexually inappropriate behavior during their ministry. Few people who enter the ministry in their 20s in North America will retire from ministry; they burn out and leave the ministry, never to return. Most seminary graduates who go straight into the ministry leave within five years, never to return. What is the main reason for these statistics? Too many put the Great Commission ahead of the Great Commandment. They are released into ministry (or release themselves) before they are affirmed as heirs. The dry rot has never been removed; and when the power is turned up, it threatens to blow their rear end off and sink their ministry.

Don't be in a rush to take your inheritance now. For if you take it before you have learned to be a son or a daughter, you may simply waste it, consuming it on your own lusts. Be patient. Displace the orphan heart and embrace the spirit of sonship. Humble yourself in subjection to parental and spiritual authority, learning obedience through the things you "suffer." Allow your heavenly Father to affirm you in His love and in your sonship. In His time—at the right time—He will release you into your destiny.

God is in charge of deciding human destiny. (James 4:12 MSG)

PRAYER TO ENCOUNTER YOUR FATHER

Timing is everything, as many people know. But I know that Your timing is perfect, and in Your perfect timing I will be release into my destiny! Exciting.

SEPTEMBER 22
EITHER OR

Throughout the previous months, the orphan heart and the heart of sonship has been discussed, particularly how we must move from being orphans who have closed off our hearts to love, to being sons and daughters secure in the love of Father God and to both receive and give love to others. Making this transition ushers us into the inheritance Father God has prepared for us and which is rightfully ours as heirs with Christ.

You may ask, "But how do I know if I have the heart of an orphan or the heart of an heir? How can I tell the difference? What are the identifying characteristics?" These are good and valid questions because recognizing and acknowledging your orphan heart is the first thing necessary toward embracing sonship. Over the next few days, I will outline twenty basic contrasts between the spirit of an orphan and the spirit of sonship. As you review the contrasting characteristics, think about them carefully and ask yourself, *Which of these applies to me?* You may find that in some areas you have the heart of an orphan and in others the heart of a son or daughter.

> *...And so you will inherit a double portion in your land, and everlasting joy will be yours.* (Isaiah 61:7 NIV)

PRAYER TO ENCOUNTER YOUR FATHER
I look forward to contemplating the characteristics between an orphan and an heir. I hope and pray that I identify more with an heir than an orphan. Be with me, Father, as I look into myself from Your perspective.

EITHER OR
(CONTINUED)

1. Image of God

Orphans see God as a Master whom they must appease continually. They feel that they must pray more, read the Bible more, or work harder to earn God's notice and favor. They are often left with a feeling that there is something more they must do or put in order before God will be pleased with them. To an orphan, God is not just Master, but also a taskmaster.

Heirs, on the other hand, see God as a loving Father who accepts them unconditionally. They know that unconditional love is never based upon the performance of the one receiving it but upon the nature of the One giving it. Therefore, they do not have to strive or act in any certain way to "earn" Father's love; in Christ He loves them anyway, fully and completely, just as they are.

Instead of your shame you will receive a double portion, and instead of disgrace you will rejoice in your inheritance. (Isaiah 61:7 NIV)

PRAYER TO ENCOUNTER YOUR FATHER

Considering the image of You, God, sometimes I do see You as a taskmaster, but most days I see You as a loving Father who loves me…just as I am. Thank You!

EITHER OR
(CONTINUED)

2. Dependency

Orphans are independent and self-reliant. They depend on their gifts, talents, intellect, and anointing. They are convinced that they cannot trust anyone else. If they want anything, they must get it for themselves. "If anything is going to get done right, I'll just have to do it myself!"

Heirs are interdependent; they know they need the community of love that God and the Body of Christ offer. This interdependency allows them to be open and ready for Father's love to flow through them to others. Heirs also know they are completely dependent on their heavenly Father, just as Jesus said, *"...the Son can do nothing of Himself, unless it is something He sees the Father doing; for whatever the Father does, these things the Son also does in like manner"* (John 5:19).

Calamity chases the sin-chaser, but prosperity pursues the God-lover. (Proverbs 13:2)

PRAYER TO ENCOUNTER YOUR FATHER

Well...again I find myself identifying with both of these descriptions. Regarding some parts of my life I'm an orphan, but yet the majority of decisions and attitudes are based on being dependent on You, Lord. I pray that 100 percent of me will be consumed by You, Father.

EITHER OR
(CONTINUED)

3. Theology

Orphans live by the love of law. Like the Pharisees of Jesus' day, orphans try to relate to God on the basis of adherence to laws, principles, rules, and regulations. Orphans value obedience more than relationship. Heirs, however, live by the law of love. They value truth, knowing that the greatest truth of all is living to receive Father's love and giving it away to the next person they meet. Heirs understand the biblical truth that *"love is the fulfillment of the law"* (Romans 13:10).

4. Security

Orphans are insecure, but usually become quite adept at covering their insecurity. They often strive to act right and do enough to please God and earn His blessings. Therefore, they rarely experience an inward peace and rest. Life for an orphan is often filled with uncertainty and fears of trusting, abandonment, and intimacy. Heirs, in contrast, are at peace and rest in Father's embrace. They know that their security in God does not depend on their behavior but is based on the grace of God and on the saving work that Jesus did on the Cross.

Let no debt remain outstanding, except the continuing debt to love one another, for whoever loves others has fulfilled the law. (Romans 13:8 NIV)

PRAYER TO ENCOUNTER YOUR FATHER

Father God, I pray for Your wisdom as I try and unshackle myself from being a superficial rule follower more than a genuine lover of others. I feel safe and secure in Your embrace, Lord.

EITHER OR
(CONTINUED)

5. Need for Approval

The need for approval is universal; we all desire acceptance. Orphans, however, are addicted to and strive for the praise, approval, and acceptance of people. But these counterfeit affections will not satisfy and instead lead to the fear of failure and rejection, which pulls an orphan heart farther away from God. Heirs are not influenced by this turmoil and fear because they know that they are totally accepted in God's love and justified by His grace. They don't have to strive for approval because in Christ they already have it.

6. Motive for Service

Orphans serve out of a sense of need for personal achievement as they seek to impress God and others. This often takes the form of hyper-religious activity. Some orphans then become so tired or cynical with the struggle that they lose motivation for serving and end up in apathy. Heirs, on the other hand, joyfully serve out of a motivation driven by a deep sense of gratitude for God's unconditional love and acceptance. Orphans serve expecting something in return; heirs serve out of love and are giving-oriented.

But if a widow has children or grandchildren, these should learn first of all to put their religion into practice by caring for their own family and so repaying their parents and grandparents, for this is pleasing to God.
(1 Timothy 5:4 NIV)

PRAYER TO ENCOUNTER YOUR FATHER

It is good feeling to know that the only approval I need is Yours. My deepest longing is to serve You, Lord God, with genuine gratitude and love.

Either Or
(Continued)

7. Motive behind Christian Disciplines

While some orphans are apathetic and possess no motivation for observing Christian discipline, there are those who do pursue the Christian disciplines— prayer, Bible reading and study, fasting, etc.—out of a sense of duty and a hope of earning God's favor. They often evaluate how spiritual they and others are by how much time they spend each day in prayer and Bible reading and how often they fast. Many orphans can quote the Bible extensively and pray for hours at a time, yet have never known personally the affectionate love and acceptance of God. Jesus chastised the Pharisees in John 5:39-40. Because their motivation is wrong, orphans who practice the Christian disciplines easily miss the love and intimacy of God.

Heirs find the Christian disciplines a pleasure and a delight rather than a duty. Those who receive a deep revelation of Father's love often discover that many of the things they used to do "religiously" either lose their importance or take on a whole new meaning for them. A new motivation of love replaces the old motivation of duty, obligation, and fear. For heirs, all the things of the Spirit, including the Christian disciplines, become sources of joy and pleasure because love brings life where duty and the letter of the law bring death.

> *You search the Scriptures because you think that in them you have eternal life; it is these that testify about Me; and you are unwilling to come to Me so that you may have life."* (John 5:39-40)

Prayer to Encounter Your Father

When I consider Your disciplines, Father, I know they are for my benefit, not my demise. I consider it a pleasure and delight to honor You with my obedience. So I give You permission to show me the areas I am not aware of that need discipline so that I can live life in Your plan.

Either Or
(Continued)

8. Motive for Purity

Orphans believe they must be holy to be accepted by God; they must be completely pure in order to win His favor and avoid His judgment and wrath. The only way they know to achieve in these areas is to work and strive for them. Therefore, they live with an increasing sense of guilt and shame over their continuing failure to achieve perfect purity and holiness.

Heirs want to be holy out of love for their Father. It is natural for heirs, especially sons, to take after their fathers; they want to be "just like Dad." Heirs who are secure in their Father's love don't want anything to hinder their intimate relationship. They don't want to grieve Him; they just want to be a resting place for God's love and His presence. Unconditional love is a greater motivator for purity than fear and intimidation.

9. Self-image

Orphans generally possess a low self-image and an attitude of self-rejection, which results from comparing themselves to others and feeling that they come out on the short end of the stick. Others seem more blessed. Others seem more loved. Others seem to get all the breaks.

Heirs feel positive and affirmed because they know how valuable and precious they are to their Father. No matter what they do or how many times they mess up, they know that Father loves them anyway. They can pick themselves up and keep going because, feeling secure in Father's love, they know that they can do or be anything.

Do not grieve the Holy Spirit of God, by whom you were sealed for the day of redemption. (Ephesians 4:30)

PRAYER TO ENCOUNTER YOUR FATHER

Guilt, shame, and rejection are not part of my life anymore, Father. Thanks to You I have a positive life outlook that will keep me moving forward toward knowing You more intimately. I refuse to act in the behaviors that used to grieve You but I know I need Your help to overcome my habits.

EITHER OR
(CONTINUED)

10. Source of Comfort

Because they have shut a portion of their heart off from expressed love, orphans seek comfort in counterfeit affections: addictions, compulsions, escapism, busyness, hyper-religious activity, etc., believing that the busier they are, the happier they are and the more worthy they are of Father's love. And because they have an independent spirit and depend on themselves, orphans find a false sense of comfort in their own good works. Heirs find true comfort in times of quietness and solitude as they rest in Father's presence and love. They have discovered that once having tasted of that place of rest, everything that the world or religiosity has to offer pales in comparison. Nothing compares with the comfort and joy of an heir basking in the unconditional love of His Father.

11. Peer Relationships

Orphans often relate to their peers through competition, rivalry, or jealousy toward others' success and position. They believe they have to fight and scramble for every advantage and desire. Orphans cannot genuinely rejoice over the success or advancement of others. They fear that if they are not "on top," they will not be valued or respected. For heirs, on the other hand, peer relationships are all about humility and unity as they honor and value others and sincerely rejoice in their blessings and success. Heirs are secure in their own identity and position, and therefore need not fear the success or advancement of others.

How then will you vainly comfort me, for your answers remain full of falsehood. (Job 21:34)

PRAYER TO ENCOUNTER YOUR FATHER

One by one, Father, You have helped me kick addictions and bad habits. I can now discern relationships that are sent and formed by You for me—and I shun those who would be my downfall.

Either Or
(Continued)

12. Handling Others' Faults

Orphans generally resort to accusation and exposure of other people's faults—while denying or trying to hide their own. They seek to build themselves up by tearing others down and destroy relationships with issues of control, criticalness, possessiveness, or the lack of respect and honor. Heirs are relationship-oriented. In love, they cover (not hide) others' faults as they seek to restore those individuals in a spirit of love and gentleness. Covering protects a person from humiliating and destructive exposure until the conflict or fault can be resolved. Covering up a fault is an effort to deceive, which is a sign of orphan thinking.

13. View of Authority

Because of the abuse and mistreatment they may have suffered at the hands of authority figures in their lives, orphans will see authority as a source of pain and are therefore suspicious of any other authority, except their own. They are distrustful of the motives of those in authority, at home, work, church, or anywhere else. This is due at least in part to their lack of a heart attitude of humility and submission. Orphans resent and fear suggestions from anyone. Heirs, however, look at authority differently. Heirs are respectful and honoring of legitimate authority, seeing authority figures as ministers of God for good in their lives. Heirs are teachable, but orphans are not.

How blessed is he whose transgression is forgiven, whose sin is covered! (Psalm 32:1)

Prayer to Encounter Your Father

Everyone has faults and I try not to point out those faults—as I definitely have faults of my own. You have taught me, heavenly Father, that submitting to authority is showing respect for You and leads me into Your favor.

EITHER OR
(CONTINUED)

14. View of Admonition

Orphans have difficulty receiving admonition, even godly admonition, because they have difficulty acknowledging when they are wrong. In their own minds, they must be right, so when admonition comes, they receive it as personal offense or rejection. To justify their conclusions, they focus on others' faults, blame other people, etc. Heirs receive admonition as a blessing and a need in their lives because it exposes faults and weaknesses that they may not be aware of. They seek to put these weaknesses to death before they become relationship-threatening problems. They recognize it as valuable correction and an opportunity for growth. Without growth, there is no maturity; and without maturity, there is no inheritance.

15. Expression of Love

Orphans are guarded and conditional in their expressions of love. Expressed love by an orphan is based on others' performance and agreement. Because orphans have closed their hearts to love, they neither know how to give unconditional love nor how to receive it.

For heirs, love is open, transparent, and affectionate. They lay down their own agendas to meet the needs of others. Love for an orphan is built on the question, "What can you do for me?" while love for an heir is built around the question, "What can I do for you?" Love for an orphan is self-love; love for an heir is selfless love. It means showing affection or affirmation simply because they know the other person is in need of it.

> *But who can discern their own errors? Forgive my hidden faults.* (Psalm 19:12 NIV)

PRAYER TO ENCOUNTER YOUR FATHER

Father, please show me how to be more willing to grow, to mature spiritually in Your sight. May I extend love to others without any hidden agendas.

OCTOBER 2

Either Or
(Continued)

16. Sense of God's Presence

For orphans, God's presence, if they sense it at all, is conditional and distant. If everything goes all right, if they feel they've appeased the Master, then they may sense God's presence. But even then, He often seems far away because their hearts are closed to intimacy. Heirs enjoy the close and intimate presence of God because they know that His presence and nearness do not depend on their behavior. All they have to do is stop, return to the center of their heart where God's love dwells, and He is always right there. Heirs know from personal experience the truth of the Scripture that says, *"Never will I leave you; never will I forsake you"* (Heb. 13:5b NIV). Orphans question whether God loves them; heirs know that God is crazy about them.

17. Condition

Orphans are in bondage. They are slaves to their fear, their mistrust, their independence and self-reliance, their sense of self-righteousness and self-justification, and most of all, to their loneliness. Heirs, on the other hand, live in the condition of liberty. Love has set them free from fear, shame, humiliation, guilt, and the constant need to prove themselves. They are free not only to receive love, but also to give it away in abundance without running out. Heirs are free to become everything their Father created them to be.

The reward of humility and the fear of the Lord are riches, and honor and life. (Proverbs 22:4)

PRAYER TO ENCOUNTER YOUR FATHER

Even when I don't feel Your arms around me, Father, I know You are there. I will wait patiently for You to whisper in my ear, "I'm here, My child, have faith." Thank You, Father, for Your ever-present presence.

EITHER OR
(CONTINUED)

18. Position

Orphans live life as if they don't have a home. They feel like servants or slaves. Their spirit is unsettled because they are away from safe harbor and don't know how to get back. They are frozen in numb-numbville in the midst of the sea of fear. Nothing satisfies, nothing feels permanent, nowhere feels like home. Heirs are at rest and at peace in the safe harbor of their Father's love. Outside the harbor the sea may churn and the wind may blow, but inside all is calm in Father's embrace.

19. Vision

Orphans are fired by spiritual ambition. They earnestly desire some spiritual achievement or distinction and are willing to strive to achieve it. They desire to be seen and counted among the mature. With heirs there is no proving, no striving after position, power, or prestige. Instead, they are content simply to experience daily their Father's unconditional love and acceptance and then be sent as a representative of His love to family and others. Intimacy precedes fruitfulness.

But there is something that I am looking for; a person simple and plain, reverently responsive to what I say. (Isaiah 66:2 The Message Translation)

PRAYER TO ENCOUNTER YOUR FATHER

Lord God, I pray that my spiritual ambition and achievement will be a shining example for other to see Your glory. Everything I am is because of Your faith in and love for me. I thank You that I am not someone without a home, a safe place. I thank You also that I don't have to do anything but simply position myself to be responsive to You.

OCTOBER 4
EITHER OR
(CONTINUED)

20. Future

For orphans, the future, like many other things in life, is always uncertain. Their attitude is, "Fight for everything you can get!" Because they have no inheritance, orphans must compete for what they want, depending solely on their own gifts and talents to control and manipulate circumstances in their favor. And because the future is uncertain, they are most interested in what benefits them right now.

Heirs are willing to wait for their inheritance because they know that their future is as bright as it is certain. As children of a loving Father with infinite resources, they know they cannot lose and are willing to suffer now for the glory that lies ahead. Heirs know that sonship releases inheritance, and they can patiently rest in their position as children of the Father!

Know also that wisdom is like honey for you: If you find it, there is a future hope for you, and your hope will not be cut off. (Proverbs 24:14 NIV)

PRAYER TO ENCOUNTER YOUR FATHER

I remember the days when I thought I had to fight for everything I wanted, but because of my encounter with You, Father, those days are over!

OCTOBER 5
FINDING OUR WAY HOME

Remember that an orphan heart cannot be cast out; it must be displaced. It is a heart that does not feel like it has a home in a father or mother's embrace. Therefore, it is insecure with love and struggles with fears of trusting, rejection, and intimacy. Although we were created by Perfect Love so that we could receive His love and give it away, we became insecure with this unconditional love as a child. Insecurities and fears then filled the uncomforted areas of our heart. First John 4:18-19 infers that you cannot cast out these fears but you displace them by introducing the orphan to Perfect Love. Then the orphan must make a choice; he either risks opening up his heart and submits to love, or he continues to put up walls of self-protection and rejects love once more.

The important thing is to position your heart to come into alignment with Father's heart and away from the father of lies. This will require humility and a willingness to approach the whole process with the simple faith of a child. The Kingdom of Heaven is a kingdom of humility, innocence, and love; and only the childlike—those who are willing to humble themselves to become sons and daughters—will enter it. The depth of humility we embrace determines the depth of Kingdom life we will experience. These truths will take you on a path of humility—a willingness to be known for who you really are.

There is no fear in love. But perfect love drives out fear, because fear has to do with punishment. The one who fears is not made perfect in love. We love because he first loved us. (1 John 4:18-19 NIV)

PRAYER TO ENCOUNTER YOUR FATHER
You are Perfect Love, Father. I take so much comfort in that truth. I make choices today to stop aligning myself with lies that cause me to not be able to trust in You. I choose to keep my heart open to You.

OCTOBER 6
TRUTH #1: FORGIVE

How do we begin movement from living life as if we don't have a home to living life as if we do? Over the next few weeks, I present eight defining truths from my own journey that helped me begin displacing my orphan heart. These eight principles are the personal revelation that I needed to stop feeling like an orphan and start feeling secure and at rest as a favored son. Do not use these eight steps in a legalistic way or as a "formula." Everybody is different, and each person's approach to transformation will be unique.

#1. Forgive your parents for misrepresenting Father's love to you.

The process of moving from slavery to sonship begins with forgiveness. Specifically, it begins with forgiving your parents for the way they have misrepresented Father's love to you. Without forgiveness, there can be no progress. None of us are perfect parents, and none of us have had perfect parents. However, maybe your parents were great, and maybe you are not aware of any unforgiveness issues with them. If that's the case, that's wonderful; you are truly blessed. Let me encourage you, however, to examine your heart on this matter. Simply ask the Holy Spirit to reveal any pockets of anger, hurt, or disappointment that you may have toward them. It doesn't have to be something "big." Sarah's perceived rejection by me when she was 5 was all it took for her to close her heart to me for twelve years.

> In prayer there is a connection between what God does and what you do. You can't get forgiveness from God, for instance, without also forgiving others. If you refuse to do your part, you cut yourself off from God's part. (Matthew 6:15 MSG)

PRAYER TO ENCOUNTER YOUR FATHER
I have learned to forgive, Father but maybe not yet as fully or as compassionately as You do, Father, but I do know that forgiveness is Your perfect will for my life, so I do my best to obey.

A CLOSED HEART

If your childhood experiences with your parents were anything like mine, however, you may have several lingering issues. My mom and dad were pillars of the community and highly regarded in their fields. Dad was well loved and honored as a local club tennis professional, and Mom was one of the most highly respected teachers in the state of Florida. They were great people; they just did not know how to be a mom and a dad or how to express love, affection, and affirmation at home.

I endured verbal, emotional, and some physical abuse from my parents, brought on mostly by alcohol. I felt that nothing I did was ever good enough; all I did was disappoint them. As I mentioned before, by the age of 12, I had closed my heart to my parents. I became a rebellious and dishonoring teenager who also became addicted to drugs, alcohol, and pornography. When it came to forgiving my parents, I had a lot of issues.

Forgiveness does not mean forgetting what your parents did, neither does it mean divorcing them in your heart. It means letting go of your identity of brokenness and dysfunction that you brought from your parents' house. It means taking up a new identity, the identity of a son or daughter in Father's Kingdom of love. This is a deliberate choice that you can make right now. You don't have to wait.

Forget your people and your father's house; then the King will desire your beauty. Because He is your Lord, bow down to Him. (Psalm 45:10-11)

PRAYER TO ENCOUNTER YOUR FATHER

Father, please show me anywhere in my heart where it may be closed to my parents for pasts issues. Then please show me how to forgive and assume my new identity in Your Kingdom of love. I give You permission to forgive through me when I can't the same way You did for the world when Jesus ask You to forgive through Him.

GOD'S WILL BE DONE

The Kingdom of God is characterized by love, joy, peace, patience, kindness, goodness, faithfulness, gentleness, and self-control (see Gal. 5:22-23); this is our inheritance in Christ. We simply begin by focusing our life on what Jesus focused His life on—doing the will of His Father. Father God has commanded us to forgive, and forgiveness begins at home.

There was something inside me that wanted my parents to come to me and say, "Jack, forgive me for being a poor parent," and for them to specifically take ownership of the individual ways they hurt me. But in order for me to forgive my parents, it meant letting go of any expectation for them to make things right with me. Otherwise, it was as though I was reaching up for Father's love with one hand but keeping my other hand gripped tightly around my parents' throats until they made things right with me.

Then I was caught in the middle, frozen in numb-numbville, and unable to move in any direction. Instead, I decided to let go of the blame I held against my parents. I chose to let them off the hook and give them a gift they didn't deserve—the gift of honor, understanding that they, like most parents, were probably also spiritual orphans possessing most of the orphan characteristics. They could not give to me what had never been given to them.

Your kingdom come. Your will be done, on earth as it is in heaven.
(Matthew 6:10)

PRAYER TO ENCOUNTER YOUR FATHER
Father, am I secretly expecting my parents to make things right with me—even though they might not even know I'm hurting? This is illogical,, help me sort out my motives.

OCTOBER 9
FORGIVENESS AND HEALING

Forgiving your earthly parents is critical to becoming a son or daughter; for when you rejected your natural parents, you also rejected the heart attitude of a son or daughter and became a spiritual orphan. Now, in order to displace that orphan thinking, you must be introduced (or reintroduced) to a loving Father. I'm not talking about re-bonding with your earthly mother and father necessarily; in many cases that may not be possible due to death or other circumstances. What I am talking about is letting go of the residual pain from life in your earthly parents' house so that you can reach up and receive God as your loving heavenly Father and trust Him to meet the deepest needs of your life.

Forgiveness does not guarantee healing. Forgiveness opens the door to healing, but forgiveness and healing are not the same thing. Why? Because forgiveness and trust are two different things. As an adult you may have prayed your heart out, gone through hundreds of hours of counseling, and done everything you know to do to forgive, even reaching a place of peace in knowing you have forgiven them; yet whenever anyone or anything reminds you of the offending parent, you get agitated or withdraw. You may have forgiven them, but you still don't fully trust them yet because you have not been fully healed. The important thing here is to begin movement toward sonship by forgiving.

But if you do not forgive others, then your Father will not forgive your transgressions. (Matthew 6:15)

PRAYER TO ENCOUNTER YOUR FATHER
Forgiveness is the first step toward healing. Thank You for the reminder, Father. You always know exactly what I need to hear from You, each and every day. I worship Your Fathering heart for me.

OCTOBER 10

TRUTH #2: ASK FOR FORGIVENESS

#2. Ask your parents to forgive you for hurting or disappointing them.
Forgiving your parents is the first step toward sonship. But sometimes forgiving them is not enough to set you free. Depending on your particular circumstances, it may be necessary for you to seek forgiveness from your mother and/ or father. It's easy to remember and rehash all the bad things they did and the way they mistreated you, but it's a lot harder to own up to all the ways you may have hurt or disappointed them. Many times the process of forgiveness calls for the ministry of restitution—offering restitution for your attitudes, behavior, and actions that have hurt others.

The ministry of restitution states that if our actions or attitudes have brought hurt to another person, there may be a need to go to that person and make right any wrong to break the destructive patterns in our relationships. Although God forgives us for each specific wrong the first time we ask, we may continue to reap what we have sown; so, in order to break that cycle and begin restoring trust, it is often necessary to make every effort to bring healing to others and to seek to restore the fractured relationship. Even if we feel the other person is 98 percent wrong and we are only 2 percent wrong, we are 100 percent responsible to walk in forgiveness and repentance for our 2 percent.

> *But I [Jesus] tell you that anyone who is angry with a brother or sister will be subject to judgment. Again, anyone who says to a brother or sister, 'Raca,' is answerable to the court. And anyone who says, 'You fool!' will be in danger of the fire of hell."* (Matthew 5:22-26 NIV)

PRAYER TO ENCOUNTER YOUR FATHER
Father, as I ask my parents to forgive me, I also ask You to forgive me for being a disobedient child of Yours. My human nature gets in the way of my spiritual nature— but less and less as I focus on You, Lord. I release my parents for the pain that they have brought into my life. I break agreement with the pain of my past that they have caused me and I choose to move forward into life where forgiveness is my focus.

OCTOBER 11
THE PAIN OF THOSE YOU HURT

It may not be enough for another person to forgive you. You may still carry unconscious guilt or shame for the offense and have a need to ask for forgiveness to be free. There can also be a block in the relationship until you acknowledge to them that you have wronged them. The other person may have forgiven you, but their trust in you has been violated. Until you acknowledge your offense, it is difficult for them to trust you again because forgiveness and trust are two different things.

When I began dealing with the matter of forgiveness toward my parents, I knew I had many issues to resolve. As prayer counselors began helping me walk through those issues, God began restoring a degree of wholeness to my life. But I still had a long way to go. The day finally came when I realized, with the help of one of my counselors, that I needed to ask my parents to forgive me for everything I had put them through. At first I resisted. After all, with the pain I had experienced at their hands, why should I have to go to them for forgiveness? They ought to come to me! In my anger over the pain they had caused me, I was blinded to how much pain I had caused them.

For they persecute those you wound and talk about the pain of those you hurt. (Psalm 69:26 NIV)

PRAYER TO ENCOUNTER YOUR FATHER
Father, I am asking that You bring to my mind anyone I have caused pain in any way. I want to change my actions or words today. Thank You.

OCTOBER 12

FALSE JUSTIFICATION

Orphans know only their own pain; they don't see the pain they inflict on others, or if they do realize it, they don't care because they feel that pain is justified. I didn't consider the pain I had brought to Captain Kline's heart, leaving him in the lurch when the situation no longer served my advantage. All I saw was my own disappointment, and that (at least in my own mind) justified my betrayal and my negative behavior.

One of my dad's greatest disappointments came the day I told him I was leaving the sea and going to Bible school. You should have seen the look he gave me! "With all the money you're making at the top of your business, you're giving it up to go to Bible school!?" He was a man who wanted nothing to do with church or with Christians. He had attended church as a boy, but only until he was seven because he had to. After his father abandoned him, everybody in the church rejected him because he was the only kid in town with no father. Dad had no use for the God I knew and represented, and for eight years after I was saved, he wouldn't let me talk to him about the Lord.

All this I saw, as I applied my mind to everything done under the sun. There is a time when a man lords it over others to his own hurt. (Ecclesiastes 8:9 NIV)

PRAYER TO ENCOUNTER YOUR FATHER
I have disappointed people and people have disappointed me, God. But today I will put that all aside and start fresh by forgiving and asking forgiveness. A clean slate for them and for me!

RECONCILIATION

Despite all this baggage and background, when I resolved to approach my parents about forgiving me, I thought Dad would be easier to deal with than Mom, so I went to him first. We both liked golf, so one day when we were together on the golf course, I plunged in.

"Dad, I want to ask you to forgive me for the pain I put you through in my teenage years."

He stopped the golf cart, looked at me, and said, "What? Where did you get this crap from?"

I said, "Dad, at twelve years old, I closed my heart off to you and started treating you with all this resentment and anger. Dad, I want to ask you to forgive me." He just sat there stupefied. "Forgive me for the pain I put you through and for the times you came and bailed me out of jail, for the times you came to the hospital when I was overdosed on drugs. Dad, you don't know half the things I was involved in. I was a pornography addict and a drug addict. You don't know all the times I was taken into custody by the police and all the other things I've done wrong, but Jesus Christ has completely forgiven me. I realize how much pain I've caused you through the years, and I'm asking you to forgive me, because Jesus forgave me. Dad, please forgive me."

Now all these things are from God, who reconciled us to Himself through Christ and gave us the ministry of reconciliation. (2 Corinthians 5:18)

PRAYER TO ENCOUNTER YOUR FATHER

Laying all my sins out in front of the person I wronged is hard, really hard. But with Your strength and faith in my, Lord, I will seek reconciliation.

RECONCILIATION
(CONTINUED)

Dad was speechless. After about ten seconds, my dad said, "No, Son, I won't forgive you."

"Why, Dad? I really need you to look me in the eye and tell me you forgive me." My dad who couldn't say the words "I love you," my dad who couldn't hold me, my dad who didn't want anything to do with God or any "religious stuff," my dad who never once apologized for the physical or emotional abuse, my dad now over 70 years of age, said, "I won't forgive you, son, until you forgive me."

I was in shock. He was a hard man who had never shed a tear, but now he was weeping. He continued, "You're asking me to forgive you when I'm the one who was so harsh and unmerciful. I put you through hell on the tennis courts. You became what you became only because I demeaned you, screamed at you, and called you names. Jack, I never knew how to be tender with you; I never knew how to be kind. My dad left me when I was seven years old, and I was raised under harshness and anger and the shame of the community. I need to ask you to forgive me because I was angry that you didn't play tennis the way I wanted you to, and I took out all my agitations on you. I shamed you. Please, Jack, will you forgive me?"

For if their rejection is the reconciliation of the world, what will their acceptance be but life. (Romans 11:15)

PRAYER TO ENCOUNTER YOUR FATHER

What a happy ending! Father I thank You, that all of my attempts at reconciliation will end happily as well. With Your guidance, I know they will!

OCTOBER 15
FATHER GOD'S MISSION

"Of course, I forgive you, Dad!"

As long as I was subject to my own mission—self-protection, blame-shifting, nursing my pain—nothing ever happened between Dad and me; nothing ever changed. But when I came to him and asked for his forgiveness, I became subject to Father God's mission—the ministry of reconciliation. And when I became subject to Father God's mission, I also became subject to my own earthly father. Every earthly father, no matter how much they've hurt their kids, longs for it to be made right. But many of them have no idea how to apologize. They don't know where to start.

My father never humbled himself to me until I first got underneath and was subject to his mission. Then he looked me in the eye and said, "Jack, I love you." It was the first time I heard him say that since I was 19 and in the hospital for a drug overdose, and he had come and embraced me and told me he loved me.

Now, on that golf course nineteen years later, my father reached out, put his arms around me, and with tears in his eyes said, "Son, I love you. Thank you for forgiving me." And we cried together as we both asked forgiveness specifically and in detail for things we had done to each other. There was a lot of weeping, but oh, the joy! I experienced a homecoming and a dad with an open heart to me!

Now all these things are from God, who reconciled us to Himself through Christ and gave us the ministry of reconciliation. (2 Corinthians 5:18)

PRAYER TO ENCOUNTER YOUR FATHER
Father, I want to love people in a way that deepens joy in people's hearts. I have known that joy, but only when I am in Your will for my life. I pray You help keep me there daily.

TO SAVE SINNERS

A year went by, and then one Sunday the phone rang. It was Dad. "Jack," he said, "I want you to know I went to church yesterday."

"It was a men's breakfast," he continued. "One of my old partying buddies came over to the house Friday night and said, 'I'm taking you to church tomorrow.' I said, 'But there's no church on Saturday.' He said, 'It's a men's breakfast, and I'm the speaker.' 'You're speaking at church?' I asked. 'You were one of the biggest party animals in town!' He said, 'That was my other life.'

"So I went with him. At the end of the breakfast, he shared his testimony of recently accepting Christ at his wife's deathbed. Then the pastor prayed for those who didn't know Jesus to accept Jesus. Jack, I want you to know that yesterday I accepted Jesus as my Savior, but it wasn't because of anything my friend said at the breakfast. It was because a year ago you came and forgave me, and I realized that day that there must be a God. And when I looked at your life, I knew that only God could do in you what happened that day. That same day I started reading my mother's old Bible and have read it every day since. Ever since that day, I've just been waiting for the right moment to accept Him. It was your forgiving me that transformed my life."

> It is a trustworthy statement, deserving full acceptance, that Christ Jesus came into the world to save sinners, among whom I am foremost of all. (1 Timothy 1:15)

PRAYER TO ENCOUNTER YOUR FATHER

Only You know the effect my obedience to You will affect others, Father God. Please use me as an instrument of Your love throughout my sphere of influence.

RECONCILIATION
(PART TWO)

Even after he was saved, my dad was never really keen on church because of all the personal pain he associated with it, but for the next ten years he was really keen on the love of God. He'd read his mother's Bible every day. Every phone call we had, he would tell me he loved me and that I was his hero. Dad is with the Lord now, but before he died, the two of us were completely reconciled. What peace that brings to my heart. It's truly amazing what can happen when you become subject to Father's mission.

Having experienced such unexpected and complete success in being reconciled with Dad, I felt more optimistic about talking to Mom. So not long after that day on the golf course, I said, "Mom, I want to ask you to forgive me for all the pain that I put you through in my teenage years."

"It's about time you came to me," she snapped. "Do you know how much you hurt me?" She really lit into me. Her angry, bitter response blew me away. No, I didn't know how much I had hurt her. At that time, I had not yet received the revelation of Father's love or entered into the spirit of sonship. I was still walking as an orphan who need everybody to say all the right things, or they put walls to keep people out. When Mom attacked me like that, I simply cut off the conversation.

And see if there be any hurtful way in me, and lead me in the everlasting way. (Psalm 139:24)

PRAYER TO ENCOUNTER YOUR FATHER

I know how that feels, Lord, when I expect the perfect response to my perfect statement or question. It's not a pleasant experience. Help me to see the answer from the other person's point of view before assuming.

OCTOBER 18

SAFE AND SUPERFICIAL

For the next ten years, I was very careful always to honor my mother in accordance with Paul's instructions in Ephesians 6:2-3. I was always polite and cordial. I honored her, but at the same time kept her at arm's length emotionally. My interaction with her was on a superficial level as I continued to protect myself from her criticalness and hurting me again.

Then I received the revelation of Father's love and began learning to walk in that truth. Opportunities for ministry began opening up, and I moved also into teaching and leading conferences on Father's love.

One summer I was visiting Mom again, as I had every year. She and Dad divorced when I was a teenager and now lived five miles apart. Every Christmas and every summer I would drive 400 miles to see them, usually staying at Mom's house. One morning Mom got up early, ready for the little verbal swordplay we engaged in every morning. She would try to get inside me, and I would try to keep her out: thrust, parry, thrust, parry. I loved her, I honored her, I blessed her, I sought to think good thoughts about her. I had even led her to the Lord. But I could not trust opening my heart up to her. So every time she tried to find an opening through my shell, I deflected her and kept things on a safe, superficial level.

Honor your father and mother (which is the first commandment with a promise), so that it may be well with you, and that you may live long on the earth. (Ephesians 6:2-3)

PRAYER TO ENCOUNTER YOUR FATHER

Father, there are many relationships in my life that are on that safe, superficial level. I pray that I can open up and also allow others to open up to me. There may be friends who really need me to listen and help them through tough times—reveal them to me, Lord.

MAKING AMENDS

About this time, Dad walked in and rescued me, immediately saying all these wonderful things about how proud he was of me. For many years, this man had always pointed out everything I had done wrong, and now…I could do no wrong in his eyes. For my part, as soon as Dad walked in the room, I lit up and came alive.

He had invited me to play golf with him, and as we got ready to leave, I glanced at Mom out of the corner of my eye. Although I noticed she was crying and wiping away tears, I still had an orphan heart to a degree, and it didn't register to me emotionally that I was the reason she was crying. I just wanted to escape. So Dad and I left.

A little later, after my wife got up, Mom asked her, "Why is it that Jack has such a wonderful relationship with his father, but when I try to have a conversation with him, it's like pulling teeth?"

Trisha, in her impeccable wisdom, said, "That's between you and your son. I'm not getting in the middle of it." Later, however, when we were driving home, Trisha told me about it. I just blew it off. I was honoring my mom to the best of my ability; what more did she want? I knew the Father's love but had not yet made the complete transition from orphan to son.

> …if their uncircumcised heart becomes humbled so that they then make amends for their iniquity. (Leviticus 26:41)

PRAYER TO ENCOUNTER YOUR FATHER

During times of my insensitivity toward others, Father, please nudge me—or hit me over the head—to get my attention so I can right the wrong. Thank You!

OCTOBER 20
THE MISSING KEY

A few months later, I spoke at a large international conference on the Father's love. It was the largest gathering with top-tier speakers I had been invited to, and I was afraid I would not be able to minister effectively. By His grace, God blessed mightily anyway.

About two weeks later, during our "family reunion" (the yearly gathering of our team, intercessors, and supporters), the speaker, James Jordan, addressed the subject of the spirit of sonship and asked us, "When did you cease being your father and mother's son?" He went on to add, "When you rejected your mother and father, you rejected a spirit of sonship, and God will deal with you only as a son."

As soon as he said that, I knew I had found a missing key. I realized that I needed to go to my mother and ask her one more time to forgive me. To make sure I didn't chicken out, I told my wife my intentions. Mom would be visiting in a few weeks for Christmas, and I would talk to her then. I needed to practice the ministry of restitution with Mom because I was beginning to realize how much my attitudes had hurt her. I loved her, I had forgiven her to the greatest degree I knew how, and I practiced honoring her to the best of my ability. But something was still missing because my love was guarded around her.

They, meanwhile, will be making amends for their iniquity, because they rejected My ordinances and their soul abhorred My statutes. (Leviticus 26:43)

PRAYER TO ENCOUNTER YOUR FATHER
As an heir to Your Kingdom, Father, I cherish that role. May You always deal with me as one of Your blessed children.

OCTOBER 21
DEAL FALSELY

I planned to talk to Mom the first night she was there, but I couldn't bring myself to do it. Or the next night, or the next. Finally, on the fifth and last night of her visit, I was getting ready to go to bed when Trisha confronted me. "Are you going to talk to your mother or not?"

Taking a deep breath, I went to her and said, "Mom, I need to talk to you a minute." Here I was, a man of supposed faith and power, secure in Father's love, trembling in my mother's presence. I was scared to death.

We sat down in my study and I said, "Mom, this summer when I was home, and Dad came in and we had such a wonderful time together, I saw you crying out of the corner of my eye because Dad and I shared a depth of relationship that you and I have not possessed. Mom, I need to ask you to forgive me for the pain I have brought to your life through the years."

Immediately the sword thrusts began. "Do you know how much you've hurt me? You have done this to me since you were twelve years old, and I've never done anything to hurt you. How could you treat me like this?"

"Mom, I'm asking you to forgive me."

"I won't forgive you until you tell me what I've done wrong. I've been the perfect mother to you."

Now therefore, swear to me here by God that you will not deal falsely with me or with my offspring or with my posterity. (Genesis 21:23)

PRAYER TO ENCOUNTER YOUR FATHER
Perspective and relativity—people have their own perspective based on many factors. And situations are all relative—especially with relatives. Father help me to understand the pain that others might be feeling before I decide to confront anyone. May I receive Your wisdom to deal with things truthfully!

OCTOBER 22

RESPECT

I sat there in shock. Ten years earlier I had shut down because I lacked basic trust in Father's love to meet my need when I was attacked. My heart was closed. There was no revelation of Father's love. I was living life like a spiritual orphan. This time it was different. I knew Father's love and was beginning to embrace a heart of sonship. I knew that I had to become subject to my mother's mission as a son and acknowledge how badly my closed heart had hurt her.

When I was about eight or ten years old, my mother and father stopped living together, even though they stayed in the same house. Dad moved into the furnace room and stopped speaking to my mother, and any communication between them passed through either my brother or me. Dad turned his attention to other things and people, and it destroyed my mother. She turned to bitterness and medicating her pain with alcohol.

As Dad poured every bit of his life into his oldest son, who was a real champion and one of the best youth league tennis players in the nation in those years, I spent all my time with my mother. I became her only source of sanity and love. But when I was 12, I had had enough and I closed my heart to her. This injured her even more because now all she knew was rejection and pain from every family member.

> *Do not rebuke an older man harshly, but exhort him as if he were your father. Treat younger men as brothers, older women as mothers, and younger women as sisters, with absolute purity.* (1 Timothy 5:1-2 NIV)

PRAYER TO ENCOUNTER YOUR FATHER

Dependency on anyone or anything other than You, Lord, is a fatal addiction. People will always let people down—that I've learned the hard way. You, though, heavenly Father are with us for the long haul…for eternity.

OCTOBER 23
SINGLE MOTHERS

Sitting with her that night, listening to the familiar barrage and bitter tirade, I knew that Father would meet my need even as my mother was attacking me. Instead of shutting down, I felt something like waves of compassionate liquid love pouring over me, securing me in His love. Softly and gently I said, "Mom, this isn't about you; this is about me. I'm asking you to forgive me."

"I'll not forgive you until you tell me what I've done wrong. I was the perfect mother. I've never done anything but love you."

That's when I realized that she had no memory of the abuse. Monday through Friday she was a teacher and sought to be a good mother. Although she was not a nurturer, at least she was there. But on Fridays and all weekend she would try to drink away the pain of being rejected by her husband and sons. When she drank, she became violent, often venting her anger at her husband by taking it out on us. And more than once, I found her covered in her own blood from self-inflicted falls or wounds.

"Mom," I said, "tell me one memory you have of one weekend from the time I was eight until I was 18 and left home." She couldn't. She had no memory of those weekends. She asked me what had happened, and when I told her of nights of being awakened and beaten for no reason, she said, "I don't believe it."

Never will I forsake you, never will I leave you. (Hebrews 13:5b)

PRAYER TO ENCOUNTER YOUR FATHER

Even during the greatest pain of my life, when I could not understand the pain of those causing me pain Your presence came to me and protected me from abusers. Father I want to say thank You to You and I ask You to remind me of where You are and were anytime I need to process my past.

OCTOBER 24

THE POWER OF
FORGIVENESS AND LOVE

"Holy Spirit," I prayed silently, "please show her." I picked up the phone, handed it to her, and said, "Call your other son."

She wouldn't do it. Then she looked at me and asked, "Did those things really happen?" Right then the Holy Spirit dropped into her mind memories of her beating my brother and me. Suddenly, she started crying as memory after memory flowed. And for the first time she said through her tears, "Well, I did have an alcohol problem." Then she said the words I never thought I would hear her say to me: "Would you forgive me?" Just as with my father, this breakthrough with Mom did not come until I got underneath in submission to her as a son. Once I opened my heart to her again and dared to risk loving again, release came for her as well as for me.

That I became my mother's hero. Her criticism turned to praise. This was a woman who, up until this time, had never apologized to me, never accepted blame for anything, and never even acknowledged her drinking problem. For the first time in thirty-six years, I had a mother again. That's the power of forgiveness. That's the power of Father's love. That's the power of a heart of sonship. Mom also went to be with the Lord, and I am at peace in knowing that we had closure before she was promoted to glory.

For the Spirit God gave us does not make us timid, but gives us power, love and self-discipline. (2 Timothy 1:7)

PRAYER TO ENCOUNTER YOUR FATHER
Addictions come in so many forms, Lord. Break any addiction I have that prevents me from seeing reality. Hold me close, Father.

OCTOBER 25
DEVIL'S HOLE

Dealing with forgiveness issues covers the first two truths in our quest to move from slavery to sonship. Extending forgiveness (Truth #1) involves humility in laying aside our hurt and our perceived "right" to hold another person responsible. Seeking forgiveness (Truth #2) also involves humility, requiring us to lay aside our pride, acknowledge our sins and mistakes, and open our hearts with no guarantee of being accepted. Humility makes us vulnerable and can sometimes be the difference between life and death.

———※———

Barry was a friend I knew in our home church. He knew I was a licensed fishing boat captain and loved hearing me tell deep-sea fishing stories. One of Barry's long-time dreams was to catch a giant Warsaw grouper. As a commercial fisherman, I had caught more giant grouper on hook and line than about any other fisherman on the East Coast. In fact, I caught over 100 of these monstrous fish, which averaged about 175 pounds; ten were over 300 pounds, and one was a 450-pounder.

Barry started to hound me, "Jack, will you take me out to catch Warsaw grouper?" There are several good spots for Warsaws right off Myrtle Beach, near where we live; one is 62 miles offshore. We called it Devil's Hole because of the number of boats and fishermen who had disappeared while fishing there, including some friends. Barry knew that I once had caught 28 grouper that totaled 5,000 pounds in one night at Devil's Hole.

Wisdom's instruction is to fear the Lord, and humility comes before honor.
(Proverbs 15:33 NIV)

PRAYER TO ENCOUNTER YOUR FATHER
It's nice to receive accolades from people, but it is better to receive favor from You, Father! I ask You for Your favor to always be upon my life.

ABANDONMENT SCARS

Barry finally persuaded me to go fishing with him, a few years after I was no longer working as a boat captain. By that time, the giant Warsaw grouper had been classified as endangered on the East Coast. So, any Warsaw we caught we would have to release, which rarely did much good. These fish come out of deep water and when brought up from 300–400 feet below, they often die from the pressure change. So I was already in violation of governmental authority, which was about to prove to be very unprofitable for both Barry and me.

Barry was and is a great guy, friend, and young man who really loves the Lord. But he had had a problem with abandonment. His father had died suddenly when he was 8 years of age, and he had never gotten beyond the rejection and shame. Barry was a true orphan. The abandonment issue left Barry with a fear of trusting and a dislike for authority and anyone telling him what to do. He was independent and self-reliant and had never received revelation to the truth of submission to spiritual authority or authority at work. With the orphan characteristics operating in his life, Barry was often right in the center of any discontent that occurred in the church or in his workplace.

Since God assured us, "I'll never let you down, never walk off and leave you." (Hebrews 13:5-6 MSG)

PRAYER TO ENCOUNTER YOUR FATHER

An independent spirit can be a good thing when it comes to personal accomplishment—I want my life to be a reflection of You.

RISKY BUSINESS

The only boat I could find to borrow was a 25-year-old, poorly maintained, 35-foot-long tub. Supposedly, it was a cursed boat; every person who had ever captained it had ended up divorced, bankrupt, or injured. It just sat at the dock; nobody would go near it. Fishermen as a whole are very superstitious, and they thought I was crazy to take it out. But for me, a curse without a cause can't land. After all, I was walking in Christ. I knew we'd be fine.

So, Barry and I loaded up enough gear for a three-day trip and headed out to Devil's Hole. The weather forecast was calling for mild winds and calm seas, and our outbound trip went fine. That first day we reached Devil's Hole and caught several hundred pounds of red snapper and grouper. One giant Warsaw hooked up but broke off.

The next day, a low-pressure area began building off the coast. As the seas slowly built in height, Barry started turning a little green around the gills (seasick), and by nightfall, the wind velocity at Frying Pan Shoals light tower was 39 knots. The rest of the fishing fleet had returned to safe harbor, but I stubbornly remained trying to catch a Warsaw. We were 62 miles offshore; and by evening, seas began running about 12 feet, and here we were in this old 35-foot scow that seemed ready to fall apart.

We get our bread at the risk of our lives because of the sword in the desert.
(Lamentations 5:9 NIV)

PRAYER TO ENCOUNTER YOUR FATHER
Taking risks is not in my nature, Father, but some people take risks and are very fortunate. Help me discern what risks You are advocating for me.

ROGUE WAVE!

With over 2,000 days captaining vessels at sea, I knew the ocean well and weathered many storms. In the early morning darkness, I saw every seaman's nightmare—the "rogue wave"— often formed when two waves converge into one, increasing the height by up to 50 percent and doubling in destructive power. Rogue waves are deadly and can take a boat to the ocean floor in seconds.

Terror threatened to overwhelm me as the wave rose to about 20 feet and broke across the bow right into the face of the wheelhouse. There was nothing I could do but scream, "Rogue wave!" It smashed into us with such tremendous force that it shattered the safety glass in all three forward windows, tearing window framing loose, and tearing off the starboard wall and windows from the wheelhouse. Shards of glass exploded into me from my neck down, ripping off my shirt. Blood poured from dozens of small lacerations, and a fragment of window framing was embedded in my throat and right arm.

The wave impact threw Barry hard onto the deck, breaking or bruising several ribs and fingers. The wave washed the antennas off the roof, drowned out our radio, and swept thousands of fragments of safety glass and debris into the engine room, clogging the bilge pumps that normally automatically pump any excess water overboard. We were still twenty-two miles from land and with the radio disabled, nobody knew where we were or that we were fighting for our lives.

Seas have lifted up, Lord, the seas have lifted up their voice; the seas have lifted up their pounding waves. (Psalm 93:3 NIV)

PRAYER TO ENCOUNTER YOUR FATHER
Father, when the waves of work and home life overwhelm me, I pray that You will hold me tightly, keep me from falling overboard.

WE'RE GOING TO DIE!

We were fighting for our lives! If we stopped making headway and turned sideways into the heavy seas we would capsize. In the water, hypothermia would render us unconscious in a few minutes with death soon following—that is, if the sharks didn't get us first.

Wracked with pain, I screamed at Barry, "BARRY! Climb below and unclog the pumps in the engine room. We have to get the water out of the boat!"

"I can't, Jack," he moaned as he rolled around on the deck in pain. "I'm too busted up."

"BARRY!" I screamed louder, "I can't leave the wheel or we'll capsize! You've got to do what I tell you!"

"I can't! It hurts too much to move!"

"BARRY, GET BELOW AND UNCLOG THOSE PUMPS RIGHT NOW, OR WE ARE GOING TO DIE!"

Somehow Barry managed to get the engine room hatch off and went below. With his hands and broken fingers, he dug shattered glass and debris away from the bilge pumps. He filled buckets, climbed out of the engine room, threw it overboard, and climbed back in, repeating the process over and over. For the next two hours, Barry overcame his fears and pain to get the bilge pumps working again. Then, using the same buckets, he bailed water until the boat was empty and stability was restored.

The waves may roll, but they cannot prevail; they may roar, but they cannot cross it. (Jeremiah 5:22 NIV)

PRAYER TO ENCOUNTER YOUR FATHER

What a harrowing experience! I've never faced a rogue wave or had glass shattered into me, but, Lord God, I have had harrowing experiences. Knowing You were with me every minute brought peace throughout my body and spirit.

OCTOBER 30
A MIRACLE

With the immediate crisis over, I determined that it would be difficult to make headway in heavy seas without a windshield to block the water that often broke over the bow from the waves, so we anchored during the remaining few hours of darkness. Barry lay down in the back of the boat torn with pain and paralyzed with fear. I passed the night worshiping and singing in the Spirit in order to keep fear from consuming me. In all my years at sea, this was perhaps the closest to death I had ever come.

The next morning, the wind and seas eased up, and we limped into port. Barry was still in numb-numbville, frozen to the rear deck in fear. As we began to pull into the marina, fishermen at the docks saw the unbelievable damage to the Bronco and came running from every direction to help secure the dock lines. No one had ever seen a boat as mangled as ours come in under its own power. A later inspection revealed that the boat was not even worth salvaging but was junked. It truly was a miracle that Barry and I even survived.

He performs wonders that cannot be fathomed, miracles that cannot be counted. (Job 9:10 NIV)

PRAYER TO ENCOUNTER YOUR FATHER

You shower Your children with miracles daily, Father. Some dramatic, others beautifully life-sustaining. I'm so very grateful for every miracle including every breath of fresh air, and everything of Your creation.

FROM SLAVE TO SON

As soon as we docked, Barry crawled on shore and got down on his hands and knees and kissed the ground. While I went to the hospital to get sewn up, Barry drove to our pastor's house and told him, "Forgive me for rebelling against you and stirring up discontent." Then on Sunday, he stood before the whole church and asked them to forgive him. As he lay on the deck through that long and terrifying night, he saw with crystal clarity how his whole life had been of independence and rebellion. But that night on the deck, he learned obedience by the things he suffered.

Barry had never been able to hold down a decent job and lived in poverty. After our close call at sea, however, he went back to work with a new spirit. He apologized to his boss. In that first week, he led three people to Christ by telling them about our ordeal. Within a year, he was promoted to the safety manager over the plant because instead of whining and complaining about everything, he got underneath and supported his company and his boss, just like he had done with me that night on the raging sea. Barry has grown and prospered financially and spiritually ever since. He became a man who lives to dispense gifts of honor and blessing to others. He moved from slavery to sonship.

> *For you have not received a spirit of slavery leading to fear again, but you have received a spirit of adoption as sons by which we cry out, "Abba! Father!"* (Romans 8:15)

PRAYER TO ENCOUNTER YOUR FATHER

Almost everyone I know has had a moment when God's light shines too brightly to ignore and they succumbed humbly into Your loving arms. Thank You for pursuing me!

NOVEMBER 1

TRUTH #3: SUBJECT
TO FATHER'S MISSION

#3. Focus your life on being a son or daughter.

The only subject Barry could talk about after we returned was how I had saved his life at sea in the bloodied and wounded state I was in. But it was his getting underneath my authority as the boat captain that saved my life as well as his. A heart of sonship recognizes its need for interdependence. So often, we see the bloodiness of our pastor or our boss and use their faults and weaknesses to justify our inaction instead of getting underneath, supporting, and saving both their lives and ours.

Sonship is a heart attitude of submission that brings self-redemption. When Barry and I were on that sinking boat, one of us had to submit to the other who was more knowledgeable and experienced in order for both of us to survive and overcome. Somebody had to be a son. Somebody had to get underneath and push up. Somebody had to get his or her hands dirty, even if those hands were broken. Somebody had to lift up in support to ensure the success of our mission—to find our way home. And with the success, both of us survived, had a change of heart, prospered, and ended up with an adventurous story to tell.

Then you shall say to your son, "We were slaves to Pharaoh in Egypt, and the Lord brought us from Egypt with a mighty hand." (Deuteronomy 6:21)

PRAYER TO ENCOUNTER YOUR FATHER

Heavenly Father, You know the beginning from the end. You know how my story ends. I can't make it to my destiny without Your guidance and the support of trusted friends You put in my life.

NOVEMBER 2
WHOSE CHILD ARE YOU?

In a gathering of like-minded ministers, most of whom had been mentored by Jack Winter, a twenty-minute conversation revolved around Jack and his life as a spiritual father to many of us. During this time, he remained very quiet and seemingly uninterested, and finally he spoke up and said, "I do not want to be anyone's father. I want to focus my life upon what Jesus focused His life upon. Jesus focused His life upon being a son. Until I am more secure in being a son, I think I would just like to focus my life there."

He went on to say, "When you focus your life on being a leader, it becomes very easy to become controlling or authoritarian. That is characteristic of an orphan heart. Then you produce children after your kind. Instead, why don't we all start focusing on being a son or daughter who seeks to do only what the Father does, and lives to serve, honor, and bless others? When you do this, people around you will start living and acting like sons and daughters too."

Something in my heart sung out in agreement. "That is what I want! Who do I seek to honor and get underneath and push up, making their lives and ministry a blessing? Whose son am I?"

But as many as received Him, to them He gave the right to become children of God, even to those who believe in His name. (John 1:12)

PRAYER TO ENCOUNTER YOUR FATHER
Because I receive You, Lord, I have the right to become one of Your children—I believe in who You are and the relationship we have where You call me Your child and I call You Abba.

NATURAL, THEN SPIRITUAL

No one can be a father who has not first been a son. No one can be a mother who has not first been a daughter. Sonship begins in the natural before it moves to the spiritual because the natural precedes the spiritual according to Paul in First Corinthians 15:46. Before you can be a son or daughter in the spiritual, you must be one in the natural.

You do not come into your inheritance or become an effective influencer in the lives of others by focusing on being a leader or even by focusing on being a spiritual parent. You come into maturity by focusing on being a child of God. That is what Jesus did. Jesus focused on being a son the entire time He was on the earth, first as a son to His earthly parents, and then as the Son of His heavenly Father. Everything Jesus did and said was from the perspective and mindset of a son. Jesus was the man He was, because of the Father He had. Whose child are you?

Scriptural support for this whole idea is found in Hebrews 13:17: *"Obey your leaders and submit to them, for they keep watch over your souls as those who will give an account. Let them do this with joy and not with grief, for this would be unprofitable for you."* We must acknowledge our need to be a son or a daughter to someone else, or it will become unprofitable for us.

However, the spiritual is not first, but the natural; then the spiritual.
(1 Corinthians 15:46)

PRAYER TO ENCOUNTER YOUR FATHER

Father, I am my parents' child because You allowed them to birth me; I respect them for that role in my life. I am also Your child and I desire to just have time to be with You enjoying Your presence!

WHAT DO THEY THINK?

What thoughts do you think arise in your pastor's mind when your name is mentioned? Would it be, *Oh, yes! His/her heart is given to bringing honor and blessing to others!* or *Oh, no! What is she/he agitated and discontent with now?* How about your boss? Does your boss see you as someone who chooses to stoop underneath and push up, doing everything to honor him/her and make the business succeed, or does the boss try to avoid you? It is your future at stake. What you reap in life next year is often determined by how the authority figures in your life see you right now. Are you an orphan with your own mission, or are you a son or daughter committed to their mission? Your future inheritance depends on whether you have a sonship or an orphan heart. There is no inheritance for orphans.

The heart of sonship is a heart that has learned to honor all people! Blessings in life are promised if we honor our mother and father (see Eph. 6:1-3). Answered prayer and intimacy with God is promised to husbands who honor their wives (see 1 Peter 3:7). Favor with God is found by honoring those in authority as well as honoring every person you come across (see 1 Peter 2:17-20). Sonship, humility, submission, being subject to Father's mission—these character qualities are often interchangeable and are a natural manifestation of a heart that has had a personal revelation of honor.

> *And if you have not been faithful in the use of that which is another's who will give you that which is your own?* (Luke 16:12)

PRAYER TO ENCOUNTER YOUR FATHER

I wonder what others think when they hear my name, Lord. I pray they think first how much I love You and honor You. I don't have to wonder what You think of me, Father, as in Your Book You tell me that I am made in Your image and that You love me.

HONOR

Honor involves a decision that is made to put love into action, to give a person a position of high value and worth. Even when we have been disappointed, hurt, or wounded by someone, honor chooses to make a decision not to respond in kind. No matter what is felt coming from another person, honor chooses to not expose but speak words that give grace to the hearer. Honor views each person as a precious gift of God's creation and grants them a position that is worthy of great respect. Honor chooses not to respond with an unwholesome word or tone.

Not to give honor is to assign dishonor. Judgment, resentment, anger, exposure, sarcasm, criticism, comparisons, favoritism, jealousy, selfishness, envy, and racism are weapons of dishonor that are used against those who are considered of little value or worth.

Each time we have a point of contact or interaction with another person, we have a decision to make. We will either arm ourselves with a weapon of dishonor, or we will give an unmerited gift of honor. Have you noticed there's no middle ground? We can be 100 percent right in our evaluation of a person's faults or weaknesses or how they've disappointed us or how they have not matched up to our expectations, but love covers and does not expose others' weaknesses or whine about them.

Honor your father and your mother, as the Lord your God has commanded you, that your days may be prolonged and that it may go well with you on the land which the Lord your God gives you. (Deuteronomy 5:16)

PRAYER TO ENCOUNTER YOUR FATHER

Whine, yes, Lord, that's what I do when someone disappoints me. Instead of whining I know I must choose to cover that person and my disappointment with Your love and favor, especially when my mom or dad or a spiritual authority.

NOVEMBER 6
THE ACID TEST

What are we communicating when we talk to other people? Do people feel value and worth being spoken by us about those whom others may feel have little worth? Genuine sonship gives honor, while an orphan heart takes honor and dispenses dishonor. Not to honor can actually become a self-imposed curse and may result in a cloud or shadow of judgment hanging over our home, workplace, church, or relationships. Dishonor does not serve our personal interests and values, even if our judgment is accurate. It is unprofitable, and our inheritance in the Kingdom of God is delayed.

Probably my greatest pitfall in walking in honor is that I am often right in my evaluation of others' attitudes, behavior, and weaknesses and the way they have let me down or disappointed me. But is my body language covering or uncovering them? Is my conversation bringing exposure, or is it leading to restoration? When the name of someone who has disappointed me comes up in a conversation, do my words, tone, or body language bring honor, or do I draw out a weapon of dishonor? Is that person's redemption at the root of my words, or do I want to make myself look innocent by uncovering the fault? Honor is the acid test for a heart of sonship.

Honor everyone. Love the brotherhood. Fear God. Honor the emperor. Servants, be subject to your masters with all respect, not only to the good and gentle but also to the unjust. For this is a gracious thing, when, mindful of God, one endures sorrows while suffering unjustly. (I Peter 2:17-19 ESV)

PRAYER TO ENCOUNTER YOUR FATHER
Sometimes my motives aren't as clear to me as they should be, Father. Expose the unrighteousness in me so I can interact righteously with people who have frustrated me.

NOVEMBER 7
SUBMIT TO HUMAN AUTHORITY

Some Christians have trouble focusing their life upon being a son or daughter because their past experiences with authority have been negative. But the sonship that we're talking about here really has little to do with authority in our life. It is an issue of honor. Sonship is not for the benefit of authority. Getting underneath and pushing up and being subject to another person's mission isn't about that person. It is about honor and whether or not you choose to be subject to Father's mission.

I feel like one of the central themes of this whole discussion is found in verse 17 in the phrase, *"Show proper respect* [honor] *to everyone."* A heart of submission is a heart that honors all people. Honor begins at home. Do you honor your spouse? Do you honor your children? Or do you inflict emotional pain on them with weapons of dishonor?

Do you honor the waiter at the restaurant and the checkout clerk at the grocery store? Do you honor the people who deliver your mail, pick up your garbage, or baby-sit your kids? Do you honor your coworkers, including those under your authority?

> *Submit yourselves for the Lord's sake to every human authority.... Live as free people, but do not use your freedom as a cover-up for evil; live as God's slaves. Show proper respect* [honor] *to everyone, love the family of believers, fear God, honor the emperor.* (1 Peter 2:13,16-17)

PRAYER TO ENCOUNTER YOUR FATHER
I admit that it is easier to honor some people over other people. Thinking that, Lord God, I am using my warped sense of judgment and that is wrong. All people are loved by You, and I will follow Your example.

BIG FISH AND LITTLE FISH

Do you honor the "little fish" who cross your path day by day? Or do you honor only the "big fish"? I never wanted my picture taken with little fish. They had no value and didn't give me bragging rights. But when I caught a big fish, I made sure I got a picture to show the world. There was plenty of meat to eat on the big fish and money to be made from selling them.

If we give a gift of honor to the "big fish" who have the power to promote us or give us something we want, but we do not dispense gifts of honor to the "little fish," those we feel have no value to us, then the honor we give to the big fish is actually manipulation and control, as we try to get something we want from them. In other words, if we are nice to the person buying us lunch but not nice to the one serving us lunch, then we are not a nice person, and we lack a heart of honor, humility, and sonship.

Sonship is not something you measure only by the way you respond to those in authority. Sonship is also demonstrated by the attitude we exhibit toward the little fish—the person who cuts us off in rush-hour traffic. At church, do you give out gifts of honor to the nursery or maintenance worker as much as you do to the pastor?

He [Jesus] also saw a poor widow put in two very small copper coins. "Truly I tell you," he said, "this poor widow has put in more than all the others. (Luke 21:2-3 NIV)

PRAYER TO ENCOUNTER YOUR FATHER

Father, the rain falls on both the just and the unjust. You created us as equals. Father, each person has worth in Your eyes—and so it will be in my eyes.

CLOSING OPEN DOORS

Every person on the face of the earth is a member of the "walking wounded." There is not one of us who has not been hurt by the words, actions, or indifference of another person. And all of us are guilty of inflicting wounds on others, most often those closest to us. We have criticized, demeaned, belittled, ridiculed, humiliated, intimidated, manipulated, controlled, exploited, or otherwise abused or misused others; and others have done the same to us.

Sad to say, Christians can be just as guilty of this as anybody else. Church leaders can control or abuse their members, and church members verbally attack their leaders. Many of these wounds can last a lifetime. This is why the principles of forgiveness and restitution are so important in the process of moving from slavery to sonship. Whether our sonship is genuine can often best be measured by the honor or dishonor we dispense to the little fish in everyday life.

Moving into this stage of the process often awakens in us awareness of other problem areas that we may need to deal with if we don't want to become stalled by the three basic fears: the fear of trusting, the fear of rejection and abandonment, and the fear of opening our heart to love. Many have unresolved issues with authority figures beyond our parents—at home, at church, at work, and in the world. This awareness leads us to the fourth truth in our journey from slavery to sonship.

Stand up in the presence of the aged, show respect for the elderly and revere your God. I am the Lord. (Leviticus 19:32 NIV)

PRAYER TO ENCOUNTER YOUR FATHER

I want to move forward in life, toward the goals You have set before me, Father. Do not allow fear to stall me in any way. Thank You in Jesus' precious name, amen.

TRUTH #4: FORGIVE AUTHORITIES

#4. Forgive spiritual and governmental authorities.

Is there any Christian who has never been hurt by church authority? Is there anyone who has never been taken advantage of by a boss, a coworker, or a friend? Unfortunately, that's life in our fallen world. There really never has been a universal revelation of Father's love on the earth. We've had a revelation of Jesus, a revelation of the Holy Spirit, and a revelation of power; and many ministries have been built upon the anointing of God, but few have been built upon a revelation of Father God's unconditional, affirming, and compassionate love.

That is why in moving toward sonship, we must forgive governmental authorities, forgive our coworkers, and forgive those within the church who have hurt us, disappointed us, or misrepresented Father's love to us in the past.

Malachi 4:5-6 prophesies that in the end time a fathering spirit will be released on the earth; but before there can be fathers, there must be sons, and before there can be mothers, there must be daughters. Those who embrace sonship today and "suffer" through the time of training and preparation for maturity, are the ones who will embody the fathering spirit on earth tomorrow. In the meantime, it is important to be willing to walk in a heart attitude of honor and submission to all legitimate earthly authority.

See, I will send the prophet Elijah to you before that great and dreadful day of the Lord comes. He will turn the hearts of the parents to their children, and the hearts of the children to their parents; or else I will come and strike the land with total destruction. (Malachi 4:5-6 NIV)

PRAYER TO ENCOUNTER YOUR FATHER

Father, loving my parents and my children are Your commands. I will turn my heart toward them and toward You daily—praying that Your Fathering heart will guide me.

In Subjection

Paul makes our role regarding authorities abundantly clear in this passage from Romans 13. "Subjection" means underneath and dependency. Who was Paul writing to? The Christians in Rome. He told the Roman believers to submit to the authority of the Roman government, a government rife with corruption, assassination, immorality, idolatry, brutality, destruction, and death. How could Paul call on followers of Christ to submit to such an ungodly system? I don't begin to understand, but I do know that Paul had a revelation of sonship. He understood the importance of believers having a heart attitude of humility, honor, servanthood, and submission.

Did the Christians subject themselves to everything the government decreed? No. Rome required that once a year every citizen and resident of the empire kneel before a statue of Caesar and declare, "Caesar is lord." It was a political loyalty test, and those who refused were regarded as traitors to the empire. Most Christians refused, acknowledging only one Lord—Jesus Christ. As a result, many believers were persecuted severely, and some were killed in the arena or executed. What Rome never understood was that the Christians who understood sonship, their refusal to bow to Caesar notwithstanding, were the most faithful, law-abiding, and productive subjects in the empire.

> *Every person is to be in subjection to the governing authorities. For there is no authority except from God, and those which exist are established by God. Therefore whoever resists authority has opposed the ordinance of God; and they who have opposed will receive condemnation upon themselves.* (Romans 13:1-2)

Prayer to Encounter Your Father

It is hard to understand why I should be subject to ungodly authorities, but the Bible tells me it is right, so I will comply, God. Yet with limitations when it comes to ever denying Your name!

NOVEMBER 12

ALSO TO THOSE WHO ARE HARSH

With us, as with them, displacing the orphan heart begins in the natural by adopting the heart attitude of a son, not only toward our parents, but also toward all legitimate earthly authority, both governmental and spiritual. If we do not have the heart of sonship toward authorities in the natural realm, how will we ever have it toward God? As Paul says in these verses, all existing authority has been established by God; therefore, those who resist are opposing God and inviting condemnation on themselves. How can we be in sonship toward God if we are opposing Him?

This goes right along with Peter's instruction to *"Show proper respect to everyone."* *"Everyone"* certainly includes those in authority. Peter continues in the very next verse to *"submit yourselves to your masters, not only to those who are good and considerate, but also to those who are harsh."* Harsh? It's easy to be in subjection to someone like Captain Kline, who was always there for me, who never criticized me, never demeaned me, never devalued me, and poured his life into me to make me a fishing boat captain. But what about the unreasonable authority figures in my life—the overdemanding boss, the controlling pastor, the authoritarian, and demeaning teacher—those who just want to use me or take from me? Even then, God's established principle applies of honoring them and making what is important to them important to me.

> *Slaves, in reverent fear of God* **submit yourselves to your masters**, *not only to those who are good and considerate, but* **also to those who are harsh**. (1 Peter 1:18 NIV)

PRAYER TO ENCOUNTER YOUR FATHER

This is a hard one, Father because I have not always known how to set healthy boundaries in my life where authorities are concerned. I know You have exampled to us respect and honor for those in position of authorities while not allowing abuse for Your kids. Show me when I am to know the difference between authorities who You have not positioned. Talk about ignoring my pride and accepting a humbling experience! I know people who can do this and I admire them.

NOVEMBER 13
SELF-IMPOSED CURSES

When we dishonor authority, it is though we are saying, "If God put this authority in my life, then what a poor manager He is!" Whenever we do not have a heart attitude of honor to those in authority, we dishonor God. We may think He has given us a raw deal, never realizing that God puts authority in our lives as a minister of good.

Consequently, those who oppose God will *"receive condemnation upon themselves."* Does God condemn us? No, the Father judges no one (see John 5:22). He doesn't have to judge us; we take pretty good care of opening the door to self-imposed curses; for when we oppose authority, we come into agreement with the first spiritual orphan—the father of lies who is a legalist. When we oppose authority, we come into agreement with the law, and we bring condemnation upon ourselves. God doesn't curse us; rather the enemy has been looking for every open door through which to come in and steal, kill, and destroy. If he can align us with orphan thinking by our agitated resistance against authority, it will give him a key to our front door, and then the enemy has legal ground to come and go in our house as he pleases.

Moreover, the Father judges no one, but has entrusted all judgment to the Son. (John 5:22 NIV)

PRAYER TO ENCOUNTER YOUR FATHER
Satan will not enter my home because I will not give him the key! I will come into agreement with Your law, Lord God, and come under the authorities You place in my life.

A MATTER OF CONSCIENCE

The sonship principle of humility, honor, and submission applies even to unreasonable authority; in Rome's case, it was murderous, immoral, and corrupt authority. When we submit to unreasonable authority, we position ourselves to see God bless, honor, and elevate us in the midst of and in spite of that unreasonable authority. Inheritance is for children, and God can release inheritance under any circumstances to children who are subject to Father's mission.

Why does God want us to submit to unreasonable authority? Following the principle of submitting to all authority helps us learn to respect legitimate authority in spite of their personal blind spots. Every person in authority in our lives has character flaws, and it is easy for us to use those character flaws as justification for rejecting their authority. We need to learn to honor all people, and with our love fulfill the whole law. Submitting to all authority also helps uncover orphan thinking that may remain in us so that we can bring it to the Cross.

> *For rulers hold no terror for those who do right, but for those who do wrong. Do you want to be free from fear of the one in authority? Then do what is right and you will be commended. For the one in authority is God's servant for your good. But if you do wrong, be afraid, for rulers do not bear the sword for no reason. They are God's servants, agents of wrath to bring punishment on the wrongdoer. Therefore, it is necessary to submit to the authorities, not only because of possible punishment but also as a matter of conscience.* (Romans 13:3-5 NIV)

PRAYER TO ENCOUNTER YOUR FATHER

Romans 13:3-5 is very clear, heavenly Father. If I want to do right, which I do, I must submit to authority that You have placed in my life and in the government. This will take more willpower than I have, God, strengthen me with Your power.

TRUTH #5: SEEK FORGIVENESS FROM AUTHORITIES

#5. You may need to seek forgiveness from those in authority.

As with parental authority, simply forgiving earthly or spiritual authority for wounding you may not be enough to break destructive patterns in your life. If you realize that you have caused others pain through weapons of dishonor or brought defilement through ungodly attitudes or behavior, you may find it necessary to go to them for forgiveness and, perhaps, restitution.

When I resigned as a Salvation Army Officer, I left with a good spirit. I had had a bad spirit for two years, but Phillip, a pastor in the area who had begun to mentor me, said, "You can't leave with a bad spirit." So before I resigned, I called headquarters and asked forgiveness from them for my agitated resistance against their policies.

After I left, I went back to the sea, captaining a sport-fishing boat out of Murrell's Inlet, South Carolina, and began attending Pastor Phillip's church, a small Spirit-filled church of about 75 (at that time). I aligned myself to Pastor Phillip, who was like a brother to me and a year older. In addition, our children were the same ages. I positioned myself underneath Pastor Phillip, supporting and helping him in any way I could.

Let no debt remain outstanding, except the continuing debt to love one another, for whoever loves others has fulfilled the law. (Romans 13:8 NIV)

PRAYER TO ENCOUNTER YOUR FATHER

It was easy to walk away from certain situations without making amends, but it left a "bad taste" in my mouth and a nagging in my mind. Holy Spirit, thank You for the nagging and the subsequent asking for forgiveness that returned sweetness to my mouth and mind.

NOVEMBER 16
THE LAST, FIRST

When I left the Salvation Army, the church I had pastored was the fastest-growing church in our division. We were helping the poor and down-and-out, and many people were saved. Being aligned with Pastor Phillip, I asked, "Phillip, is there anything I can do? I just want to get underneath; I just want to serve you." "Yes, there is," he replied. "There's a sign-up sheet to clean the church and the bathrooms every week. Why don't you sign up?"

I thought, *Don't you know that I was near the top of my class in Bible school and was elected lifetime president? And you want me to clean toilets? I've grown beyond that.* But what I actually said was, "Well, I'll think about it." So I got in my car and left. Then the Holy Spirit said, "Uh-huh, just look what you're full of." So I went back to the church and put my wife's name on the list. She made sure I was right beside her as we cleaned the church together.

I was willing to do anything Pastor Phillip needed. If the usher didn't show up, I ushered. If the nursery worker didn't show up, I volunteered. I held babies and got puked on. I did anything I could to get underneath Pastor Phillip and push up. And it is funny how quickly you find out what you are full of when doing commode ministry. Toilet ministry offers some great opportunities for growth!

> *Sitting down, Jesus called the Twelve and said, "Anyone who wants to be first must be the very last, and the servant of all." (Mark 9:35 NIV)*

PRAYER TO ENCOUNTER YOUR FATHER
Jesus' statement to His disciples is directed to me as well. I will put others' needs first and stand in line last if it means being obedient to Your will, Lord God. I ask You to show me the times when I am to do this so I don't confuse this with law.

NOVEMBER 17
MOVING UP

After 18 months serving at Pastor Phillip's church, I learned that his father, also a pastor, was looking for a new staff member. Pastor Miles' church had grown to a couple thousand people who were moving into a new sanctuary. A few months earlier, the worship leader had become discontent and walked off with over 100 people. The rift had wounded the soul of the church, and Pastor Miles needed somebody new, somebody who had not been around during the split, to come in and help restore trust.

To feel me out before making a commitment, Pastor Miles asked me to go to Japan and China with him and Phillip for three weeks. As we were preparing to return home from China, I could not stop weeping as my heart was moved with compassion for so many broken and impoverished people who didn't know Christ. I felt it was time to leave the sea once more and return to ministry. Pastor Miles said, "Jack, I want you to move to Spartanburg, South Carolina where I live and help at the church."

I acknowledged that I was open to it. He wanted to know what I felt I had to offer the church and what position I should take. My response was, "I believe I need to start on maintenance. I'll serve in the church, but my heart is not mature enough for a staff position." He said he would sleep on it.

Humble yourselves in the presence of the Lord, and He will exalt you.
(James 4:10)

PRAYER TO ENCOUNTER YOUR FATHER
You are always true to Your promises and Your Word, Father. When I humble myself, good things happen in my life. When I exalt You, then You are pleased.

Subtle Pride

The next morning at breakfast, Pastor Miles said, "Jack, because you are willing to start in a low place, I believe your character is mature enough to start as an associate pastor. I want you to be pastor over evangelism and missions. I also need you to help restore trust in the men in the church and to focus your time upon ministering to them." So, we decided I would go on staff at the largest Spirit-filled church in South Carolina.

Because of the heart of sonship I had toward Pastor Phillip and because I sought to make what was important to him important to me, a staff position at Evangel Cathedral was offered to me rather than to others more educated and experienced. It was my inheritance; I was willing to scrub toilets and make what was important to my authority important to me.

I'd had such a spirit of sonship with Pastor Phillip who was like a brother, and now I was dealing with his father 24 years older than me. Dealing with a brother figure and relating to a father figure were two different things to this spiritual orphan, and I was about to find out what my heart was full of. Remember, I would act like a son as long as someone was making decisions to benefit me. Outwardly, I appeared humble and honoring, but inwardly I unconsciously valued authority for what they could do for me.

Catch the foxes for us, the little foxes that are ruining the vineyards, while our vineyards are in blossom. (Song of Solomon 2:15)

PRAYER TO ENCOUNTER YOUR FATHER

The sayings, "Look out for number one first" and "It's all about me" ring too true in my life at times. I'm looking good on the outside but inside my goodness is rotting. I repent right now, Father, please forgive me and show me those little "behaviors" foxes that try to kill my character.

ORPHAN HEART EXPOSED

For a year, I never failed to make what was important to Pastor Miles important to me, and he began entrusting me to fill the pulpit more and more on Sundays when he was out of town. I became one of the congregation's favorite speakers and staff members. Within six months, Pastor Miles placed me on the ruling executive board of the church. Decision after decision was made that benefited me and helped fulfill my dreams. I was moving up, and my soul reveled in the attention and affirmation!

I was one of nine associate pastors, and I moved into sibling rivalry and competition with other staff members for Pastor Miles' attention and speaking opportunities. I was a man of integrity, purity, and of the Spirit, yet I still classically followed the orphan thinking. There is nothing easier than self-deception, which I never saw coming.

A new staff member came on the team who was struggling with orphan issues himself. It was obvious that he was seeking to move his way to the top and become the favored son in Pastor Miles' eyes and the favored staff member to the church. It appeared to me that more and more decisions were being made that benefited him, and I began to receive it as personal offense. Consequently, I closed my heart to Pastor Miles and began the downward spiral along the twelve steps of the spiritual orphan.

> Be of sober spirit, be on the alert. Your adversary, the devil, prowls around like a roaring lion, seeking someone to devour. (1 Peter 5:8)

PRAYER TO ENCOUNTER YOUR FATHER

Just when I think I'm doing all the right things and saying all the right words, an orphan heart or pridefulness surfaces. Father, alert me to arrogance when it slithers into my actions and speech.

RELIGIOUS MASK

I started noticing Pastor Miles' faults and weaknesses and could not get my focus off them.

Pastor Miles would ask, "Jack, is everything all right?" And I would respond as if things were fine. Orphan hearts are usually pretty dysfunctional. They don't trust people enough to talk about their feelings. I began to think that everyone else was missing God, and I was the only one hearing clearly from Him. Months went by, and our relationship went from very open and transparent to closed, because I had shut the door on my end.

Pastor Miles had been in ministry more than forty years. He was a man of honor, integrity, consistency, and great wisdom. He knew that I was no longer being honest and real, but I did not know that he knew it; so, I kept wearing my religious mask and aggressively striving to achieve recognition and favor.

With the loss of trust in me, Pastor Miles rotated me off the executive board, which I received as rejection. The more I closed my heart, the harder I worked, because now I felt that I had to earn my way back into his graces through hyper-religious activity. But the harder I labored, the more deeply into orphan thinking I sank. It began to consume me every waking moment. I no longer valued the unheralded aspects of ministry but hungered to be seen and heard and to have greater authority.

Do not harden your hearts… (Psalm 95:8)

PRAYER TO ENCOUNTER YOUR FATHER
Strip any mask off me, Father, so I can be honest with myself, others, and You. Hiding behind hyper-religious activity sours everyone involved.

FATHER OF LIES

Feeling like I was on the outside looking in, the father of lies led me unconsciously into self-deception. My words were often directed at influencing people to see how caring, wise, and right I was. I often said things in such a way that put me in a better light in the congregation's eyes than other staff members. People with whom I was in relationship with began to believe that I cared more about them than Pastor Miles did.

Totally unaware of it at that time, I stepped into marginal deception. This does not involve a direct lie; rather, it is sharing information or speaking in such a way that influences a person to form conclusions that are beneficial to me. Marginal deception occurs when I give only partial information or relate circumstances in a way that influences people to come into agreement with my point of view.

Due to my unhealed need for love and affirmation that manifested as an orphan heart, I unknowingly was influencing others to form wrong conclusions about the senior pastor to which I never sought to bring correction or proper clarity. This was also done by the absence of deflected praise. Deflected praise occurs when someone speaks words of honor or affirmation to me and I, in turn, share the glory with others who are part of the team. When I did not deflect praise, it resulted in my taking illegitimate praise unto myself.

You are of your father the devil, and you want to do the desires of your father. He was a murderer from the beginning, and does not stand in the truth because there is no truth in him. Whenever he speaks a lie, he speaks from his own nature, for he is a liar and the father of lies. (John 8:44)

PRAYER TO ENCOUNTER YOUR FATHER

The devil can slip into any conversation or situation when I give him the opportunity, like twisting the truth to my benefit or absorbing praise when it should be given to You, Lord. I ask You father to make me sensitive to times when I allow him to slip into my life.

NOVEMBER 22
MISREPRESENTATION

One of my duties was to visit the hospitals and people's homes each week. Often the people I visited would say something like, "Oh, you have such a caring and pastoral heart! Pastor Miles used to visit, but he doesn't have time for me anymore. But you take time from your busy schedule every week. God bless you!"

I would often respond, "He is very busy, but I will be sure to visit and pray with you, and if you need anything, just call me." I would illegitimately take praise for myself by not deflecting it back to Pastor Miles. I thought I was 100-percent loyal, when in reality I was unconsciously relishing in drawing the hearts of the people to myself. Deflected praise would have responded, "As the church began to grow, Pastor Miles sent me to you. I am personally representing him and know that he is praying for you. Next time you see him, thank him for sending me to visit you."

People with Orphan hearts unconsciously become manipulative in our pursuit for affirmation, acceptance, and achievement. We are often left with a sense of heaviness or guilt and feel insecure in our relationships. This binds others to us in an unhealthy, codependent relationship, because we want them to need and admire us and to think that we are more mature and wiser than we really are.

In all things show yourself to be an example of good deeds, with purity in doctrine, dignified. (Titus 2:7)

PRAYER TO ENCOUNTER YOUR FATHER

Father in Heaven, I never want to misrepresent You or Your servants. Keep the door shut where deception may want to wander in.

MARGINAL DECEPTION AND DEFLECTED PRAISE

These two areas—marginal deception and deflected praise—in which I struggled revealed how deeply the orphan heart had deceived me. I was subject to my own mission and was illegitimately winning hearts, and I never saw it. Even though I had integrity and thought that I was being totally loyal, it was such an easy thing to unknowingly draw people's hearts to myself. This held me back from maturity, promotion, and favor with God and people. In the church, I unconsciously caused tension and division in the spiritual realm because of my lack of maturity and my need to feel accepted and liked.

Over the next year and a half, I experienced some of the worst emotional pain and confusion that I had known since my childhood. During this time, I was being trained in every type of deliverance and prayer counseling ministry. I was leading prayer counseling sessions with men and ministering to pastors and their families. I could set others free but was becoming more and more personally bound by orphan thinking.

There was a lot of betrayal and hurt from another staff member who brought division to the staff. Something inside me needed Pastor Miles to put me back into a high-profile place before the people. It was my orphan heart, always striving but never achieving, always longing but never satisfied.

Beware that your hearts are not deceived, and that you do not turn away and serve other gods and worship them. (Deuteronomy 11:16)

PRAYER TO ENCOUNTER YOUR FATHER
Sometimes emotional pain and confusion is worse than physical pain. When my mind is unsettled, it can turn a beautiful day into a day of torment. Only You, Father, can heal minds that are torn. Thank You.

NOVEMBER 24
CRAZINESS

People would come and say, "You're my favorite speaker on staff; why don't you speak much anymore?" It was like getting kicked in the gut to have to say, "Well, Pastor Miles just wants to give others an opportunity," while inwardly I was seething with hurt and disappointment. And of course, I felt that I didn't have a problem; it was all Pastor Miles' fault! As an orphan I could not recognize my own closed spirit. Every time Pastor Miles came around, I would run to him with my "IV system," telling him all the wonderful things I was doing, hoping he would pat me on the back and tell me how wonderful I was. Do you see what kind of craziness an orphan spirit will drive you to?

I started turning in reports on all the ministry I was accomplishing so he would know how hard I was slaving for him in the church. After all, an orphan is a slave, not a son. During this time, I slaved away seventy hours a week. I was one of the favorite pastoral care persons on staff, but I'd lost trust in Pastor Miles' eyes because I lacked an open heart and wasn't honest with him, and he could feel it. Every time he asked how I was doing, I continued to assure him that everything was fine. No problems. But I wasn't real, and I didn't know he could see through my religious mask as easily as he did.

Do not withhold good from those to whom it is due, when it is in your power to do it. (Proverbs 3:27)

PRAYER TO ENCOUNTER YOUR FATHER
The only pat on the back I really need is from You, Father. There are times when I yearn to hear praise from my spouse or boss, but when I turn to You in prayer—You give me more than a pat, You embrace me! Help me to be aware when it is within my power as Your child to not to withhold affirmation from others, pointing out their strengths.

NOVEMBER 25
SENT OUT BLESSED

Things at the church for me just slowly leveled out, but we never talked through this issue. I wanted to resign many times, but my mentor, Pastor Phillip, would not agree to me leaving. He told me, "You do not leave when you feel that the chips are down, or you will repeat the pattern in the next place you go. You leave only when you are sent out blessed."

Finally, things balanced out. The other staff member fueling dissension was exposed. I received some restoration of recognition and authority, and then I felt released to leave. I went to Pastor Miles and said, "You know, I'm getting so caught up in prayer ministry to leaders and pastors that I really feel like this is what I'm to do with my life."

He said, "I agree; that's where your anointing lies, and that is what you need to do. I'll bless you and send you out. I'll give you three months' pay to get the ministry off the ground, and I'll even take up an offering for you." Despite my orphan heart, he did everything he could to bless me. Pastor Miles is known to be a man of impeccable character who is generous and full of grace. He has never had a moral or ethical compromise in his life or ministry.

Help us, O God of our salvation, for the glory of Your name; And deliver us and forgive our sins for Your name's sake. (Psalm 79:9)

PRAYER TO ENCOUNTER YOUR FATHER
There are many godly role models in Your Kingdom, Lord. Unfortunately, the news is only full of the people who fall into sin. May I lift up those who are faithful and lead people into their destinies. —for Your glory.

NOVEMBER 26
MOVING ON

So we started Shiloh Place Ministries and lived in poverty for the next seven years. We had a particular anointing for prayer counseling ministry, so I went into churches and conducted prayer counseling seminars. Pastor Miles was now Bishop Miles, and overseer of a growing ministers' fellowship. Twice a year I attended the pastors' meeting with Bishop Miles, but he never promoted my ministry as he did others.

I was seething because he was promoting others and not me. My orphan thinking went something like this: I've got more integrity than they do. I've not had a moral failure like some have. And besides, I'm the guy who's been helping many of these folks' marriages! I was on my own mission and was mad because I felt nobody was underneath pushing me up.

I had an effective ministry. God had used my wife and me to help save many marriages, but Bishop Miles wouldn't promote me. All he had to do was bring me up on that platform one time in front of the ministers' fellowship and say, "Jack Frost has an incredible ministry; you need to get him in your church," and financial prosperity would have come to us practically overnight. But he never did it. He did it with those, who in my eyes, had less integrity than me, but he wouldn't do it with me. No sonship, no inheritance! No sonship, no influence!

For jealousy enrages a man, and he will not spare in the day of vengeance.
(Proverbs 6:34)

PRAYER TO ENCOUNTER YOUR FATHER
Bitterness and jealousy and envy can knock me down just as quick as pride. Please help me to keep my mind and spirit free of these sins, Father.

NO FAITH OR TRUST

In my weakest hour, when orphan thinking threatened to sink my boat, God's love found me, and I received a deep personal revelation of Father's love that transformed my life as much as when I received Christ. The anointing on my life and ministry increased greatly. Yet, I still had never talked with Pastor Miles. I had let seven years pass with no closure—seven years of the enemy having a key to my front door.

Then I went to a church pastored by a friend of mine named Roger to conduct an Experiencing Father's Embrace Encounter. Roger was one of the ruling elders and closest friends of Pastor Miles and had been a mentor to me. After driving me and my team to the motel and dropping the others off to go inside, Roger asked me to stay behind. When we were alone in the car, he said, "Jack, do you realize that EFI elders and Pastor Miles do not have faith and trust in your ministry?"

I had suspected it for a long time but never had any facts, just an undercurrent of feeling. I just couldn't see that I was at fault. Instead, I wanted to justify, blame-shift, and make myself look innocent. Roger said, "They feel like you just relate to EFI and the pastors for what they can do for you. You have never yet sought to be honest with Pastor Miles and resolve your issues with him from when you were on staff."

Trust in the Lord and do good; dwell in the land and cultivate faithfulness. (Psalm 37:3)

PRAYER TO ENCOUNTER YOUR FATHER
Leaving the door open only even a tiny crack is enough for the evil one to slither in and make himself at home. Not reconciling and not closing the door tightly allows problems to escalate. I know this from experience, Father, You've seen it too in my life. Help me, Holy Spirit, to kick the door shut hard!

SEEING THE LIGHT

I went home and called my friend and brother, Pastor Phillip. "Phillip, are you aware that your dad and the elders of EFI do not have trust in my ministry?" "Yes, I am, Jack." "You and I are in covenant together. Why haven't you told me before?" "Because I didn't think you were mature enough to handle it, and your angry attitude is revealing that you apparently aren't."

I honestly could not see what I had been doing wrong. So, I did what I had learned to do in times of crisis—I went into solitude for several days to pray and fast. About the fourth day, I felt the Holy Spirit prompt me to write down every way that I had valued people and the church for what they could do for me. I wrote down the emotions and attitudes that I had struggled with for ten years.

One thing about fasting—three or four days into it and you'll find out what you're full of! I saw it. And it was one of the ugliest things I have ever seen! I had typed nine, single-spaced pages of self-centered, self-consuming, and self-referential behavior. I realized that my relationships were built upon what others could do for me and that I had been subject to my own mission all these years. I defiled the church and EFI because I was not there to get underneath and push up Bishop Mile's vision, only my own.

He has redeemed my soul from going to the pit, and my life shall see the light. (Job 33:28)

PRAYER TO ENCOUNTER YOUR FATHER

Revelation of my ugliness is not anything I like to do routinely. Yet, Father, that is exactly what I should do to ensure Your will is being accomplishing in my life. I only do this to allow You to search me and see if I have any way in me that would wound others. I give You permission to reveal that to me so I can deal with those issues.

RESTITUTION

When I finally saw the ugliness of my orphan heart, I immediately went to my mentor and said, "Phillip, please forgive me; I see now what you're saying." Then I called Roger and asked, "What do I need to do?" I knew it was not enough just to forgive and be forgiven; I needed to make restitution.

I was terrified to approach Bishop Miles because I was intimidated by authority. It was pure orphan thinking. So, Roger went with me. I had sent a copy of my nine-page confession to Bishop Miles in advance so he could read it before we met. As we sat down at lunch together, we chatted, and he was as friendly as could be. That helped set me more at ease. I asked Bishop Miles, "You received the letter that I sent you?"

"Yes, I did." "Did you read it?" "Every word."

"Bishop Miles," I said, "I want to ask you to forgive me for all these years that I valued you for what you could do for me." I also confessed to him that I had put a demand on our relationship—I wanted him to be my source of affirmation and promotion, and not God. It resulted in me operating in control and manipulation, trying to get my unhealed need met. Furthermore, I confessed the defilement I had brought into his church and all the people I drew to myself who had gotten underneath me instead of deflecting praise to him.

And all the country of Judea was going out to him, and all the people of Jerusalem; and they were being baptized by him in the Jordan River, confessing their sins. (Mark 1:5)

PRAYER TO ENCOUNTER YOUR FATHER

Confession is good for the soul, they say. I know that's true as I confess to You daily, Father, and I praise and thank You for understanding me, even when I don't know what to say.

NOVEMBER 30
FORGIVEN

Bishop Miles said, "Jack, I forgave you years ago. I tried to talk to you about it, but every time I tried, you insisted everything was fine. I lost trust in you because you weren't honest with me."

And we wonder why promotion doesn't seem to come our way in the workplace or in our church. Promotion is often delayed for orphans; or it is illegitimately taken at a high price to our relationships, character, and integrity. Orphans feel the need to fight and wrangle for everything they want. That's probably one reason why there is so much strife and division in our churches. Spiritual orphans are competing with each other for position, any morsel of affirmation, or the praise of people.

We wonder why much of the church is powerless in our nations and our cities, and why many flock to other religions or cults. Could it be because of so many orphan hearts that misrepresent Father's love to their families and to the world?

Bishop Miles forgave me, blessed me, and sent me on my way with these words, "Jack, you have really matured. I do not know many men who would have humbled themselves the way you have. I am proud of you, and I believe in you. God is about to do something great through your life!"

He touched my mouth with it and said, "Behold, this has touched your lips; and your iniquity is taken away and your sin is forgiven." (Isaiah 6:7)

PRAYER TO ENCOUNTER YOUR FATHER
I thank You Father for the grace You seem to have for Your children as You take away our iniquities. When I am honest with myself and You and others, only then can You work something great in my life. This is my hope and prayer, Lord, that I will be honest and forthright.

DECEMBER 1

RESTORATION

God told me that I would take healing and restoration to the nations of the earth. Later, Bill Hamon and five or six other prophets confirmed it prophetically. For seventeen years, I had slaved to make that word come to pass, but it never did. I worked, I labored, I did everything to build the ministry, and yet few people in authority would get behind me. Few would promote me, even though I helped thousands of people. I struggled, had no money, and little backing. It was not until I confessed and renounced my orphan heart, made restitution to the authorities I had defied and defiled, and embraced the spirit of sonship that the prophecy began to be fulfilled. No sonship, no influence. No sonship, no inheritance.

There may be a need for you to go to pastoral or other authority and make restitution to them for being an orphan toward them instead of a child. Don't do it because I did it; do it because the Holy Spirit convicts you to do so. Take a few minutes to sit quietly and ask God to show you anyone in authority whom you may need to go to and make things right. It may be a past or present boss, pastor, or teacher. Write their names down then begin to move toward bringing closure in those relationships. As you do, you will also progress in your journey from slavery to sonship.

If you return to the Almighty, you will be restored: If you remove wicked-ness far from your tent. (Job 22:23 NIV)

PRAYER TO ENCOUNTER YOUR FATHER

I will write down the names that come to me, Father of those I have wounded. Then I will take the steps necessary to restore those relationships, in Jesus' name.

DECEMBER 2
COME, FOLLOW ME

Jack's Bank was the name that a few fishermen gave to one of the hottest grouper fishing spots ever found off the Outer Banks of North Carolina. Every time I hit this super-secret spot, I was heading to the bank when I got home. One winter, I caught 75,000 pounds of snowy grouper on hook-and-line on one shipwreck in a two-month period. It was over $80,000 in fish sales, and my captain's pay was over $25,000. Not bad for two months of the most adventurous fishing I have ever known.

I had received Christ as my Savior only two years earlier when I felt that God was speaking to me to leave my life as a commercial fishing captain and attend Bible school to lay a foundation for taking the message of healing and restoration to the nations. I was very insecure with that idea because my whole identity had been wrapped up in being Top Hook. Bible school and ministry had too many intimidating uncertainties.

So I bargained with God, "If in the next few months, You pay off all my debts and provide the money my wife and I need for us both to attend two years of Bible school, I will receive that as confirmation that I need to step out of my comfort zone and into faith." I was willing, but I thought I found a way out of leaving the sea and obeying God.

Come, follow me," Jesus said, "and I will send you out to fish for people."
(Matthew 4:19 NIV)

PRAYER TO ENCOUNTER YOUR FATHER
I would rather not bargain with You, Father. Knowing that You know best is all that I need. But I do thank You when in my immaturity You presented Your will in my life clearly, and I chose to follow You.

DECEMBER 3

SO THANKFUL

The very next commercial fishing trip following that deal with God was fishing for red snapper. We fished all night and boated about a thousand pounds, and then headed east to fish for deep-water snowy grouper during the day hours. As we motored to the east, I put the boat on auto-pilot and fell asleep at the wheel and went several miles farther east than planned. When I awoke and looked at my fish-finding scope, I saw the largest school of grouper that I had ever seen sitting on top of a wreck in 840 feet of water.

As we anchored on this previously undiscovered and uncharted wreck, we caught 9,000 pounds of snowy grouper within the next thirty hours. Every fish weighed between 50 and 60 pounds. It took a day to return to the dock and another day to unload and sell those fish. We turned the boat around and went right back and caught another 9,000 pounds in less than another thirty hours. I made $7,400 captain's share in just six days.

It was my inheritance. I was willing (though skeptical) to give up everything that had made me secure in life—my identity at sea—and be obedient to the word that I felt God had given me to follow Him. I was so thankful that God had set me free from drug and porn addiction that I wanted to be subject to God's mission, not mine.

Singing with thankfulness in your hearts to God. (Colossians 3:16)

PRAYER TO ENCOUNTER YOUR FATHER
I have so very many people and things and places to be thankful for, heavenly Father. At the top of the list is Jesus. Thank You!

DECEMBER 4
PASSION AND FAITH

It is difficult to put into words the passion and faith that I found in God during this season of reaping the harvest that He had prepared for me. I knew beyond a shadow of a doubt that the discovery of Jack's Bank was a supernatural God thing and that He was providing everything I needed to transition my life on the sea to a life seeking the Kingdom of God and making it known to the world.

When at port, I would keep my boat fully equipped with fuel, bait, ice, fishing gear, and food, and wait until a winter storm passed through. Then on the last day of a freezing gale, at 2 o'clock in the morning, I would sneak the boat away from the dock while others were in their warm and cozy beds. By the time the weather was nice enough for others to go, I would have beaten my way through 8- to 12-foot seas and be ready to fish as soon as the sea died down. Within 24 hours, I had my boat loaded with snowy grouper and on my way home while the rest of the fleet was on their way out. I must say that I wasn't driven only by the calling of God on my life, but also by a boatload of pride and ego at slyly outsmarting the fleet. Even now, many years later, my emotions can feel the glory of those weeks.

Be exalted, O Lord, in Your strength; we will sing and praise Your power.
(Psalm 21:13)

PRAYER TO ENCOUNTER YOUR FATHER
Father, my passion and faith is in You, for You are the only steady light in my life. I know You will always be with me, hear me, comfort me, and love me. That is so very reassuring.

DECEMBER 5
TRUTH AND LIGHT

So many Christians have received Christ and have the right to be joint heirs with Him. Everything we see in Christ we are an heir too, but sometimes jealousy, shame, or feeling that others are more blessed seem to hold us back. At other times, it just seems that the thief steals the blessings of God right out from under us. Whatever it may be, many people do not receive their inheritance because of two important truths that were robbing me for years of provision and fruitfulness in my life and family. Let's see how much they may be hindering you from being subject to Father's mission.

An orphan heart is bound up and steeped in lies and ungodly beliefs that have their source in the father of lies. Consequently, an orphan does not legitimately receive an inheritance. Orphans live in the realm of untruth and darkness while inheritance belongs to the realm of truth and light. This contrast between truth and lies leads us to the sixth truth in our quest to move from slavery to sonship.

So Jesus was saying to those Jews who had believed Him, "If you continue in My word, then you are truly disciples of Mine; and you will know the truth, and the truth will make you free." (John 8:31-32)

PRAYER TO ENCOUNTER YOUR FATHER
My desire is to keep all open doors and windows shut tight against the thief who comes to steal my joy, peace, and my blessings. Father, would You station Your angels around my home and protect us from evil.

TRUTH #6: RENOUNCE
ORPHAN THINKING

#6. Daily renounce ungodly beliefs and hidden lies of orphan thinking.
Proverbs 23:7 says that we become according to what we think in our hearts. A
key truth to displacing orphan thinking is to expose the lies and ungodly beliefs
that are at its core and let light dispel the darkness. It is a daily battle that we all
fight. In fact, Paul describes it in blatantly warlike terms in Second Corinthians
10:4-5; this Scripture refers to a fortress of thought that includes lies against
what God has revealed about Himself. It is a habit structure of thinking that
exalts itself above the knowledge of God's love. The fortress of thought gives the
enemy ground to traffic in your life. If you cast out the demonic influence but
let the fortress of thought remain, then the demonic influence has a legal right
to return and to reoccupy the fortress.

Our minds are either influenced by the Father of Creation or the father of
lies. There is a 12-step downward spiral that orphan thinking takes that culmi-
nates in a stronghold of oppression. Only in daily walking in the truth of Christ
can such a stronghold be displaced. One of the biggest dangers in all of this is
the fact that so often lies and ungodly beliefs creep into our thoughts so subtly
that we don't recognize them as orphan thinking.

For as he thinks in his heart, so is he. (Proverbs 23:7 NKJV)

PRAYER TO ENCOUNTER YOUR FATHER
*What is in my heart right now, Father, is the warmth and calmness that comes
from knowing You intimately. I give You permission to show me the strongholds of
thinking that keeps me involved with the orphan issues of my heart.*

TWISTED THOUGHTS

A couple of months after my act of confession and restitution with Bishop Miles, Trisha said to me, "I had a dream last night about your upcoming trip to Poland." I was scheduled to attend a pastors' conference in northern Poland during May of that year. Trisha continued, "I dreamed that Bishop Miles was with you. Why don't you call him and invite him to go with you?"

"He doesn't have time for me," I replied. Do you see how orphan thinking twists our thought life? True, Bishop Miles was a very busy man who regularly traveled internationally. His time was precious, and I immediately assumed that I had no value to him and he could spare none of his time for me. So I left it alone.

The next day Trisha said, "I had that dream again. You really need to call Bishop Miles."

"He's booked years in advance," I protested, "He's not going to take time for me." Again I was thinking like I was a little bitty nothing, an orphan nobody values or would promote. Nobody was going to favor me; nobody cared about me. Do you see how quickly and easily we can come into agreement with the accuser of the believers—the first spiritual orphan?

For the accuser of our brothers and sisters, who accuses them before our God day and night, has been hurled down. (Revelation 12:10 NIV)

PRAYER TO ENCOUNTER YOUR FATHER
Father, I pray to never agree with the evil one again. I don't want to be influenced by anyone or anything other than You, Lord.

DECEMBER 8
GRACIOUSNESS

Finally, I picked up the phone and called his office, "I'd like to schedule a phone appointment with Bishop Miles for any time he is available." Bishop Miles got on the phone. "Hello, Jack. How are you doing?"

"Things are going pretty well," I said. "In fact, they're going great. We have a pastors' conference in Poland coming up in May, and I was wondering if you would come with me and be one of the key speakers."

He said excitedly, "Two years ago, I felt that God told me to go to Poland. I don't know anybody there, and I've been praying ever since for an open door to Poland. I'll adjust my schedule and come with you." And just like that, Bishop Miles went to Poland. As we walked to the baggage claim area of the airport, this man who had been faithful in ministry for over 40 years, and whom I had served under for three, put his hand on my shoulder and said, "Now, Jack, I'm here to serve you."

"But Bishop Miles," I protested, "you're the apostle. You're the one who…"

"This is your conference, Jack. You're the host and you invited me. I don't even need to speak. I just want to be here to help you with anything you need." I'm thinking, *And my orphan heart had trouble receiving this humble man's servant heart all these years?*

Let your speech always be with grace, as though seasoned with salt, so that you will know how you should respond to each person. (Colossians 4:6)

PRAYER TO ENCOUNTER YOUR FATHER

Father, help me to destroy any orphan heart thinking and accept the good, godly people You have placed in my life. Show me how You feel about them and set a watch to my speech to never criticize especially when I don't know their pain.

DECEMBER 9

BREAKTHROUGH

We went to the conference and I taught on Father's transforming love. The central European pastors wept in travail as Bishop Miles watched in amazement. By the fourth day, most of the ninety pastors present were on their faces on the floor in repentance. Having observed and absorbed this all week, Bishop Miles asked, "How soon can you come back to Evangel Cathedral and conduct an Experiencing Father's Embrace Encounter? How soon can you come to the ministers' fellowship and teach this to all the ministers?"

Since I had left Bishop Miles' church, he had never invited me back to speak. "Whenever you want," I replied. "As soon as we get home, I'm going to call all the elders of the ministers' fellowship and tell them that they need to get this revelation in their church."

Bishop Miles asked me to speak on the first night, which was always a night of honor at the fellowship. He introduced me to the 275 pastors who were there and told them that what I had to say was one of the most needed revelations of our day, a vital word for the end times. This was the same place where for years I could hardly get a speaking slot or promotion to save my life! But back then, I was an untrustworthy orphan, and now I was moving toward sonship.

Now, my son, the Lord be with you, and may you have success and build the house of the Lord your God, as he said you would. (1 Chronicles 22:11 NIV)

PRAYER TO ENCOUNTER YOUR FATHER

Success is earned through humility and an open heart. Lord, thank You for the successes I have known in life. I pray You will bring more my way as I yield more of my feeling that I don't have value to You.

DECEMBER 10
COMING CLEAN

I stood before 275 ministers and confessed, "I joined this fellowship in its second year when there were only eighteen of us. Now there are hundreds, and for the last twelve years, I have done everything to promote myself and manipulate you to further my ministry. I have related to this fellowship based upon what you could do for me rather than on how I could get underneath and be a blessing to Bishop Miles and to Evangel Fellowship. In my immaturity, I tried to use you. Please forgive me." Needless to say, everyone was shocked.

Then I shared my testimony of receiving an experiential revelation of Father's love. When the altar ministry began, many of the very same elders who had no trust in my life or ministry before were the first ones at the altar weeping. In fact, some ended up in my arms as we wept together and they asked forgiveness for judging me harshly. Later several pastors from large churches asked, "How soon can you come to my church and teach on Father's love?"

If I had not cast down the ungodly beliefs and invited Bishop Miles to come to Poland with me, the reconciliation of relationships, restoration of trust, and promotion to areas of greater influence might never have happened. Acknowledging and renouncing the ungodly beliefs and hidden lies are vital to displacing an orphan heart with the truth of God's transforming love.

> *Therefore confess your sins to each other and pray for each other so that you may be healed. The prayer of a righteous person is powerful and effective.* (James 5:16 NIV)

PRAYER TO ENCOUNTER YOUR FATHER
Fessing up to sin and wrongdoing is the most refreshing and burden-lifting feeling! Having a clear conscious and right heart before You, Father, is worth more than any type of praise from any person on earth.

TRUTH #7: SOW INTO YOUR INHERITANCE

#7. Begin sowing into your inheritance.

As this revelation of orphans and sons became real to me, I discovered another important truth in displacing orphan thinking when I realized that it was time to begin to sow into my inheritance. Prior to this, each December we would get a letter from Evangel Fellowship International (EFI), that invited us to participate in a Christmas offering for Bishop Miles. I knew what his salary was, and how often he spoke at other churches, which collected nice offerings for him. And here I was trying to raise a family of five on less than $30,000. "Why didn't they take up an offering for me?" Definitely orphan thinking.

God began to reveal to me how I was dishonoring authority with orphan thinking whenever I felt that authority didn't need a blessing they were receiving as much as I did. I had no honor toward authority. Heirs recognize the power of sowing into their inheritance by blessing those who have blessed them as well as blessing others as they have been blessed.

As I encountered Romans 15:27 in my new mindset of a son, I realized that I had a debt to all the people who had put up with me in my "teenage" years, my years of spiritual immaturity when I did more taking from people than giving. How much grief and pain had I caused Bishop Miles and other people in my life because of my immaturity in not valuing them?

For if the Gentiles have shared in their spiritual things, they are indebted to minister to them also in material things. (Romans 15:27)

PRAYER TO ENCOUNTER YOUR FATHER

I will start sowing into my inheritance, Father, by blessing those who blessed me. Thank You for the opportunity and the resources to do this—for Your glory.

DECEMBER 12

INDEBTED

Think about all the people to whom you owe a spiritual debt. Who nurtured you in the faith? Who mentored you? Who matured you in the things of God? Who modeled Father's love for you sincerely, regardless of how imperfectly? Who tolerated being valued by you for what they could do for you rather than for relationship's sake? Have you sowed materially into their lives and ministries? Are you making what is important to them important to you?

> *Nevertheless, the one who receives instruction in the word should share all good things with their instructor. Do not be deceived: God cannot be mocked. A man reaps what he sows. Whoever sows to please their flesh, from the flesh will reap destruction; whoever sows to please the Spirit, from the Spirit will reap eternal life.* (Galatians 6:6-8 NIV)

PRAYER TO ENCOUNTER YOUR FATHER

Father, these are good questions that I will consider prayerfully. Bring people to mind who helped me along the way and bring occasions for me to repay them in kind. In the mean time I speak a blessing over them.

SOWING HONOR

I realized that receiving an offering for Bishop Miles and sowing into his life and ministry was not about meeting his need but about revealing my own heart issues. God really grabbed hold of my heart with this. I sat down with my wife, "Trisha, we've never joyfully blessed those in authority who put up with us in our years of immaturity. And look how much we have struggled." We gave to the poor, to missions, here and there; but because we felt our authority didn't need it or deserve it, we failed to honor them. But it wasn't about their need, it was about our need to sow honor so that we might reap honor and become influencers for the Kingdom of God.

I told Trisha, "I want us to start giving to the people who have put up with us all through the years and helped us mature." Together we made a list of about five people and began praying for seed to sow: "Father, we don't have any money. We don't have any way to bless these folks. So, Father, in accordance with Romans 15:27, First Corinthians 9:11, and Galatians 6:6-8, we ask You to supply seed for the sower, bread for food, that You might multiply a harvest. Bring increase that we will be prosperous in everything for liberality." We started claiming this daily, and financial increase began to occur.

If we have sown spiritual seed among you, is it too much if we reap a material harvest from you? (1 Corinthians 9:11)

PRAYER TO ENCOUNTER YOUR FATHER

Honoring those who have influenced by spiritual growth will be more of a priority of mine, Lord. Thank You for this nudge. I ask for creative idea and witty inventions on how to bless them.

DECEMBER 14
GIVE GENEROUSLY

We decided to not make sowing into our inheritance just about finances, but also about our time, focus, and loyalty. We looked for other ways to bless Bishop Miles and Pastor Phillip. Whatever was important to them, we were going to make important to us and all our team at Shiloh Place Ministries. We searched out every possible way to honor, bless, support, and promote their families, work, and ministry.

When Trisha and I received this revelation about sowing into our inheritance, our income at Shiloh Place Ministries went up 78 percent in the first year. The second year it went up 76 percent, then another 74 percent. After 9-11-2001, many ministries' finances began to decline worldwide, yet ours continued to climb. Everywhere we go, we are astounded at the honor and finances that people entrust us with.

Our tithe belongs at our local church, but beyond that, we continue to sow materially into the people who have ministered to us. It is a biblical principle. We have a debt, and it is an honor to discharge that debt by blessing materially and with our loyalty and emotional support, each of those who have put up with us when we had orphan hearts. That is sowing into our inheritance, and it is helping to displace orphan thinking with a heart of sonship!

If it is to encourage, then give encouragement; if it is giving, then give generously; if it is to lead, do it diligently; if it is to show mercy, do it cheerfully. (Romans 12:8 NIV)

PRAYER TO ENCOUNTER YOUR FATHER
Giving generously and cheerfully is one of my goals, Lord God. May Your Holy Spirit instill the gift of generosity in me toward all I have—through Your blessings.

DECEMBER 15

Truth #8: Entering Your Inheritance

#8. Entering into your inheritance.

On our quest for movement from slavery to sonship, the final truth that I have to impart to you is the transformation that I have seen in my life, family, relationships, and ministry. The following are some of the lasting fruit that has sprung forth from sonship being worked through our heart.

First, I began to discover God's rest. For most of my life, I struggled with the inability to rest and enjoy life. Something always seemed to grip me and pull me into restlessness. Some words to describe how I felt inside were tension, agitation, striving, or stressed. Let's try to give definition to this restlessness—the feeling that there is something more that I have to do or put in order to feel valued, affirmed, accepted, or loved.

Our competitive culture tends to define rest as a place of idleness or being unproductive. But the biblical rest found in sonship is not a place without activity or fruitfulness. Rest is a posture of the heart of sonship that feels so sheltered in Father's love that it does not allow itself to be pulled into a place where we strive to feel valued, affirmed, or secure. Abiding in rest is the place where all people will be drawn to us because everyone is searching for rest.

> But I said to you, "You will possess their land; I will give it to you as an inheritance, a land flowing with milk and honey." I am the Lord your God, who has set you apart from the nations. (Leviticus 20:24 NIV)

Prayer to Encounter Your Father

Father, You know that I definitely get caught up in the "must be productive" cycle of thinking. Help me find rest in Your embrace, Father God.

PERFECT LOVE

Second, feeling more secure and at rest in Father's love displaced much of my fear—fear of authority, fear of trusting, fear of rejection, and fear of intimacy. When around those in authority or even in a group of people, I no longer feel like I am on the outside looking in and wondering what I have to do to get on the inside. Perfect love has displaced so much of the insecurity and fear of being hurt again.

Third, with fear displaced, our relationships have become much more open, real, and meaningful, and are becoming the community of love that Christ intended for them to be. We are surrounded by true friends who are there for us, no matter what, and we seek to be there for them. We have seen the yoke of independence broken and embraced interdependent friendships.

Just then a man came up to Jesus and asked, "Teacher, what good thing must I do to get eternal life?" (Matthew 19:16 NIV)

PRAYER TO ENCOUNTER YOUR FATHER

Thank You, Father for the lessons I've learned along the way this year, and previous years walking with You. I thank You that You have created an atmosphere for me to rest, learn and feel safe to change in.

MATURITY

Fourth, I helped my mom and dad receive the Lord, and I experienced closure when they passed away. There is much to say of seeing them pass on to be with the Lord, and your heart feeling innocent of the sins that they committed against you and the dishonor you committed against them. Forgiveness and restitution prevents the accuser of believers from binding you with a guilt or victim mentality.

Fifth, the hearts of my children have been restored to my heart. When my heart was full of orphan thinking toward my parents and spiritual authorities, I reaped from my children the same attitudes and relationship. All three of my children are now seeking to walk in a spirit of sonship with me. Can you imagine the joy and fulfillment that I, as a father, feel in that?

Instead, speaking the truth in love, we will grow to become in every respect the mature body of him who is the head, that is, Christ. (Ephesians 4:13 NIV)

PRAYER TO ENCOUNTER YOUR FATHER

Every day Father, I pray that I will take steps to become more and more mature in my spiritual life—bring me closer and closer to You so that Your nature can heal any damaged image I have of You.

DECEMBER 18
TO THE NATIONS

Sixth, all three of my children and the spouses of the two married ones are walking with God and seeking to make His love known to the world. In my orphan years, my children went through their years of rebellion and being seduced by the world. They all have come home to God's love, motivated by the transformation they have seen in their mom and dad.

Seventh, over the last eight years we have seen great favor, honor, and promotion released upon our lives and ministry. Following the act of confession and restitution with Bishop Miles, we have steadily matured into primary influencers in Evangel Fellowship International. We have been made elders in the fellowship and are regular speakers in their ministers' meetings. Outside of EFI, we are looked to as respected apostolic leaders in the nations for the revelation of God as a loving, affectionate, affirming Father.

> *Now if you obey me fully and keep my covenant, then out of all nations you will be my treasured possession.* (Exodus 19:5 NIV)

PRAYER TO ENCOUNTER YOUR FATHER
Father I thank You that fulfilling Your word to me has been my desire. I thank You for my destiny, my everything has always been planned successfully by You.

THE APPOINTED TIME

Eighth, financial provision and increase have been supernatural over the last eight years both in our ministry and personal lives. After fifteen years of poverty, the heart of sonship has made a way for us to give hilariously and to be a financial blessing to our children's and grandchildren's future.

Ninth, as we began to focus our life upon being a son and daughter to those in authority in our lives, many of our staff and team members began to do likewise with us and Shiloh Place. As promotion came to us, promotion began to occur in them, and we now have over seventy ministry team members who are traveling the world with the message of God's transforming love and deeply impacting families, churches, and ministers.

We praise you, God, we praise you, for your Name is near; people tell of your wonderful deeds. You say, "I choose the appointed time; it is I who judge with equity." (Psalm 75:1-2 NIV)

PRAYER TO ENCOUNTER YOUR FATHER

Father I pray the prayer of Jabez now and ask You to continue to enlarge my sphere of influence and I continue to pursue any hindrance that has caused increase to not be a part of my life. I thank You that Your timing for my increase in my life is perfect.

DECEMBER 20
HEARTS HEALED

Tenth, in eight years we went from a little impoverished, nobody-has-heard-of-us ministry, to an international ministry that is touching the world through our schools, encounters, and resource materials. Many people are coming to know Christ, and many more are having families transformed and hearts healed.

All ten of these things have occurred without self-assertion and aggressive striving to try and make them happen. We settled into God's rest, focused our life upon being a son and daughter, and His love has produced the inheritance. Intimacy preceded fruitfulness. Sonship preceded inheritance and the fulfillment of the word that God gave—"Leave your identity at sea, and you shall take healing and restoration to the nations."

> Oh, that You would bless me indeed, and enlarge my territory, that Your hand would be with me, and that You would keep me from evil, that I may not cause pain.' So God granted him what he requested." (2 Chronicles 4:10)

PRAYER TO ENCOUNTER YOUR FATHER
Father I thank You that it is desire for us to prosper and our lives to go well without us striving to attain success.

MINISTRY OF RESTITUTION

If our actions or attitudes have brought hurt to another person, there may be a need to go to that person and make right any wrong to break the destructive patterns in our relationships. Although God forgives us for each specific wrong the first time we ask, we may continue to reap what we have sown; so, in order to break that cycle and begin restoring trust, it is often necessary to make every effort to bring healing to others and to seek to restore the fractured relationship.

> But I tell you that anyone who is angry with a brother or sister will be subject to judgment. Again, anyone who says to a brother or sister, "Raca," is answerable to the court. And anyone who says, "You fool!" will be in danger of the fire of hell. Therefore, if you are offering your gift at the altar and there remember that your brother or sister has something against you, leave your gift there in front of the altar. First go and be reconciled to them; then come and offer your gift. Settle matters quickly with your adversary who is taking you to court. Do it while you are still together on the way, or your adversary may hand you over to the judge, and the judge may hand you over to the officer, and you may be thrown into prison. Truly I tell you, you will not get out until you have paid the last penny. (Matthew 5:22-26 NIV)

> If you are pure and upright, even now he will rouse himself on your behalf and restore you to your prosperous state. (Job 8:6 NIV)

PRAYER TO ENCOUNTER YOUR FATHER

Thank You for restoring my relationships and life. For forgiving me the first time I ask! Help me to bring healing to others and to restore fractured relationships, in Jesus' name.

DECEMBER 22
SELF-PITY OR REPENTANCE

It may not be enough for another person to forgive you. You may still carry unconscious guilt or shame for the offense and have a need to ask for forgiveness to be free. There can also be a block in the relationship until you acknowledge to them that you have wronged them. The other person may have forgiven you, but trust has been violated. Until you acknowledge your offense, it is difficult for them to trust you again because forgiveness and trust are two different things. You will then either respond with self-pity (feelings of sorrow over our suffering) or repentance in action that begins to rebuild trust with those who were offended.

Self-pity seldom leads to transformed behavior or restored relationships. Rather, self-pity:

- Diminishes, in our eyes, the gravity of each sin we commit against love and honor toward others.

- Hinders godly repentance when we feel that life has not been fair with us and believe that others are the cause of our frustrations. Thus, we do not look to God but people to meet our need.

- Places the primary fault upon others for relational conflicts because we feel that we have been treated unfairly. If they would not have done that to me…or…If only they would have done this for me, then life would be better and I would not be forced to act in such a way!

Yet now I am happy, not because you were made sorry, but because your sorrow led you to repentance. …At every point you have proved yourselves to be innocent in this matter. (2 Corinthians 7:9-11 NIV)

PRAYER TO ENCOUNTER YOUR FATHER
Father I take this self-pity to Your cross and ask Jesus to remind me of who I am and who I belong to. Crash into those self-absorbed parties that I tend to give myself. Transform my behavior to reflect You and Your grace.

SELF-PITY
(CONTINUED)

Self-pity:

- Excuses our negative attitudes by seeing the weaknesses in others and feeling that our rightness justifies our judgmentalism or actions.

- Attempts to persuade others to feel sorry for us and to acknowledge that we have been treated unfairly (defilement) thus strengthening the stronghold of self-pity within.

- May try to compensate for our relational failures with increased hyper-religious activity, aggressively striving to earn self-worth or acceptance, or we may take on a false sense of responsibility and place all the blame upon ourselves for relational conflicts thus denying others the opportunity to deal with their own issues.

- Often leads to others feeling manipulated or demeaned by closing our heart to those who will not come into agreement with our self-pity, thus leaving others feeling that they have little value or honor in our presence.

- May result in hidden anger at our feelings of loss or unmet expectations. This increases our blame toward others and results in deeper feelings of anger, insecurity, shame, isolation, apathy, self-condemnation, addictive compulsive behavior, and/or depression.

- Leaves us dissatisfied at work, church, and at home, and we want to escape to a place where we can find rest.

A happy heart makes the face cheerful, but heartache crushes the spirit." (Proverbs 15:13)

PRAYER TO ENCOUNTER YOUR FATHER

Again and again, Lord, I'm whining to myself about this or that or him or her. I'm sorry, please forgive my self-pity moments. Help me to move on. I thank You that You gave me a happy heart so forgive me for trying to make it sad through focus on my situational circumstances.

DECEMBER 24
REPENTANCE
(CONTINUED)

On the other hand, godly repentance always involves action. It is not just emotions and tears. Godly repentance:

- Is so grieved at the wounding and stress our actions and attitudes have brought to others that we are now willing to humble ourselves and do whatever it takes to restore healthy relationships.

- Hates the destructive habit patterns that have misrepresented God's love and grace to others.

- Becomes more concerned with others' needs than our own pride and walls of self-protection.

- Is willing to lay down the need to be right in order to see healing in those whom we have hurt or offended.

- Chooses to walk in openness and transparency, and willingly comes forward and acknowledges our sin against love and how we have hurt or offended others.

- Does not seek to make excuses, seek to put the blame on others, or diminish the depth of our self-deception or fear of intimacy with which we have struggled.

- Takes the focus off ourselves (self-pity) and begins to focus our energy upon humility, confession, forgiveness, repentance, and healing the pain that we have caused others.

This is what the Sovereign Lord, the Holy One of Israel, says: "In repentance and rest is your salvation, in quietness and trust is your strength." (Isaiah 30:15 NIV)

PRAYER TO ENCOUNTER YOUR FATHER
I pray that godly repentance will become an active part of my life, Lord God. I will focus my energy on You and others—me last.

PRACTICING THE MINISTRY OF RESTITUTION

To practice the ministry of restitution, follow these suggestions:

1. Ask God to reveal to you each way you have brought hurt or offense to another person (see Ps. 139:23-24).
   - What is the basic offense? How did you demean, devalue, dishonor, or hurt that person?
   - Ask the Holy Spirit to bring conviction and repentance to each individual issue (see Rom. 2:4).

2. Ask mature spiritual leaders who know you personally to speak admonition into your blind spots.
   - Review with them the offenses that you have noted (see James 5:16; Ephs. 4:15).
   - Give them permission to speak the truth in love to you, about what they have seen in you that could be perceived as offensive or defiling.
   - Ask for input as to how you can approach the offended person and bring restoration to the relationship.

Make this your common practice: Confess your sins to each other and pray for each other so that you can live together whole and healed. (James 5:16 MSG)

PRAYER TO ENCOUNTER YOUR FATHER

Heavenly Father, in obedience to You and Your Word, I will practice the ministry of restitution daily. I ask You for input when I have hurt another. I give You permission to speak the truth to me through Your spirit but also Your children. Thank You for looking on our hearts and never throwing us away.

PRACTICING THE MINISTRY
OF RESTITUTION
(CONTINUED)

3. Ask forgiveness for how your immaturity, attitudes, actions, or neglect has caused hurt or offense.

- Be thankful for this opportunity for growth. God is using this situation to help expose hidden destructive habit patterns and to bring them to death.

- Call on the phone to schedule a meeting with the offended party. A letter is not the best way because it does not give opportunity for them to respond, plus it documents instead of removes the offense. Approach them with humility and respect.

- Schedule the meeting during the best time of day for them. Allow plenty of time to discuss the issues.

- Begin the meeting by telling the person that God has been revealing to you how your attitude and actions have misrepresented God's love to them. Example: "God has brought to my attention how wrong I was (tell them the basic offense without going into detail). It would mean a lot to me if you would forgive me. Will you forgive me?" Do not go into too much detail, thereby giving the enemy something to work with and an opportunity to stir up bitterness, resentment, or defilement in the other person.

If you, God, kept records on wrongdoings, who would stand a chance? As it turns out, forgiveness is your habit, and that's why you're worshiped. (Psalm 130:3-4 MSG)

PRAYER TO ENCOUNTER YOUR FATHER

It is true that over the years my immaturity, attitude, actions, and neglect has caused hurt or offense to family members, coworkers, and even friends and neighbors. I ask for forgiveness and wisdom to set things right with others.

PRACTICING THE MINISTRY
OF RESTITUTION
(CONTINUED)

3. Ask forgiveness for how your immaturity, attitudes, actions, or neglect has caused hurt or offense—continued:

- Do not expect them to forgive you. They may, but do not require it, as it does not always happen.
- At this time, do not mention their faults. Just take ownership of your own. (Later, if your spiritual authority thinks it wise, and some trust is restored with the person, you may go to them about hurts you have received from them.)
- Do not try to diminish your offense by blame-shifting, justifying your behavior because of past hurts, or try to make an excuse because you were having a bad day. That only serves to diminish godly repentance. Take full ownership of your dishonor and misrepresentation of God's love.
- Ask the person if there are other areas they have personally seen that have brought offense to them or others. Ask forgiveness and apologize for each area they mention.
- You may want to do this individually with each family member you may have offended or defiled.
- If your attitudes or actions have brought offense or defilement to the whole family, workplace, or church, then after you have gone to them individually, you may want to gather the group together and ask them corporately to forgive you and to give you grace while you are attempting to make some changes in life.

Smart people know how to hold their tongue; their grandeur is to forgive and forget. (Proverbs 19:11 MSG)

PRAYER TO ENCOUNTER YOUR FATHER

Admitting a fault or mistake can be really hard, Father. But with Your support, the comfort of the Holy Spirit, and the love of Christ, I will take responsibility and make amends each time.

JUDGING OURSELVES

4. Ask a spiritually mature person, to whom you are accountable, to meet with you weekly or monthly.

- Be sure that this individual is mature and not afraid to speak the truth in love to you and that the person does not come into agreement (defilement) with the issues you are having with others, but that they know how to help you judge yourself in each matter (see 1 Cor. 11:31).

- Discuss any other blind spots that are being exposed and have the person pray with you over issues.

- Ask the person how you can grow and mature relationally.

But if we judged ourselves rightly, we would not be judged. (1 Corinthians 11:31)

PRAYER TO ENCOUNTER YOUR FATHER

Judging myself is not as easy as it sounds. Sometimes I'm too hard on myself and other times I let actions and words slip by that are harsh or sinful. Father God, bring into my life a spiritually mature person who can reveal Your righteous judgment to me.

ALIVE AGAIN

As long as I tried to build my identity and ministry through orphan thinking, I felt like the angry older brother slaving in the fields and thought that the father had never given me anything for which to be merry.

> *Meanwhile, the older son was in the field. When he came near the house, he heard music and dancing. So he called one of the servants and asked him what was going on. "Your brother has come," he replied, "and your father has killed the fattened calf because he has him back safe and sound." The older brother became angry and refused to go in. So his father went out and pleaded with him. But he answered his father, "Look! All these years I've been slaving for you and never disobeyed your orders. Yet you never gave me even a young goat so I could celebrate with my friends. But when this son of yours who has squandered your property with prostitutes comes home, you kill the fattened calf for him!"* (Luke 15:25-30 NIV)

I saw little lasting fruit and was left in a state of agitated resistance against authority and in disappointment and frustration. But as I began to sow into my inheritance by getting underneath and blessing others and earnestly seeking to be faithful with that which was another's, I began to receive the promises of God for my life, family, and ministry.

> *"My son," the father said, "you are always with me, and everything I have is yours. But we had to celebrate and be glad, because this brother of yours was dead and is alive again; he was lost and is found."* (Luke 15:31-32 NIV)

PRAYER TO ENCOUNTER YOUR FATHER

Thank You, Holy Father, for welcoming me into Your family where each person is a favored child of Yours. I praise You and worship You with all my heart and soul and mind.

DECEMBER 30
WONDERING

Have you wondered why you have not seen more lasting fruit in your life? Do you wonder why you don't have more influence in your workplace? Do you wonder why you haven't come into the place that God has called you to in your local church and that you know He wants you to move into? Are you sowing into your inheritance? Or do you cop an attitude when it's time to take up an offering or to bless your pastor or boss at Christmastime?

Your inheritance, the word God has given you, is delayed until you learn obedience from the things that you suffer by becoming a son or a daughter. Then you begin to become a representative of God's transforming love to your family and others. It is all wrapped up in the principles of honor and submission, of humbling yourself to become faithful with that which is another's, of getting underneath and pushing up, of serving unselfishly and whole- heartedly to build up another with no personal agenda or ulterior motives.

As always, Christ is our example, who said that He *"did not come to be served, but to serve, and to give His life as a ransom for many"* (Matt. 20:28). God opposes the proud. He is not opposed to you, but He is opposed to anything of the orphan heart in you that tries to exalt itself or promote itself.

> *Whoever can be trusted with very little can also be trusted with much, and whoever is dishonest with very little will also be dishonest with much. So if you have not been trustworthy in handling worldly wealth, who will trust you with true riches? And if you have not been trustworthy with someone else's property, who will give you property of your own?* (Luke 16:10-12 NIV)

PRAYER TO ENCOUNTER YOUR FATHER
Father, I choose to be trustworthy with what You have placed in my hands. That includes Your kids and how You love them. I ask You to help me example Your nature and image to them.

FATHER'S TRANSFORMING LOVE

It's time for sons and daughters to come into our inheritance, but it will not come without a repentant heart that is moved to action. This is what God is releasing on the earth in our generation. Father's transforming love and the heart of sonship—this is the message that the church and the world needs to hear before the end comes.

Don't keep living as an orphan in constant frustration, agitation, and fear—no love, no trust, no home, and no influence. What would your life be like if you had no fear? It would be like the life of Jesus, of whom Father said, *"This is My beloved Son, in whom I am well pleased."* Surrender your orphan heart for a heart of sonship. Enter the embrace of the Father who loves you more than you can possibly imagine. Hold close your identity as a son or daughter of the Father of Creation and explore it to your heart's content.

Your inheritance is waiting for you. Don't let orphan thinking deny you what is rightfully yours as an heir with Christ. Be subject to Father's mission and experience life and peace, allowing Him to bring you into fruitfulness. Your family and the nations are waiting for you to enter into your inheritance!

> *Whenever, though, they turn to face God as Moses did, God removes the veil and there they are—face-to-face! They suddenly recognize that God is a living, personal presence, not a piece of chiseled stone. And when God is personally present, a living Spirit, that old, constricting legislation is recognized as obsolete. We're free of it! All of us! Nothing between us and God, our faces shining with the brightness of his face. And so we are transfigured much like the Messiah, our lives gradually becoming brighter and more beautiful as God enters our lives and we become like him.* (2 Corinthians 3:18 MSG)

PRAYER TO ENCOUNTER YOUR FATHER

With Your blessing and encouragement, Father, I am ready to accept my inheritance, to advance Your mission, and to enjoy life of peace and fruitfulness. All glory and honor to You—Almighty God, Lord Jesus, and Holy Spirit.

About Jack and Trisha Frost

Jack Frost, well-known minister, loving husband and father, died on March 5, 2007, after a heroic battle with cancer. His wisdom and spiritual insights live on through his writings and Shiloh Place Ministries.

Jack Frost grew up in Daytona Beach, Florida, not far from the beach and the intercoastal waterway. During his childhood years, his days were spent fishing, boating, and surfing. In his late teens, he became lost in the hippie and drug culture for a few years. After a couple of scrapes with the law, he fled to Columbia, South Carolina, where he met his future wife, Trisha, who was born and raised in Columbia. They eventually moved back to the Daytona Beach area where they were married in 1975.

Jack worked fishing boats all through his 20s, and he earned a captain's license allowing him to captain boats up to 100 tons, or about 125 feet in length. Jack was one of the most successful commercial snapper fishermen in the late 1970s and early 1980s on the southeast coast of the United States.

In 1980, at 27 years of age, Jack had a miraculous encounter with God's love while fishing alone at sea for three days. This experience set him free from ten years of drug and alcohol problems and fifteen years of pornography addiction. His passion for the sea was exchanged for a desire to see others healed from their brokenness.

Trisha and Jack entered The Salvation Army College for Officer's Training in 1982 and graduated in 1984. For the next two years they served in command of The Salvation Army in the Myrtle Beach, South Carolina, area. As pastors and heads of their social work programs, they experienced great success even in the midst of family problems, depression, and burnout. This led to their resigning the ministry, and Jack returned to the sea for twenty months as captain of a sport fishing boat that fished for marlin, sailfish, Wahoo, tuna, mackerel, and Maui Maui.

In 1988, they accepted a position as associate pastors at Evangel Cathedral in Spartanburg, South Carolina. Old patterns of burnout and depression once more caught up with them, and they resigned in 1991. They spent several months in solitude and prayer as they sought to know God for who He is, not just for what He can do through them in ministry. They also sought out ministers of healing prayer to help them walk through past hurts and disappointments.

Out of their own experience of healing and restoration, they founded Shiloh Place Ministries in 1991 as a safe place for leaders to come and experience personal ministry and equipping them to bring healing to others. Through the years, many pastors, missionaries, and leaders have had their marriages and ministries transformed at Shiloh Place.

SHILOH PLACE MINISTRIES
PO Box 5
Conway, SC 29528
Phone: 843-365-1905
Website: www.shilohplace.org

FREE E-BOOKS?
YES, PLEASE!

Get **FREE** and deeply discounted **Christian books** for your **e-reader** delivered to your inbox **every week!**

IT'S SIMPLE!

VISIT lovetoreadclub.com

SUBSCRIBE by entering your email address

RECEIVE free and discounted e-book offers and inspiring articles delivered to your inbox every week!

Unsubscribe at any time.

SUBSCRIBE NOW!

LOVE TO READ CLUB

visit **LOVETOREADCLUB.COM** ▶